MW00465628

India : What can it teach us?

BESTSELLING NON-FICTION

- Abraham Lincoln by Lord Charnwood, ISBN: 9789387669147
- Annihilation of Caste by Dr B.R. Ambedkar, ISBN: 9789390492756
- Be What You Wish by Neville Goddard, ISBN: 9789388118163
- Civilization and Its Discontents by Sigmund Freud, ISBN: 9789388118279
- Guerrilla Warfare by Ernesto Che Guevara, ISBN: 9789391181932
- How I Made 2 Million in the Stock Market by N. Darvas, ISBN: 9789389440218
- Jail Diary and Other Writings by Bhagat Singh, ISBN: 9789390492084
- Man-eaters of Kumaon by Jim Corbett, ISBN: 9789354990038
- My Experiments with Truth by Mahatma Gandhi, ISBN: 9789387669277
- Relativity by Albert Einstein, ISBN: 9789387669185
- Reminiscences of a Stock Operator by Edwin Lefevre, ISBN: 9789390492244
- Scientific Healing Affirmations by P. Yogananda, ISBN: 9789354990137
- The Art of War by Sun Tzu, ISBN: 9789387669321
- The Book of Five Rings by Miyamoto Musashi, ISBN: 9789389440553
- The Diary of a Young Girl by Anne Frank, ISBN: 9789387669208
- The Game of Life and How to Play It by F.S. Shinn, ISBN: 9789388118316
- The Law of Success by Napoleon Hill, ISBN: 9789389157949
- The Origin of Species by Charles Darwin, ISBN: 9789387669345
- The Power of Your Subcon. Mind by Joseph Murphy, ISBN: 9789387669222
- The Psychopathology of Everyday Life by Sigmund Freud, ISBN: 9789388118231
- The Richest Man in Babylon by George S. Clason, ISBN: 9789388118354
- The Science of Getting Rich by Wallace D. Wattles, ISBN: 9789387669239
- The World as I See It by Albert Einstein, ISBN: 9789388118248
- Why I am an Atheist and Other Works by Bhagat Singh, ISBN: 9789354992667
- Zen in the Art of Archery by Eugen Herrigel, ISBN: 9789354990298

Search the book by its ISBN

INDIA

WHAT CAN IT TEACH US?

*A Course of Lectures Delivered before
the University of Cambridge*

F. Max Müller

GENERAL PRESS

Published by
GENERAL PRESS
4805/24, Fourth Floor, Krishna House
Ansari Road, Daryaganj, New Delhi - 110002
Ph : 011-23282971, 45795759
E-mail : generalpressindia@gmail.com

www.generalpress.in

© General Press

First Edition : 2023

ISBN : 9789354995385

Published by Azeem Ahmad Khan for General Press

Contents

Dedicated

To E. B. COWELL M.A., LL.D.,
PROFESSOR OF SANSKRIT AND FELLOW OF
CORPUS CHRISTI COLLEGE IN THE UNIVERSITY
OF CAMBRIDGE

My dear Cowell: As these Lectures would never have been written or delivered but for your hearty encouragement, I hope you will now allow me to dedicate them to you, not only as a token of my sincere admiration of your great achievements as an Oriental scholar, but also as a memorial of our friendship, now more than thirty years old, a friendship which has grown from year to year, has weathered many a storm, and will last, I trust, for what to both of us may remain of our short passage from shore to shore.

I must add, however, that in dedicating these Lectures to you, I do not wish to throw upon you any responsibility for the views which I have put forward in them. I know that you do not agree with some of my views on the ancient religion and literature of India, and I am well aware that with regard to the recent date which I have assigned to the whole of what is commonly called the Classical Sanskrit Literature, I stand almost alone. No, if friendship can claim any voice in the courts of science and literature, let me assure you that I shall consider your outspoken criticism of my Lectures as the very best proof of your true and honest friendship. I have through life considered it the greatest honor if real scholars, I mean men not only of learning, but of judgment and character, have considered my writings worthy of a severe and searching criticism; and I have cared far more for the production of one single new fact, though it spoke against me, than for any amount of empty praise or empty abuse. Sincere devotion to his studies and an unswerving love of truth ought to furnish the true scholar with an armor impermeable to flattery or abuse, and with a visor that shuts out no ray of light, from whatever quarter it may come. More light, more truth, more facts, more combination of facts, these are his quest. And if in that quest he fails, as many have failed before him, he knows that in the search for truth failures are sometimes the condition of victory, and the true conquerors often those whom the world calls the vanquished.

You know better than anybody else the present state of Sanskrit scholarship. You know that at present and for some time to come Sanskrit scholarship means discovery and conquest. Every one of your own works marks a real advance, and a permanent occupation of new ground. But you know also how small a strip has as yet been explored of the vast continent of Sanskrit literature, and how much still remains *terra incognita*. No doubt this exploring work is troublesome, and often disappointing, but young students must learn the truth of a remark lately made by a distinguished member of the Indian Civil Service, whose death we all deplore, Dr. Burnell, "that no trouble is thrown away which saves trouble to others." We want men who will work hard, even at the risk of seeing their labors unrequited; we want strong and bold men who are not afraid of storms and shipwrecks. The worst sailors are not those who suffer shipwreck, but those who only dabble in puddles and are afraid of wetting their feet.

It is easy now to criticise the labors of Sir William Jones, Thomas Colebrooke, and Horace Hayman Wilson, but what would have become of Sanskrit scholarship if they had not rushed in where even now so many fear to tread? And what will become of Sanskrit scholarship if their conquests are forever to mark the limits of our knowledge? You know best that there is more to be discovered in Sanskrit literature than *Nalas* and *Sakuntalâs*, and surely the young men who every year go out to India are not deficient in the spirit of enterprise, or even of adventure? Why, then, should it be said that the race of bold explorers, who once rendered the name of the Indian Civil Service illustrious over the whole world, has well-nigh become extinct, and that England, which offers the strongest incentives and the most brilliant opportunities for the study of the ancient language, literature, and history of India, is no longer in the van of Sanskrit scholarship?

If some of the young candidates for the Indian Civil Service who listened to my Lectures, quietly made up their minds that such a reproach shall be wiped out, if a few of them at least determined to follow in the footsteps of Sir William Jones, and to show to the world that Englishmen who have been able to achieve by pluck, by perseverance, and by real political genius the material conquest of India, do not mean to leave the laurels of its intellectual conquest entirely to other countries, then I shall indeed rejoice, and feel that I have paid back, in however small a degree, the large debt of gratitude which I owe to my adopted country and to some of its greatest statesmen, who have given me the opportunity which I could find nowhere else of realizing the dreams of my life – the publication of the text and commentary of the Rig-Veda, the most ancient book of Sanskrit, aye of Aryan literature, and now the edition of the translations of the "Sacred Books of the East."

I have left my Lectures very much as I delivered them at Cambridge. I am fond of the form of Lectures, because it seems to me the most natural form which in our age didactic composition ought to take. As in ancient Greece the dialogue reflected most truly the intellectual life of the people, and as in the Middle Ages learned literature naturally assumed with the recluse in his monastic cell the form of a long monologue, so with us the lecture places the writer most readily in that position in which he is accustomed to deal with his fellow-men, and to communicate his knowledge to others. It has no doubt certain disadvantages. In a lecture which is meant to be didactic, we have, for the sake of completeness, to say and to repeat certain things which must be familiar to some of our readers, while we are also forced to leave out information which, even in its imperfect form, we should probably not hesitate to submit to our fellow-students, but which we feel we have not yet sufficiently mastered and matured to enable us to place it clearly and simply before a larger public.

But the advantages outweigh the disadvantages. A lecture, by keeping a critical audience constantly before our eyes, forces us to condense our subject, to discriminate between what is important and what is not, and often to deny ourselves the pleasure of displaying what may have cost us the greatest labor, but is of little consequence to other scholars. In lecturing we are constantly reminded of what students are so apt to forget, that their knowledge is meant not for themselves only, but for others, and that to know well means to be able to teach well. I confess I can never write unless I think of somebody for whom I write, and I should never wish for a better audience to have before my mind than the learned, brilliant, and kind-hearted assembly by which I was greeted in your University.

Still I must confess that I did not succeed in bringing all I wished to say, and more particularly the evidence on which some of my statements rested, up to the higher level of a lecture; and I have therefore added a number of notes containing the less-organized matter which resisted as yet that treatment which is necessary before our studies can realize their highest purpose, that of feeding, invigorating, and inspiriting the minds of others.

Yours affectionately,
–F. Max Müller
Oxford, December, 1882

Introduction

Professor Max Müller has been so long and widely known in the world of letters as to render any formal introduction unnecessary. He has been from his early youth an assiduous student of philology, justly regarding it as an important key to history and an invaluable auxiliary to intellectual progress. A glance at his personal career will show the ground upon which his reputation is established.

Friedrich Maximilian Müller, the son of Wilhelm Müller, the Saxon poet, was born at Dessau, December 6th, 1823. He matriculated at Leipzig in his eighteenth year, giving his principal attention to classical philology, and receiving his degree in 1843. He immediately began a course of Oriental studies, chiefly Sanskrit, under the supervision of Professor Brockhaus, and in 1844 engaged in his translation of the "Hitopadesa." He removed from Leipzig to Berlin, and attended the lectures of Bopp, Rücker, and Schelling. The next year he went to Paris to listen to Eugene Burnouf at the Collége de France. He now began the collecting of material for his great quarto edition of the "Rig-Veda Sanhita" and the "Commentary of Ságanadránja." He visited England for this purpose to examine the manuscripts in the Bodleian Library and at the Indian House. At the recommendation of H. H. Wilson, the Orientalist, he was commissioned by the East India Company to publish his edition in England at their expense. The first volume appeared in 1849, and five others followed during the next few years.

In 1850 he delivered a course of "Lectures on Comparative Philology" at Oxford, and the next year was made member of Christ Church, curator, etc., and appointed Taylorian Professor of Modern European Languages and Literature. He received also numerous other marks of distinction from universities, and was made one of the eight foreign members of the Institute of France. The Volney prize was awarded him by the French Academy for his "Essay on the Comparative Philology of Indo-European Languages and its Bearing on the Early Civilization of Mankind."

His writings have been numerous. Besides editing the translations of the "Sacred Books of the Principal Religions," he has published a "Handbook for the Study of Sanskrit," a "Sanskrit-English Dictionary and Grammar," "Lectures upon the Science of Language," "An Introduction to the Science of Religion," "Essays on Mythology," "Chips from a German Workshop," etc. He seems to have no intermission, but penetrates where others would not have ventured, or have faltered from utter weariness. In the field of philology he has few peers, while in early Sanskrit learning he has virtually taken the part of an innovator. While reverently following after Sir William Jones, Colebrooke, Windischmann, Bopp, and others of equal distinction, he sets aside the received views in regard to chronology and historical occurrences. The era of Vikramâditya and the Golden Age of Sanskrit literature, bearing a date almost simultaneous with the Augustan period at the West, are postponed by him to a later century. It may be that he has overlooked some canon of interpretation that would have modified his results. Those, however, who hesitate to accept his conclusions freely acknowledge his scholarly enthusiasm, persistent energy, and great erudition.

Sanskrit in his judgment constitutes an essential element of a liberal education. While heartily admiring the employment of some of the best talent and noblest genius of our age in the study of development in the outward world, from the first growth of the earth and the beginning of organic life to the highest stages, he pleads earnestly that there is an inward and intellectual world also to be studied in its historical development in strict analogy with the other, leading up to the beginning of rational thought in its steady progress from the lowest to the highest stages. In that study of the history of the human mind, in that study of ourselves, our true selves, India occupies a place which is second to no other country. Whatever sphere of the human mind may be selected for special study, whether language, religion, mythology, or philosophy, whether laws, customs, primitive art or primitive science, we must go to India, because some of the most valuable and most instructive materials in the history of man are treasured up there, and there only. He inveighs most eloquently against the narrowing of our horizon to the history of Greeks and Romans, Saxons and Celts, with a dim background of Palestine, Egypt, and Babylon, leaving out of sight our nearest intellectual relatives, the Aryans of India, the framers of that most wonderful language the Sanskrit, the fellow-workers in the construction of our fundamental concepts, the fathers of the most natural of natural religions, the makers of the most transparent of mythologies, the inventors of the most subtle philosophy, and the givers of the most elaborate laws. It is the purpose of historical study to enable each generation to profit from the experience of those who came before, and advance toward higher aims, without being obliged to start anew from the same point as its ancestors after the manner of every race of brutes. He who knows little of those who preceded is very likely to care little for those coming after. "Life would be to him a chain of sand, while it ought to be a kind of electric chain that makes our hearts tremble and vibrate with the most ancient thoughts of the Past, as well as with the most distant hopes of the Future."

In no just sense is this an exaggeration. Deep as science and research have explored, extensive as is the field which genius and art have occupied, they have an Herculean labor yet to perform before India will have yielded up all her opulence of learning. The literature of the world in all ages has been richly furnished, if not actually inspired, from that fountain. The Wisdom of the Ancients, so much lauded in the earlier writings of Hebrews, Greeks, and Phœnicians, was abundantly represented in the lore of these Wise Men of the East.

The first Ionian sages lighted the torch of philosophy at the altar of Zoroaster. The conquest of Asia Minor by the Persians brought Thales, Anaximenes, and Herakleïtos into contact with the Eranian dogmas. The leaven thus imparted had a potent influence upon the entire mass of Grecian thought. We find it easy to trace its action upon opinions in later periods and among the newer nations. Kant, Hegel, Stewart, and Hamilton, as well as Platô, Zenô, and Aristotle, had their prototypes in the world and antiquity beyond. Even the first Zarathustra was an exponent and not the originator of the Religion and Science of Light. We are thus carried by this route back to the ancient Aryan Home for the sources from which so many golden streams have issued. In the Sanskrit books and mantras we must look for the treasures that make human souls rich. Perhaps we have been too much disposed to regard that former world as a wonderland, a repertory of folk-lore, or a theatre of gross and revolting superstition. We are now required by candor and justice to revise such notions. These primeval peoples, in their way and in a language akin to ours, adored the Father in heaven, and contemplated the future of the soul with a sure and certain hope.

Nor did they, while observing the myriads of races intervening between man and the monad, regard the world beyond as waste and void. Intelligences of every grade were believed to people the region between mortals and the Infinite. The angels and archangels, and the spirits of the just made perfect – *devas* and *pitris* they called them – ministered about the throne of the Supreme Being, and abode in the various spheres of universal space. Much of the difference between our thought and theirs consists in the names and not in the substance of our beliefs.

We may thus be prepared to receive what India can teach us. In her classic dialect, the Sanskrit, we may read with what success the children of the men who journeyed from the ancient Aryan Home into the Punjâb and Aryavartta have ventured "to look inward upon themselves, upward to something not themselves, and to see whether they could not understand a little of the true purport of that mystery which we call life upon earth." It was perfectly natural, as well as perfectly right, that as the beholder caught a glance of the Infinite Beyond, the image impressed itself upon his sensorium, as would be the case from looking at the sun, and he would as a result perceive that Infinite in all that he looked upon. Thus to the Sanskrit-speaking Aryan, as to the enlightened mind of to-day, not to see it was utter blindness. What we call science, law, morality, religion, was in his view pervaded alike throughout by this concept of Divine presence, or else it would have been less than a dream that had not come to the awaking. He was a follower of the light, not from the senses or the logical understanding, but from the eternal world. Let us not dwell on any darker shade of the picture. Clouds are dark to those who are beneath them; but on the upper side, where the sun shines, they glow with golden splendor. Let us be willing to contemplate India fraternally, and upon that side where the radiance of the Divine sheds a refulgent illumination.

–Alexander Wilder
Newark, N. J.,
May 14th, 1883

Lecture 1

What can India Teach us?

When I received from the Board of Historical Studies at Cambridge the invitation to deliver a course of lectures, specially intended for the candidates for the Indian Civil Service, I hesitated for some time, feeling extremely doubtful whether in a few public discourses I could say anything that would be of real use to them in passing their examinations. To enable young men to pass their examinations seems now to have become the chief, if not the only object of the universities; and to no class of students is it of greater importance to pass their examinations, and to pass them well, than to the candidates for the Indian Civil Service.

But although I was afraid that attendance on a few public lectures, such as I could give, would hardly benefit a candidate who was not already fully prepared to pass through the fiery ordeal of the three London examinations, I could not on the other hand shut my eyes completely to the fact that, after all, universities were not meant entirely, or even chiefly, as stepping-stones to an examination, but that there is something else which universities can teach and ought to teach – nay, which I feel quite sure they were originally meant to teach – something that may not have a marketable value

17

before a Board of Examiners, but which has a permanent value for the whole of our life, and that is a real interest in our work, and, more than that, a love of our work, and, more than that, a true joy and happiness in our work. If a university can teach that, if it can engraft that one small living germ in the minds of the young men who come here to study and to prepare themselves for the battle of life, and, for what is still more difficult to encounter, the daily dull drudgery of life, then, I feel convinced, a university has done more, and conferred a more lasting benefit on its pupils than by helping them to pass the most difficult examinations, and to take the highest place among Senior Wranglers or First-Class men.

Unfortunately, that kind of work which is now required for passing one examination after another, that process of cramming and crowding which has of late been brought to the highest pitch of perfection, has often the very opposite effect, and instead of exciting an appetite for work, it is apt to produce an indifference, if not a kind of intellectual nausea, that may last for life.

And nowhere is this so much to be feared as in the case of candidates for the Indian Civil Service. After they have passed their first examination for admission to the Indian Civil Service, and given proof that they have received the benefits of a liberal education, and acquired that general information in classics, history, and mathematics, which is provided at our public schools, and forms no doubt the best and surest foundation for all more special and professional studies in later life, they suddenly find themselves torn away from their old studies and their old friends, and compelled to take up new subjects which to many of them seem strange, outlandish, if not repulsive. Strange alphabets, strange languages, strange names, strange literatures and laws have to be faced, "to be got up" as it is called, not from choice, but from dire necessity. The whole course of study during two years is determined for them, the subjects fixed, the books prescribed, the examinations regulated, and there is no time to look either right or left, if a candidate wishes to make sure of taking each successive fence in good style, and without an accident.

I know quite well that this cannot be helped. I am not speaking against the system of examinations in general, if only they are intelligently conducted; nay, as an old examiner myself, I feel bound to say that the amount of knowledge produced ready-made at these examinations is to my mind perfectly astounding. But while the answers are there on paper, strings of dates, lists of royal names and battles, irregular verbs, statistical figures and whatever else you like, how seldom do we find that the heart of the candidates is in the work which they have to do. The results produced are certainly most ample and voluminous, but they rarely contain a spark of original thought, or even a clever mistake. It is work done from necessity, or, let us is just, from a sense of duty, but it is seldom, or hardly ever, a labor of love.

Now why should that be? Why should a study of Greek or Latin – of the poetry, the philosophy, the laws and the art of Greece and Italy – seem congenial to us, why should it excite even a certain enthusiasm, and command general respect, while a study of Sanskrit, and of the ancient poetry, the philosophy, the laws, and the art of India is looked upon, in the best case, as curious, but is considered by most people as useless, tedious, if not absurd?

And, strange to say, this feeling exists in England more than in any other country. In France, Germany, and Italy, even in Denmark, Sweden, and Russia, there is a vague charm connected with the name of India. One of the most beautiful poems in the German language is the *Weisheit der Brahmanen*, the "Wisdom of the Brahmans," by Rückert, to my mind more rich in thought and more perfect in form than even Goethe's *West-östlicher Divan*. A scholar who studies Sanskrit in Germany is supposed to be initiated in the deep and dark mysteries of ancient wisdom, and a man who has travelled in India, even if he has only discovered Calcutta, or Bombay, or Madras, is listened to like another Marco Polo. In England a student of Sanskrit is generally considered a bore, and an old Indian civil servant, if he begins to describe the marvels of Elephanta or the Towers of Silence, runs the risk of producing a count-out.

There are indeed a few Oriental scholars whose works are read, and who have acquired a certain celebrity in England, because they were really men of uncommon genius, and would have ranked among the great glories of the country, but for the misfortune that their energies were devoted to Indian literature – I mean Sir William Jones, "one of the most enlightened of the sons of men," as Dr. Johnson called him, and Thomas Colebrooke. But the names of others who have done good work in their day also, men such as Ballantyne, Buchanan, Carey, Crawfurd, Davis, Elliot, Ellis, Houghton, Leyden, Mackenzie, Marsden, Muir, Prinsep, Rennell, Turnour, Upham, Wallich, Warren, Wilkins, Wilson, and many others, are hardly known beyond the small circle of Oriental scholars; and their works are looked for in vain in libraries which profess to represent with acertain completeness the principal branches of scholarship and science in England.

How many times, when I advised young men, candidates for the Indian Civil Service, to devote themselves before all things to a study of Sanskrit, have I been told, "What is the use of our studying Sanskrit? There are translations of *Sakuntalâ*, Manu, and the *Hitopadesa*, and what else is there in that literature that is worth reading? *Kâlidâsa* may be very pretty, and the Laws of Manu are very curious, and the fables of the *Hitopadesa* are very quaint; but you would not compare Sanskrit literature with Greek, or recommend us to waste our time in copying and editing Sanskrit texts which either teach us nothing that we do not know already, or teach us something which we do not care to know?"

This seems to me a most unhappy misconception, and it will be the chief object of my lectures to try to remove it, or at all events to modify it, as much as possible. I shall not attempt to prove that Sanskrit literature is as good as Greek literature. Why should we always compare? A study of Greek literature has its own purpose, and a study of Sanskrit literature has its own purpose; but what I feel

convinced of, and hope to convince you of, is that Sanskrit literature, if studied only in a right spirit, is full of human interests, full
of lessons which even Greek could never teach us, a subject worthy
to occupy the leisure, and more than the leisure, of every Indian
civil servant; and certainly the best means of making any young
man who has to spend five-and-twenty years of his life in India,
feel at home among the Indians, as a fellow-worker among
fellow-workers, and not as an alien among aliens. There will be
abundance of useful and most interesting work for him to do, if
only he cares to do it, work such as he would look for in vain,
whether in Italy or in Greece, or even among the pyramids of
Egypt or the palaces of Babylon.

You will now understand why I have chosen as the title of my
lectures, "What can India teach us?" True, there are many things
which India has to learn from us; but there are other things, and,
in one sense, very important things, which we too may learn
from India.

If I were to look over the whole world to find out the country
most richly endowed with all the wealth, power, and beauty that
nature can bestow – in some parts a very paradise on earth – I
should point to India. If I were asked under what sky the human
mind has most full developed some of its choicest gifts, has most
deeply pondered on the greatest problems of life, and has found
solutions of some of them which well deserve the attention even of
those who have studied Plato and Kant – I should point to India.
And if I were to ask myself from what literature we, here in Europe,
we who have been nurtured almost exclusively on the thoughts of
Greeks and Romans, and of one Semitic race, the Jewish, may draw
that corrective which is most wanted in order to make our inner life
more perfect, more comprehensive, more universal, in fact more
truly human, a life, not for this life only, but a transfigured and
eternal life – again I should point to India.

I know you will be surprised to hear me say this. I know that more
particularly those who have spent many years of active life in Calcutta,

or Bombay, or Madras, will be horror-struck at the idea that the humanity they meet with there, whether in the bazaars or in the courts of justice, or in so-called native society, should be able to teach *us* any lessons.

Let me therefore explain at once to my friends who may have lived in India for years, as civil servants, or officers, or missionaries, or merchants, and who ought to know a great deal more of that country than one who has never set foot on the soil of Âryâvarta, that we are speaking of two very different Indias. I am thinking chiefly of India such as it was a thousand, two thousand, it may be three thousand years ago; they think of the India of to-day. And again, when thinking of the India of to-day, they remember chiefly the India of Calcutta, Bombay, or Madras, the India of the towns. I look to the India of the village communities, the true India of the Indians.

What I wish to show to you, I mean more especially the candidates for the Indian Civil Service, is that this India of a thousand, or two thousand, or three thousand years ago, ay the India of to-day also, if only you know where to look for it, is full of problems, the solution of which concerns all of us, even us in this Europe of the nineteenth century.

If you have acquired any special tastes here in England, you will find plenty to satisfy them in India; and whoever has learned to take an interest in any of the great problems that occupy the best thinkers and workers at home, need certainly not be afraid of India proving to him an intellectual exile.

If you care for geology, there is work for you from the Himalayas to Ceylon.

If you are fond of botany, there is a flora rich enough for many Hookers.

If you are a zoologist, think of Haeckel, who is just now rushing through Indian forests and dredging in Indian seas, and to whom his stay in India is like the realization of the brightest dream of his life.

If you are interested in ethnology, why India is like a living ethnological museum.

If you are fond of archæology, if you have ever assisted at the opening of a barrow in England, and know the delight of finding a fibula, or a knife, or a flint in a heap of rubbish, read only General Cunningham's "Annual Reports of the Archæological Survey of India," and you will be impatient for the time when you can take your spade and bring to light the ancient Vihâras or colleges built by the Buddhist monarchs of India.

If ever you amused yourselves with collecting coins, why the soil of India teems with coins, Persian, Carian, Thracian, Parthian, Greek, Macedonian, Scythian, Roman,[1] and Mohammedan. When Warren Hastings was Governor-General, an earthen pot was found on the bank of a river in the province of Benares, containing one hundred and seventy-two gold darics.[2] Warren Hastings considered himself as making the most munificent present to his masters that he might ever have it in his power to send them, by presenting those ancient coins to the Court of Directors. The story is that they were sent to the melting-pot. At all events they had disappeared when Warren Hastings returned to England. It rests with you to prevent the revival of such vandalism.

In one of the last numbers of the *Asiatic Journal of Bengal* you may read of the discovery of a treasure as rich in gold almost as some of the tombs opened by Dr. Schliemann at Mykenæ, nay, I should add, perhaps, not quite unconnected with some of the treasures found at Mykenæ; yet hardly anyone has taken notice of it in England![3]

---

1. Pliny (VI. 26) tells us that in his day the annual drain of bullion into India, in return for her valuable produce, reached the immense amount of "five hundred and fifty millions of sesterces." See E. Thomas, "The Indian Balhará," p. 13.

2. Cunningham, in the "Journal of the Asiatic Society of Bengal," 1881, p. 184.

3. General Cunningham describes this treasure in the "Journal of the Asiatic Society of Bengal" as having been found on the northern bank of the Oxus in 1877, and containing coins from Darius down to Antiochus the Great, and Euthydemus, King of Baktria. This would seem to indicate that it had

The study of Mythology has assumed an entirely new character, chiefly owing to the light that has been thrown on it by the ancient Vedic Mythology of India. But though the foundation of a true Science of Mythology has been laid, all the detail has still to be worked out, and could be worked out nowhere better than in India. Even the study of fables owes its new life to India, from whence the various migrations of fables have been traced at various times and through various channels from East to West.[1] Buddhism is now known to have been the principal source of our legends and parables. But here, too, many problems still wait for their solution. Think, for instance, of the allusion to the fable of the donkey in the lion's skin, which occurs in Plato's Cratylus.[2] Was that borrowed from the East? Or take the fable of the weasel changed by Aphroditê into a woman who, when she saw a mouse, could not refrain from making a spring at it. This, too, is very like a Sanskrit fable; but how then could it have been brought into Greece early enough

---

been buried there in 208 B.C., when Baktria was invaded by Antiochus and Euthydemus defeated. The coins, figures, and ornaments, many of them, were manifestly Persian, and doubtless had been brought into that country and kept by the victorious generals of Alexander. Some of the works of art unearthed by Dr. Schliemann at Mykenæ are either Persian or Assyrian in character, and are like those found on the Oxus. Professor Forchhammer very plausibly supposes that they were spoils from the Persian camp which had been awarded to Mykenæ as her share after the overthrow of Mardonius.—A. W.

1. See "Selected Essays," vol. i., p. 500, "The Migration of Fables."
2. Cratylus, 411 A. "Still, as I have put on the lion's skin, I must not be faint-hearted." Possibly, however, this may refer to Hercules, and not to the fable of the donkey in the lion's or the tiger's skin. In the Hitopadesa, a donkey, being nearly starved, is sent by his master into a corn-field to feed. In order to shield him he puts a tiger's skin on him. All goes well till a watchman approaches, hiding himself under his gray coat, and trying to shoot the tiger. The donkey thinks it is a gray female donkey, begins to bray, and is killed. On a similar fable in Æsop, see Benfey, "Pantschatantra," vol. i., p. 463; M. M., "Selected Essays," vol. i., p. 513.

to appear in one of the comedies of Strattis, about 400 B.C.?[1] Here, too, there is still plenty of work to do.

We may go back even farther into antiquity, and still find strange coincidences between the legends of India and the legends of the West, without as yet being able to say how they travelled, whether from East to West, or from West to East. That at the time of Solomon there was a channel of communication open between India and Syria and Palestine is established beyond doubt, I believe, by certain Sanskrit words which occur in the Bible as names of articles of export from Ophir, articles such as ivory, apes, peacocks, and sandalwood, which, taken together, could not have been exported from any country but India.[2] Nor is there any reason to suppose that the commercial intercourse between India, the Persian Gulf, the Red Sea and the Mediterranean was ever completely interrupted, even at the time when the Book of Kings is supposed to have been written.

Now you remember the judgment of Solomon, which has always been admired as a proof of great legal wisdom among the Jews.[3] I must confess that, not having a legal mind, I never could suppress a certain shudder[4] when reading the decision of Solomon: "Divide the living child in two, and give half to the one, and half to the other."

Let me now tell you the same story as it is told by the Buddhists, whose sacred Canon is full of such legends and parables. In the Kanjur,

---

1. See "Fragmenta Comic" (Didot), p. 302; Benfey, l. c. vol. i., p. 374.
2. "Lectures on the Science of Language," vol. i., p. 231.
   The names employed in the Hebrew text of the Bible are said to be Tamil.—A. W.
3. 1 Kings 3:25.
4. The Bible story is dramatic; the other is not. The "shudder" is a tribute to the dramatic power of the Bible narrative. The child was in no danger of being cut in twain. In the Buddhist version the child *is* injured. Why does not Prof. Müller shudder when the child is hurt and cries? The Solomonic child is not hurt and does not cry. Is not the Bible story the more humane, the more dignified, the more dramatic? And no canon of criticism requires us to believe that a poor version of a story is the more primitive.—AM. PUBS.

which is the Tibetan translation of the Buddhist Tripitaka, we likewise read of two women who claimed each to be the mother of the
same child. The king, after listening to their quarrels for a long
time, gave it up as hopeless to settle who was the real mother. Upon
this Visâkhâ stepped forward and said: "What is the use of examin-
ing and cross-examining these women? Let them take the boy and
settle it among themselves." Thereupon both women fell on the
child, and when the fight became violent the child was hurt and
began to cry. Then one of them let him go, because she could not
bear to hear the child cry.

That settled the question. The king gave the child to the true
mother, and had the other beaten with a rod.

This seems to me, if not the more primitive, yet the more
natural form of the story – showing a deeper knowledge of human
nature and more wisdom than even the wisdom of Solomon.[1]

Many of you may have studied not only languages, but also the
Science of Language, and is there any country in which some of
the most important problems of that science, say only the growth
and decay of dialects, or the possible mixture of languages, with
regard not only to words, but to grammatical elements also, can be
studied to greater advantage than among the Aryan, the Dravidian,
and the Munda inhabitants of India, when brought in contact with
their various invaders and conquerors, the Greeks, the Yue-tchi, the
Arabs, the Persians, the Moguls, and lastly the English?

Again, if you are a student of Jurisprudence, there is a history of
law to be explored in India, very different from what is known of
the history of law in Greece, in Rome, and in Germany, yet both
by its contrasts and by its similarities full of suggestions to the
student of Comparative Jurisprudence. New materials are being

---

1. See some excellent remarks on this subject in Rhys Davids, "Buddhist
   Birth-Stories," vol. i., pp. xiii. and xliv. The learned scholar gives another
   version of the story from a Singhalese translation of the Gâtaka, dating from
   the fourteenth century, and he expresses a hope that Dr. Fausböll will soon
   publish the Pâli original.

discovered every year, as, for instance, the so-called Dharma or Samayâkârika Sûtras, which have supplied the materials for the later metrical law-books, such as the famous Laws of Manu. What was once called "The Code of Laws of Manu," and confidently referred to 1200, or at least 500 B.C., is now hesitatingly referred to perhaps the fourth century A.D., and called neither a Code, nor a Code of Laws, least of all, the Code of Laws of Manu.

If you have learned to appreciate the value of recent researches into the antecedents of all law, namely the foundation and growth of the simplest political communities – and nowhere could you have had better opportunities for it than here at Cambridge – you will find a field of observation opened before you in the still-existing village estates in India that will amply repay careful research.

And take that which, after all, whether we confess or deny it, we care for more in this life than for anything else – nay, which is often far more cared for by those who deny than by those who confess – take that which supports, pervades, and directs all our acts and thoughts and hopes – without which there can be neither village-community nor empire, neither custom nor law, neither right nor wrong – take that which, next to language, has most firmly fixed the specific and permanent barrier between man and beast – which alone has made life possible and bearable, and which, as it is the deepest, though often-hidden spring of individual life, is also the foundation of all national life – the history of all histories, and yet the mystery of all mysteries – take religion, and where can you study its true origin,[1] its natural growth, and it's inevitable decay better than in India, the home of Brahmanism, the birthplace of Buddhism, and the refuge of Zoroastrianism, even now the mother of new superstitions – and why not, in the future, the regenerate child of the purest faith, if only purified from the dust of nineteen centuries?

---

1. This is true of what theologians call natural religion, which is assumed to be a growth out of human consciousness; but the Christian religion is not a natural religion.—AM. PUBS.

You will find yourselves everywhere in India between an immense past and an immense future, with opportunities such as the old world could but seldom, if ever, offer you. Take any of the burning questions of the day – popular education, higher education, parliamentary representation, codification of laws, finance, emigration, poor-law; and whether you have anything to teach and to try, or anything to observe and to learn, India will supply you with a laboratory such as exists nowhere else. That very Sanskrit, the study of which may at first seem so tedious to you and so useless, if only you will carry it on, as you may carry it on here at Cambridge better than anywhere else, will open before you large layers of literature, as yet almost unknown and unexplored, and allow you an insight into strata of thought deeper than any you have known before, and rich in lessons that appeal to the deepest sympathies of the human heart.

Depend upon it, if only you can make leisure, you will find plenty of work in India for your leisure hours.

India is not, as you may imagine, a distant, strange, or, at the very utmost, a curious country. India for the future belongs to Europe, it has its place in the Indo-European world, it has its place in our own history, and in what is the very life of history, the history of the human mind.

You know how some of the best talent and the noblest genius of our age has been devoted to the study of the development of the outward or material world, the growth of the earth, the first appearance of living cells, their combination and differentiation, leading up to the beginning of organic life, and its steady progress from the lowest to the highest stages. Is there not an inward and intellectual world also which has to be studied in its historical development, from the first appearance of predicative and demonstrative roots, their combination and differentiation, leading up to the beginning of rational thought in its steady progress from the lowest to the highest stages? And in that study of the history of the human mind, in that study of ourselves, of our true selves, India occupies a place second to no other country. Whatever sphere of the human mind you may select for your special study, whether it be language, or religion, or mythology, or philosophy, whether it be laws or customs, primitive art or primitive science, everywhere, you have to go to India, whether you like it or not, because some of the most valuable and most instructive materials in the history of man are treasured up in India, and in India only.

And while thus trying to explain to those whose lot will soon be cast in India the true position which that wonderful country holds or ought to hold in universal history, I may perhaps be able at the same time to appeal to the sympathies of other members of this University, by showing them how imperfect our knowledge of universal history, our insight into the development of the human intellect, must always remain, if we narrow our horizon to the history of Greeks and Romans, Saxons and Celts, with a dim background of Palestine, Egypt, and Babylon,[1] and leave out of sight our nearest intellectual relatives, the Aryans of India, the framers of the most wonderful language, the Sanskrit, the fellow-workers in the construction of our fundamental concepts, the fathers of the most natural of natural religions, the makers of the most transparent of mythologies, the inventors of the most subtle philosophy, and the givers of the most elaborate laws.

There are many things which we think essential in a liberal education, whole chapters of history which we teach in our schools and universities, that cannot for one moment compare with the chapter relating to India, if only properly understood and freely interpreted.

In our time, when the study of history threatens to become almost an impossibility – such is the mass of details which historians collect in archives and pour out before us in monographs – it seems to me more than ever the duty of the true historian to find out the real proportion of things, to arrange his materials according

---

1. There are traces of Aryan occupation at Babylon, Rawlinson assures us, about twenty centuries B.C. This would suggest a possible interchange of religious ideas between the earlier Aryan and Akkado-Chaldean peoples.—A. W.

to the strictest rules of artistic perspective, and to keep completely
out of sight all that may be rightly ignored by us in our own passage
across the historical stage of the world. It is this power of discover-
ing what is really important that distinguishes the true historian
from the mere chronicler, in whose eyes everything is important,
particularly if he has discovered it himself. I think it was Frederick
the Great who, when sighing for a true historian of his reign,
complained bitterly that those who wrote the history of Prussia
never forgot to describe the buttons on his uniform. And it is probably of such historical works that Carlyle was thinking when he said
that he had waded through them all, but that nothing should ever
induce him to hand even their names and titles down to posterity.
And yet how much is there even in Carlyle's histories that might
safely be consigned to oblivion!

Why do we want to know history? Why does history form a
recognized part of our liberal education? Simply because all of us,
and every one of us, ought to know how we have come to be what
we are, so that each generation need not start again from the same
point and toil over the same ground, but, profiting by the experience of those who came before, may advance toward higher points
and nobler aims. As a child when growing up might ask his father
or grandfather *who* had built the house they lived in, or who had
cleared the field that yielded them their food, we ask the historian
whence we came, and how we came into possession of what we call
our own. History may tell us afterward many useful and amusing
things, gossip, such as a child might like to hear from his mother or
grandmother; but what history has to teach us before all and everything, is our own antecedents, our own ancestors, our own descent.

Now our principal intellectual ancestors are, no doubt, the *Jews*,
the *Greeks*, the *Romans*, and the *Saxons*, and we, here in Europe,
should not call a man educated or enlightened who was ignorant
of the debt which he owes to his intellectual ancestors in Palestine,
Greece, Rome, and Germany. The whole past history of the world
would be darkness to him, and not knowing what those who came

before him had done for him, he would probably care little to do anything for those who are to come after him. Life would be to him a chain of sand, while it ought to be a kind of electric chain that makes our hearts tremble and vibrate with the most ancient thoughts of the past, as well as with the most distant hopes of the future.

Let us begin with our religion. No one can understand even the historical possibility of the Christian religion without knowing something of the Jewish race, which must be studied chiefly in the pages of the Old Testament. And in order to appreciate the true relation of the Jews to the rest of the ancient world, and to understand what ideas were peculiarly their own, and what ideas they shared in common with the other members of the Semitic stock, or what moral and religious impulses they received from their historical contact with other nations of antiquity, it is absolutely necessary that we should pay some attention to the history of Babylon, Nineveh, Phœnicia, and Persia. These may seem distant countries and forgotten people, and many might feel inclined to say, "Let the dead bury their dead; what are those mummies to us?" Still, such is the marvellous continuity of history, that I could easily show you many things which we, even we who are here assembled, owe to Babylon, to Nineveh, to Egypt, Phœnicia, and Persia.

Everyone who carries a watch owes to the Babylonians the division of the hour into sixty minutes. It may be a very bad division, yet such as it is, it has come to us from the Greeks and Romans, and it came to them from Babylon. The sexagesimal division is peculiarly Babylonian. Hipparchos, 150 B.C., adopted it from Babylon, Ptolemy, 150 A.D., gave it wider currency, and the French, when they decimated everything else, respected the dial-plates of our watches, and left them with their sixty Babylonian minutes.

Everyone who writes a letter owes his alphabet to the Romans and Greeks; the Greeks owed their alphabet to the Phœnicians, and the Phœnicians learned it in Egypt. It may be a very imperfect alphabet – as all the students of phonetics will tell you – yet, such as it is and has been, we owe it to the old Phœnicians and Egyptians, and in every letter we trace, there lies imbedded the mummy of an ancient Egyptian hieroglyphic.

What do we owe to the Persians? It does not seem to be much, for they were not a very inventive race, and what they knew they had chiefly learned from their neighbors, the Babylonians and Assyrians. Still, we owe them something. First of all, we owe them a large debt of gratitude for having allowed themselves to be beaten by the Greeks; for think what the world would have been if the Persians had beaten the Greeks at Marathon, and had enslaved – that means, annihilated – the genius of ancient Greece. However, this may be called rather an involuntary contribution to the progress of humanity, and I mention it only in order to show how narrowly, not only Greeks and Romans, but Saxons and Anglo-Saxons too, escaped becoming Parsis or Fire-worshippers.

But I can mention at least one voluntary gift which came to us from Persia, and that is the relation of silver to gold in our bi-metallic currency. That relation was, no doubt, first determined in Babylonia, but it assumed its practical and historical importance in the Persian empire, and spread from there to the Greek colonies in Asia, and thence to Europe, where it has maintained itself with slight variation to the present day.

A *talent*[1] was divided into sixty *minæ*, a mina into sixty *shekels*. Here we have again the Babylonian sexagesimal system, a system which owes its origin and popularity, I believe, to the fact that *sixty* has the greatest number of divisors. Shekel was translated into Greek by *Stater*, and an Athenian gold stater, like the Persian gold stater, down to the times of Crœsus, Darius, and Alexander, was the sixtieth part of a mina of gold, not very far therefore from our sovereign. The proportion of silver to gold was fixed as thirteen or thirteen and a third to one; and if the weight of a silver shekel was made as thirteen to ten, such a coin would correspond very

---

1. See Cunningham, "Journal of the Asiatic Society of Bengal," 1881, pp. 162-168.

nearly to our florin.[1] Half a silver shekel was a *drachma*, and this was therefore the true ancestor of our shilling.

Again you may say that any attempt at fixing the relative value of silver and gold is, and always has been, a great mistake. Still it shows how closely the world is held together, and how, for good or for evil, we are what we are, not so much by ourselves as by the toil and moil of those who came before us, our true intellectual ancestors, whatever the blood may have been composed of that ran through their veins, or the bones which formed the rafters of their skulls.

And if it is true, with regard to religion, that no one could understand it and appreciate its full purport without knowing its origin and growth, that is, without knowing something of what the cuneiform inscriptions of Mesopotamia, the hieroglyphic and hieratic texts of Egypt, and the historical monuments of Phœnicia and Persia can alone reveal to us, it is equally true with regard to all the other elements that constitute the whole of our intellectual life. If we are Jewish or Semitic in our religion, we are *Greek* in our philosophy, *Roman* in our politics, and *Saxon* in our morality; and it follows that a knowledge of the history of the Greeks, Romans, and Saxons, or of the flow of civilization from Greece to Italy, and through Germany to these isles, forms an essential element in what is called a liberal, that is, an historical and rational education.

But then it might be said, Let this be enough. Let us know by all means all that deserves to be known about our real spiritual ancestors in the great historical kingdoms of the world; let us be grateful for all we have inherited from Egyptians, Babylonians, Phœnicians, Jews, Greeks, Romans, and Saxons. But why bring in India? Why add a new burden to what every man has to bear already, before he can call himself fairly educated? What have we inherited from the dark dwellers on the Indus and the Ganges,

---

1. *Sim*, the Persian word for silver, has also the meaning of one thirteenth; see Cunningham, l. c. p. 165.

that we should have to add their royal names and dates and deeds to the archives of our already overburdened memory? There is some justice in this complaint. The ancient inhabitants of India are not our intellectual ancestors in the same direct way as Jews, Greeks, Romans, and Saxons are; but they represent, nevertheless, a collateral branch of that family to which we belong by language, that is, by thought, and their historical records extend in some respects so far beyond all other records and have been preserved to us in such perfect and such legible documents, that we can learn from them lessons which we can learn nowhere else, and supply missing links in our intellectual ancestry far more important than that missing link (which we can well afford to miss), the link between Ape and Man.

I am not speaking as yet of the literature of India as it is, but of something far more ancient, the language of India, or Sanskrit. No one supposes any longer that Sanskrit was the common source of Greek, Latin, and Anglo-Saxon. This used to be said, but it has long been shown that Sanskrit is only a collateral branch of the same stem from which spring Greek, Latin, and Anglo-Saxon; and not only these, but all the Teutonic, all the Celtic, all the Slavonic languages, nay, the languages of Persia and Armenia also.

What, then, is it that gives to Sanskrit its claim on our attention, and its supreme importance in the eyes of the historian?

First of all, its antiquity – for we know Sanskrit at an earlier period than Greek. But what is far more important than its merely chronological antiquity is the antique state of preservation in which that Aryan language has been handed down to us. The world had known Latin and Greek for centuries, and it was felt, no doubt, that there was some kind of similarity between the two. But how was that similarity to be explained? Sometimes Latin was supposed to give the key to the formation of a Greek word, sometimes Greek seemed to betray the secret of the origin of a Latin word. Afterward, when the ancient Teutonic languages, such as Gothic and Anglo-Saxon, and the ancient Celtic and Slavonic languages too, came to be studied, no one could help seeing a certain family likeness among them all. But how such a likeness between these languages came to be, and how, what is far more difficult to explain, such striking differences too between these languages came to be, remained a mystery, and gave rise to the most gratuitous theories, most of them, as you know, devoid of all scientific foundation. As soon, however, as Sanskrit stepped into the midst of these languages, there came light and warmth and mutual recognition. They all ceased to be strangers, and each fell of its own accord into its right place. Sanskrit was the eldest sister of them all, and could tell of many things which the other members of the family had quite forgotten. Still, the other languages too had each their own tale to tell; and it is out of all their tales together that a chapter in the human mind has been put together which, in some respects, is more important to us than any of the other chapters, the Jewish, the Greek, the Latin, or the Saxon.

The process by which that ancient chapter of history was recovered is very simple. Take the words which occur in the same form and with the same meaning in all the seven branches of the Aryan family, and you have in them the most genuine and trustworthy records in which to read the thoughts of our true ancestors, before they had become Hindus, or Persians, or Greeks, or Romans, or Celts, or Teutons, or Slaves. Of course, some of these ancient charters may have been lost in one or other of these seven branches of the Aryan family, but even then, if they are found in six, or five, or four, or three, or even two only of its original branches, the probability remains, unless we can prove a later historical contact between these languages, that these words existed before the great *Aryan Separation*. If we find *agni*, meaning fire, in Sanskrit, and *ignis*, meaning fire, in Latin, we may safely conclude that *fire* was known to the undivided Aryans, even if no trace of the same name of fire occurred anywhere else. And why? Because there is no indication that Latin remained longer united with Sanskrit than any of the other Aryan languages, or that Latin could have borrowed such a word from Sanskrit, after these two languages had once become distinct. We have, however, the Lithuanian *ugnis*, and the Scottish *ingle*, to show that the Slavonic and possibly the Teutonic languages also, knew the same word for fire, though they replaced it in time by other words. Words, like all other things, will die, and why they should live on in one soil and wither away and perish in another, is not always easy to say. What has become of *ignis*, for instance, in all the Romance languages? It has withered away and perished, probably because, after losing its final unaccentuated syllable, it became awkward to pronounce; and another word, *focus*, which in Latin meant fireplace, hearth, altar, has taken its place.

Suppose we wanted to know whether the ancient Aryans before their separation knew the mouse: we should only have to consult the principal Aryan dictionaries, and we should find in Sanskrit *mûsh*, in Greek μῦς, in Latin *mus*, in Old Slavonic *mȳše*, in Old High German *mûs*, enabling us to say that, at a time so distant from us that we feel inclined to measure it by Indian rather than by our own chronology, the mouse was known, that is, was named, was conceived and recognized as a species of its own, not to be confounded with any other vermin.

And if we were to ask whether the enemy of the mouse, the *cat*, was known at the same distant time, we should feel justified in saying decidedly, No. The cat is called in Sanskrit mârgâra and vidâla. In Greek and Latin the words usually given as names of the cat, γαλέη and αἴλουρος, *mustella* and *feles*, did not originally signify the tame cat, but the weasel or marten. The name for the real cat in Greek was κάττα, in Latin *catus*, and these words have supplied the names for cat in all the Teutonic, Slavonic, and Celtic languages. The animal itself, so far as we know at present, came to Europe from Egypt, where it had been worshipped for centuries and tamed; and as this arrival probably dates from the fourth century A.D., we can well understand that no common name for it could have existed when the Aryan nations separated.[1]

---

1. The common domestic cat is first mentioned by Cæsarius, the physician, brother of Gregory of Nazianus, about the middle of the fourth century. It came from Egypt, where it was regarded as sacred. Herodotus denominates it

In this way a more or less complete picture of the state of civilization, previous to the Aryan Separation, can be and has been reconstructed, like a mosaic put together with the fragments of ancient stones; and I doubt whether, in tracing the history of the human mind, we shall ever reach to a lower stratum than that which is revealed to us by the converging rays of the different Aryan languages.

Nor is that all; for even that Proto-Aryan language, as it has been reconstructed from the ruins scattered about in India, Greece, Italy, and Germany, is clearly the result of a long, long process of thought. One shrinks from chronological limitations when looking into such distant periods of life. But if we find Sanskrit as a perfect literary language, totally different from Greek and Latin, 1500 B.C., where can those streams of Sanskrit, Greek, and Latin meet, as we trace them back to their common source? And then, when we have followed these mighty national streams back to their common meeting-point, even then that common language looks like a rock washed down and smoothed for ages by the ebb and flow of thought. We find in that language such a compound, for instance, as *asmi*, I am, Greek μ . What would other languages give for such a pure concept as *I am*? They may say, *I stand*, or *I live*, or *I grow*, or *I turn*, but it is given to few languages only to be able to say *I am*. To us nothing seems more natural than the auxiliary verb *I am*; but, in reality, no work of art has required greater efforts than this little word *I am*. And all those efforts lie beneath the level of the common Proto-Aryan speech. Many different ways were open, were tried, too, in order to arrive at such a compound as *asmi*, and such a concept as *I am*. But all were given up, and this one alone remained, and was preserved forever in all the languages and all the dialects of the Aryan family. In *as-mi*, *as* is the root, and in the compound *as-mi*,

---

αἴλουρος, which was also the designation of the weasel and marten. Kallimachus employs the same title, which his commentator explains as κάττος. In later times this name of uncertain etymology has superseded every other. The earlier Sanskrit writers appear to have had no knowledge of the animal; but the margara is named by Manu, and the vidala by Panini.—A. W.

the predicative root *as*, to be, is predicated of *mi*, I. But no language could ever produce at once so empty, or, if you like, so general a root as *as*, to be. *As* meant originally *to breathe*, and from it we have *asu*, breath, spirit, life, also *âs* the mouth, Latin *ôs*, *ôris*. By constant wear and tear this root *as*, to breathe, had first to lose all signs of its original material character, before it could convey that purely abstract meaning of existence, without any qualification, which has rendered to the higher operations of thought the same service which the nought, likewise the invention of Indian genius, has to render in arithmetic. Who will say how long the friction lasted which changed *as*, to breathe, into *as*, to be? And even a root *as*, to breathe, was an Aryan root, not Semitic, not Turanian. It possessed an historical individuality – it was the work of our forefathers, and represents a thread which unites us in our thoughts and words with those who first thought for us, with those who first spoke for us, and whose thoughts and words men are still thinking and speaking, though divided from them by thousands, it may be by hundreds of thousands of years.

This is what I call *history* in the true sense of the word, something really worth knowing, far more so than the scandals of courts, or the butcheries of nations, which fill so many pages of our Manuals of History. And all this work is only beginning, and whoever likes to labor in these the most ancient of historical archives will find plenty of discoveries to make – and yet people ask, What is the use of learning Sanskrit?

We get accustomed to everything, and cease to wonder at what would have startled our fathers and upset all their stratified notions, like a sudden earthquake. Every child now learns at school that English is an Aryan or Indo-European language, that it belongs to the Teutonic branch, and that this branch, together with the Italic, Greek, Celtic, Slavonic, Iranic, and Indic branches, all spring from the same stock, and form together the great Aryan or Indo-European family of speech.

But this, though it is taught now in our elementary schools, was really, but fifty years ago, like the opening of a new horizon of the world of the intellect, and the extension of a feeling of closest fraternity that made us feel at home where before we had been strangers, and changed millions of so-called barbarians into our own kith and kin. To speak the same language constitutes a closer union than to have drunk the same milk; and Sanskrit, the ancient language of India, is substantially the same language as Greek, Latin, and Anglo-Saxon. This is a lesson which we should never have learned but from a study of Indian language and literature, and if India had taught us nothing else, it would have taught us more than almost any other language ever did.

It is quite amusing, though instructive also, to read what was written by scholars and philosophers when this new light first dawned on the world. They would not have it, they would not believe that there could be any community of origin between the people of Athens and Rome, and the so-called Niggers of India. The classical scholar scouted the idea, and I myself still remember the time, when I was a student at Leipzig, and began to study Sanskrit, with what contempt any remarks on Sanskrit or comparative grammar were treated by my teachers, men such as Gottfried Hermann, Haupt, Westermann, Stallbaum, and others. No one ever was for a time so completely laughed down as Professor Bopp, when he first published his Comparative Grammar of Sanskrit, Zend, Greek, Latin, and Gothic. All hands were against him; and if in comparing Greek and Latin with Sanskrit, Gothic, Celtic, Slavonic, or Persian, he happened to have placed one single accent wrong, the shouts of those who knew nothing but Greek and Latin, and probably looked in their Greek dictionaries to be quite sure of their accents, would never end. Dugald Stewart, rather than admit a relationship between Hindus and Scots, would rather believe that the whole Sanskrit language and the whole of Sanskrit literature – mind, a literature extending over three thousand years and larger than the ancient literature of either Greece or Rome – was a forgery of those wily priests, the Brahmans. I remember too how, when I was at school at Leipzig (and a very good school it was, with such masters as Nobbe, Forbiger, Funkhaenel, and Palm – an old school too, which could boast of Leibnitz among its former pupils) I remember, I say, one of our masters (Dr. Klee) telling us one afternoon, when it was too hot to do any serious work, that there was a language spoken in India, which was much the same as Greek and Latin, nay, as German and Russian. At first we thought it was a joke, but when one saw the parallel columns of numerals, pronouns, and verbs in Sanskrit, Greek, and Latin written on the blackboard, one felt in the presence of facts, before which one had to bow. All one's ideas of Adam and Eve, and the Paradise, and the tower of Babel, and Shem, Ham, and Japhet, with Homer and Æneas and Virgil too, seemed to be whirling round and round, till at last one picked up the fragments and tried to build up a new world, and to live with a new historical consciousness.

Here you will see why I consider a certain knowledge of India an essential portion of a liberal or an historical education. The concept of the European man has been changed and widely extended by our acquaintance with India, and we know now that we are something different from what we thought we were. Suppose the Americans, owing to some cataclysmal events, had forgotten their English origin, and after two or three thousand years found themselves in possession of a language and of ideas which they could trace back historically to a certain date, but which, at that date, seemed, as it were, fallen from the sky, without any explanation of their origin and previous growth, what would they say if suddenly the existence of an English language and literature were revealed to them, such as they existed in the eighteenth century – explaining all that seemed before almost miraculous, and solving almost every question that could be asked? Well, this is much the same as what the discovery of Sanskrit has done for us. It has added a new period to our historical consciousness, and revived the recollections of our childhood, which seemed to have vanished forever.

Whatever else we may have been, it is quite clear now that, many thousands of years ago, we were something that had not yet developed into an Englishman, or a Saxon, or a Greek, or a Hindu either, yet contained in itself the germs of all these characters. A strange being, you may say. Yes, but for all that a very real being, and an ancestor too of whom we must learn to be proud, far more than of any such modern ancestors, as Normans, Saxons, Celts, and all the rest.

And this is not all yet that a study of Sanskrit and the other Aryan languages has done for us. It has not only widened our views of man, and taught us to embrace millions of strangers and barbarians as members of one family, but it has imparted to the whole ancient history of man a reality which it never possessed before.

We speak and write a great deal about antiquities, and if we can lay hold of a Greek statue or an Egyptian Sphinx or a Babylonian Bull, our heart rejoices, and we build museums grander than any royal palaces to receive the treasures of the past. This is quite right. But are you aware that every one of us possesses what may be called the richest and most wonderful Museum of Antiquities, older than any statues, sphinxes, or bulls? And where? Why, in our own language. When I use such words as *father* or *mother*, *heart* or *tear*, *one, two, three, here* and *there*, I am handling coins or counters that were current before there was one single Greek statue, one single Babylonian Bull, one single Egyptian Sphinx. Yes, each of us carries about with him the richest and most wonderful Museum of Antiquities; and if he only knows how to treat those treasures, how to rub and polish them till they become translucent again, how to arrange them and read them, they will tell him marvels more marvellous than all hieroglyphics and cuneiform inscriptions put together. The stories they have told us are beginning to be old stories now. Many of you have heard them before. But do not let them cease to be marvels, like so many things which cease to be marvels because they happen every day. And do not think that there is nothing left for you to do. There are more marvels still to be discovered in language than have ever been revealed to us; nay, there is no word, however common, if only you know how to take it to pieces, like a cunningly contrived work of art, fitted together thousands of years ago by the most cunning of artists, the human mind, that will not make you listen and marvel more than any chapter of the Arabian Nights.

But I must not allow myself to be carried away from my proper subject. All I wish to impress on you by way of introduction is that the results of the Science of Language, which, without the aid of Sanskrit, would never have been obtained, form an essential element of what we call a liberal, that is an historical education – an education which will enable a man to do what the French call *s'orienter*, that is, "to find his East," "his true East," and thus to determine his real place in the world; to know, in fact, the port whence man started, the course he has followed, and the port toward which he has to steer.

We all come from the East – all that we value most has come to us from the East, and in going to the East, not only those who have received a special Oriental training, but everybody who has enjoyed the advantages of a liberal, that is, of a truly historical education, ought to feel that he is going to his "old home," full of memories, if only he can read them. Instead of feeling your hearts sink within you, when next year you approach the shores of India, I wish that every one of you could feel what Sir William Jones felt, when, just one hundred years ago, he came to the end of his long voyage from England, and saw the shores of India rising on the horizon. At that time, young men going to the wonderland of India were not ashamed of dreaming dreams and seeing visions; and this was the dream dreamed and the vision seen by Sir William Jones, then simple Mr. Jones:

> "When I was at sea last August (that is in August, 1783), on my last voyage to this country (India) I had long and ardently desired· to visit, I found one evening, on inspecting the observations of the day, that *India* lay before us, *Persia* on our left, while a breeze from *Arabia* blew nearly on our stern.

A situation so pleasing in itself and to me so new, could not fail to awaken a train of reflections in a mind which had early been accustomed to contemplate with delight the eventful histories and agreeable fictions of this Eastern world. It gave me inexpressible pleasure to find myself in the midst of so noble an amphitheatre, almost encircled by the vast regions of Asia, which has ever been esteemed the nurse of sciences, the inventress of delightful and useful arts, the scene of glorious actions, fertile in the productions of human genius, and infinitely diversified in the forms of religion and government, in the laws, manners, customs, and languages, as well as in the features and complexions of men. I could not help remarking how important and extensive a field was yet unexplored, and how many solid advantages unimproved."

India wants more such dreamers as that young Mr. Jones, standing alone on the deck of his vessel and watching the sun diving into the sea – with the memories of England behind and the hopes of India before him, feeling the presence of Persia and its ancient monarchs, and breathing the breezes of Arabia and its glowing poetry. Such dreamers know how to make their dreams come true, and how to change their visions into realities.

And as it was a hundred years ago, so it is now; or at least, so it may be now. There are many bright dreams to be dreamed about India, and many bright deeds to be done in India, if only you will do them. Though many great and glorious conquests have been made in the history and literature of the East, since the days when Sir William Jones[1] landed at Calcutta, depend upon it, no young Alexander here need despair because there are no kingdoms left for him to conquer on the ancient shores of the Indus and the Ganges.

---

1. Sir William Jones was thirty-seven years of age when he sailed for India. He received the honor of knighthood in March, 1783, on his appointment as Judge of the Supreme Court of Judicature at Fort William, at Bengal.—A. W.

Lecture 2

Truthful Character of the Hindus

In my first Lecture I endeavored to remove the prejudice that everything in India is strange, and so different from the intellectual life which we are accustomed to in England, that the twenty or twenty-five years which a civil servant has to spend in the East seem often to him a kind of exile that he must bear as well as he can, but that severs him completely from all those higher pursuits by which life is made enjoyable at home. This need not be so and ought not to be so, if only it is clearly seen how almost every one of the higher interests that make life worth living here in England, may find as ample scope in India as in England.

To-day I shall have to grapple with another prejudice which is even more mischievous, because it forms a kind of icy barrier between the Hindus and their rulers, and makes anything like a feeling of true fellowship between the two utterly impossible.

That prejudice consists in looking upon our stay in India as a kind of *moral* exile, and in regarding the Hindus as an inferior race, totally different from ourselves in their moral character, and, more particularly in what forms the very foundation of the English character, respect for truth.

44

I believe there is nothing more disheartening to any high-minded young man than the idea that he will have to spend his life among human beings whom he can never respect or love – natives, as they are called, not to use even more offensive names – men whom he is taught to consider as not amenable to the recognized principles of self-respect, uprightness, and veracity, and with whom therefore any community of interests and action, much more any real friendship, is supposed to be out of the question.

So often has that charge of untruthfulness been repeated, and so generally is it now accepted, that it seems almost Quixotic to try to fight against it.

Nor should I venture to fight this almost hopeless battle, if I were not convinced that such a charge, like all charges brought against a whole nation, rests on the most flimsy induction, and that it has done, is doing, and will continue to do more mischief than anything that even the bitterest enemy of English dominion in India could have invented. If a young man who goes to India as a civil servant or as a military officer, goes there fully convinced that the people whom he is to meet with are all liars, liars by nature or by national instinct, never restrained in their dealings by any regard for truth, never to be trusted on their word, need we wonder at the feelings of disgust with which he thinks of the Hindus, even before he has seen them; the feelings of distrust with which he approaches them, and the contemptuous way in which he treats them when brought into contact with them for the transaction of public or private business? When such tares have once been sown by the enemy, it will be difficult to gather them up. It has become almost an article of faith with every Indian civil servant that all Indians are liars; nay, I know I shall never be forgiven for my heresy in venturing to doubt it.

Now, quite apart from India, I feel most strongly that every one of these international condemnations is to be deprecated, not only for the sake of the self-conceited and uncharitable state of mind from which they spring, and which they serve to strengthen and confirm, but for purely logical reasons also, namely for the reckless and slovenly character of the induction on which such conclusions rest. Because a man has travelled in Greece and has been cheated by his dragoman, or been carried off by brigands, does it follow that all Greeks, ancient as well as modern, are cheats and robbers, or that they approve of cheating and robbery? And because in Calcutta, or Bombay, or Madras, Indians who are brought before judges, or who hang about the law-courts and the bazaars, are not distinguished by an unreasoning and uncompromising love of truth, is it not a very vicious induction to say, in these days of careful reasoning, that all Hindus are liars – particularly if you bear in mind that, according to the latest census, the number of inhabitants of that vast country amounts to two hundred and fifty-three millions. Are all these two hundred and fifty-three millions of human beings to be set down as liars, because some hundreds, say even some thousands of Indians, when they are brought to an English court of law, on suspicion of having committed a theft or a murder, do not speak the truth, the whole truth, and nothing but the truth? Would an English sailor, if brought before a dark-skinned judge, who spoke English with a strange accent, bow down before him and confess at once any misdeed that he may have committed; and would all his mates rush forward and eagerly bear witness against him, when he had got himself into trouble?

The rules of induction are general, but they depend on the subjects to which they are applied. We may, to follow an Indian proverb, judge of a whole field of rice by tasting one or two grains only, but if we apply this rule to human beings, we are sure to fall into the same mistake as the English chaplain who had once, on board an English vessel, christened a French child, and who remained fully convinced for the rest of his life that all French babies had very long noses.

I can hardly think of anything that you could safely predicate of *all* the inhabitants of India, and I confess to a little nervous tremor whenever I see a sentence beginning with "The people of India," or even with "All the Brahmans," or "All the Buddhists." What follows is almost invariably wrong. There is a greater difference between an Afghan, a Sikh, a Hindustani, a Bengalese, and a Dravidian than between an Englishman, a Frenchman, a German, and a Russian – yet all are classed as Hindus, and all are supposed to fall under the same sweeping condemnation.

Let me read you what Sir John Malcolm says about the diversity of character to be observed by anyone who has eyes to observe, among the different races whom we promiscuously call Hindus, and whom we promiscuously condemn as Hindus. After describing the people of Bengal as weak in body and timid in mind, and those below Calcutta as the lowest of our Hindu subjects, both in character and appearance, he continues: "But from the moment you enter the district of Behar, the Hindu inhabitants are a race of men, generally speaking, not more distinguished by their lofty stature and robust frame than they are for some of the finest qualities of the mind. They are brave, generous, humane, and their truth is as remarkable as their courage."

But because I feel bound to protest against the indiscriminating abuse that has been heaped on the people of India from the Himâlaya to Ceylon, do not suppose that it is my wish or intention to draw an ideal picture of India, leaving out all the dark shades, and giving you nothing but "sweetness and light." Having never been in India myself, I can only claim for myself the right and duty of every historian, namely, the right of collecting as much information as possible, and the duty to sift it according to the recognized rules of historical criticism. My chief sources of information with regard to the national character of the Indians in ancient times will be the works of Greek writers and the literature of the ancient Indians themselves. For later times we must depend on the statements of the various conquerors of India, who are not always the most lenient judges of those whom they may find it more difficult to rule than to conquer. For the last century to the present day, I shall have to appeal, partly to the authority of those who, after spending an active life in India and among the Indians, have given us the benefit of their experience in published works, partly to the testimony of a number of distinguished civil servants and of Indian gentlemen also, whose personal acquaintance I have enjoyed in England, in France, and in Germany.

As I have chiefly to address myself to those who will themselves be the rulers and administrators of India in the future, allow me to begin with the opinions which some of the most eminent, and, I believe, the most judicious among the Indian civil servants of the past have formed and deliberately expressed on the point which we are to-day discussing, namely, the veracity or want of veracity among the Hindus.

And here I must begin with a remark which has been made by others also, namely, that the civil servants who went to India in the beginning of this century, and under the auspices of the old East India Company, many of whom I had the honor and pleasure of knowing when I first came to England, seemed to have seen a great deal more of native life, native manners, and native character than those whom I had to examine five-and-twenty years ago, and who are now, after a distinguished career, coming back to England. India is no longer the distant island which it was, where each Crusoe had to make a home for himself as best he could. With the short and easy voyages from England to India and from India to England, with the frequent mails, and the telegrams, and the Anglo-Indian newspapers, official life in India has assumed the character of a temporary exile rather, which even English ladies are now more ready to share than fifty years ago. This is a difficulty which cannot be removed, but must be met, and which, I believe, can best be met by inspiring the new civil servants with new and higher interests during their stay in India.

I knew the late Professor Wilson, our Boden Professor of Sanskrit at Oxford, for many years, and often listened with deep interest to his Indian reminiscences.

Let me read you what he, Professor Wilson, says of his native friends, associates, and servants:[1]

"I lived, both from necessity and choice, very much among the Hindus, and had opportunities of becoming acquainted with them in a greater variety of situations than those in which they usually come under the observation of Europeans. In the Calcutta mint, for instance, I was in daily personal communication with a numerous body of artificers, mechanics, and laborers, and always found among them cheerful and unwearied industry, good-humored compliance with the will of their superiors, and a readiness to make whatever exertions were demanded from them; there was among them no drunkenness, no disorderly conduct, no insubordination. It would not be true to say that there was *no* dishonesty, but it was comparatively rare, invariably petty, and much less formidable than, I believe, it is necessary to guard against in other mints in other countries. There was considerable skill and ready docility. So far from there being any servility, there was extreme frankness, and I should say that where there is confidence without fear, frankness is one of the most universal features in the Indian character. Let the people feel sure of the temper and good-will of their superiors, and there is an end of reserve and timidity, without the slightest departure from respect..."

Then, speaking of the much-abused Indian Pandits, he says: "The studies which engaged my leisure brought me into connection with the men of learning, and in them I found the similar merits of industry, intelligence, cheerfulness, frankness, with others peculiar to their avocation. A very common characteristic of these men, and of the Hindus especially, was a simplicity truly childish, and a total unacquaintance with the business and manners of life.

1. Mill's "History of British India," ed. Wilson, vol. i., p. 375.

Where that feature was lost, it was chiefly by those who had been long familiar with Europeans. Among the Pandits or the learned Hindus there prevailed great ignorance and great dread of the European character. There is, indeed, very little intercourse between any class of Europeans and Hindu scholars, and it is not wonderful, therefore, that mutual misapprehension should prevail."

Speaking, lastly, of the higher classes in Calcutta and elsewhere, Professor Wilson says that he witnessed among them "polished manners, clearness and comprehensiveness of understanding, liberality of feeling, and independence of principle that would have stamped them gentlemen in any country in the world." "With some of this class," he adds, "I formed friendships which I trust to enjoy through life."

I have often heard Professor Wilson speak in the same, and in even stronger terms of his old friends in India, and his correspondence with Ram Comul Sen, the grandfather of Keshub Chunder Sen,[1] a most orthodox, not to say bigoted, Hindu, which has lately been published, shows on what intimate terms Englishmen and Hindus may be, if only the advances are made on the English side.

There is another Professor of Sanskrit, of whom your University may well be proud, and who could speak on this subject with far greater authority than I can. He too will tell you, and I have no doubt has often told you, that if only you look out for friends among the Hindus, you will find them, and you may trust them.

There is one book which for many years I have been in the habit of recommending, and another against which I have always been warning those of the candidates for the Indian Civil Service whom I happened to see at Oxford; and I believe both the advice and the warning have in several cases borne the very best fruit. The book which I consider most mischievous, nay, which I hold responsible for some of the greatest misfortunes that have happened to India, is Mill's "History of British India," even with the antidote against

---

1. Keshub Chunder Sen is the present spiritual director of the Brahmo Samag, the theistic organization founded by the late Rammohun Roy.—A. W.

its poison, which is supplied by Professor Wilson's notes. The book which I recommend, and which I wish might be published again in a cheaper form, so as to make it more generally accessible, is Colonel Sleeman's "Rambles and Recollections of an Indian Official," published in 1844, but written originally in 1835-1836.

Mill's "History," no doubt, you all know, particularly the candidates for the Indian Civil Service, who, I am sorry to say, are recommended to read it, and are examined in it. Still, in order to substantiate my strong condemnation of the book, I shall have to give a few proofs:

Mill in his estimate of the Hindu character is chiefly guided by Dubois, a French missionary, and by Orme and Buchanan, Tennant, and Ward, all of them neither very competent nor very unprejudiced judges. Mill,[1] however, picks out all that is most unfavorable from their works, and omits the qualifications which even these writers felt bound to give to their wholesale condemnation of the Hindus. He quotes as serious, for instance, what was said in joke, namely, that "a Brahman is an ant's nest of lies and impostures." Next to the charge of untruthfulness, Mill upbraids the Hindus for what he calls their litigiousness. He writes: "As often as courage fails them in seeking more daring gratification to their hatred and revenge, their malignity finds a vent in the channel of litigation." Without imputing dishonorable motives, as Mill does, the same fact might be stated in a different way, by saying, "As often as their conscience and respect of law keep them from seeking more daring gratification to their hatred and revenge, say by murder or poisoning, their trust in English justice leads them to appeal to our courts of law." Dr. Robertson, in his "Historical Disquisitions concerning India," seems to have considered the litigious subtlety of the Hindus as a sign of high civilization rather than of barbarism, but he is sharply corrected by Mr. Mill, who tells him that "nowhere is this subtlety carried higher than among the wildest of the Irish." That courts of justice, like the English, in which a verdict was not to be obtained,

---

1. Mill's "History," ed. Wilson, vol. i., p. 368.

as formerly in Mohammedan courts, by bribes and corruption, should at first have proved very attractive to the Hindus, need not surprise us. But is it really true that the Hindus are more fond of litigation than other nations? If we consult Sir Thomas Munro, the eminent Governor of Madras, and the powerful advocate of the Ryotwar settlements, he tells us in so many words:[1] "I have had ample opportunity of observing the Hindus in every situation, and I can affirm, that they are not litigious."[2]

But Mill goes further still, and in one place he actually assures his readers[3] that a "Brahman may put a man to death when he lists." In fact, he represents the Hindus as such a monstrous mass of all vices, that, as Colonel Vans Kennedy remarked, society could not have held together if it had really consisted of such reprobates only. Nor does he seem to see the full bearing of his remarks. Surely, if a Brahman might, as he says, put a man to death whenever he lists, it would be the strongest testimony in their favor that you hardly ever hear of their availing themselves of such a privilege, to say nothing of the fact – and a fact it is – that, according to statistics, the number of capital sentences was one in every 10,000 in England, but only one in every million in Bengal.[4]

Colonel Sleeman's "Rambles" are less known than they deserve to be. To give you an idea of the man, I must read you some extracts from the book.

His sketches being originally addressed to his sister, this is how he writes to her:

"*My dear Sister*: Were any one to ask your countrymen in India, what had been their greatest source of pleasure while there,

1. Mill's "History," vol. i., p. 329.
2. Manu, VIII. 43, says: "Neither a King himself nor his officers must ever promote litigation; nor ever neglect a lawsuit instituted by others."
3. Mill's "History," vol. i., p. 327.
4. See Elphinstone, "History of India," ed. Cowell, p. 219, note. "Of the 232 sentences of death 64 only were carried out in England, while the 59 sentences of death in Bengal were all carried out."

perhaps nine in ten would say the letters which they receive from their sisters at home... And while thus contributing so much to our happiness, they no doubt tend to make us better citizens of the world and servants of government than we should otherwise be; for in our 'struggles through life' in India, we have all, more or less, an eye to the approbation of those circles which our kind sisters represent, who may therefore be considered in the exalted light of a valuable species of *unpaid magistracy* to the government of India."

There is a touch of the old English chivalry even in these few words addressed to a sister whose approbation he values, and with whom he hoped to spend the winter of his days. Having been, as he confesses, idle in answering letters, or rather, too busy to find time for long letters, he made use of his enforced leisure, while on his way from the Nerbuddah River to the Himmaleh Mountains, in search of health, to give to his sister a full account of his impressions and experiences in India.

Though what he wrote was intended at first "to interest and amuse his sister only and the other members of his family at home," he adds, in a more serious tone: "Of one thing I must beg you to be assured, that I have nowhere indulged in fiction, either in the narrative, the recollections, or the conversations. What I relate on the testimony of others, I believe to be true; and what I relate on my own, you may rely upon as being so."

When placing his volumes before the public at large in 1844, he expresses a hope that they may "tend to make the people of India better understood by those of our countrymen whose destinies are cast among them, and inspire more kindly feelings toward them."

You may ask why I consider Colonel Sleeman so trustworthy an authority on the Indian character, more trustworthy, for instance, than even so accurate and unprejudiced an observer as Professor Wilson. My answer is – because Wilson lived chiefly in Calcutta, while Colonel Sleeman saw India, where alone the true India can be seen, namely, in the village-communities. For many years he was employed as Commissioner for the suppression of Thuggee. The Thugs were professional assassins, who committed their murders under a kind of religious sanction. They were originally "all Mohammedans, but for a long time past Mohammedans and Hindus had been indiscriminately associated in the gangs, the former class, however, still predominating."[1]

In order to hunt up these gangs, Colonel Sleeman had constantly to live among the people in the country, to gain their confidence, and to watch the good as well as the bad features in their character.

Now what Colonel Sleeman continually insists on is that no one knows the Indians who does not know them in their village-communities – what we should now call their *communes*. It is that village-life which in India has given its peculiar impress to the Indian character, more so than in any other country we know. When in Indian history we hear so much of kings and emperors, of râjahs and mahârâjahs, we are apt to think of India as an Eastern monarchy, ruled by a central power, and without any trace of that self-government which forms the pride of England. But those who have most carefully studied the political life of India tell you the very opposite.

The political unit, or the social cell in India has always been, and, in spite of repeated foreign conquests, is still the village-community. Some of these political units will occasionally combine or be combined for common purposes (such a confederacy being called a grâmagâla), but each is perfect in itself. When we read in the Laws of Manu of officers appointed to rule over ten, twenty, a hundred, or a thousand of these villages, that means no more than that they were responsible for the collection of taxes, and generally for the good behavior of these villages. And when, in later times, we hear of circles of eighty-four villages, the so-called Chourasees

---

1. Sir Ch. Trevelyan, Christianity and Hinduism, 1882, p. 42.

    This will be news to many. It has been quite common to include the Thugs with the worshippers of Bhavani, the consort of Siva. The word signifies a deceiver, which eliminates it from every religious association.—A. W.

(Katurasîti[1]), and of three hundred and sixty villages, this too seems to refer to fiscal arrangements only. To the ordinary Hindu, I mean to ninety-nine in every hundred, the village was his world, and the sphere of public opinion, with its beneficial influences on individuals, seldom extended beyond the horizon of his village.[2]

Colonel Sleeman was one of the first who called attention to the existence of these village-communities in India, and their importance in the social fabric of the whole country both in ancient and in modern times; and though they have since become far better known and celebrated through the writings of Sir Henry Maine, it is still both interesting and instructive to read Colonel Sleeman's account. He writes as a mere observer, and uninfluenced as yet by any theories on the development of early social and political life among the Aryan nations in general.

I do not mean to say that Colonel Sleeman was the first who pointed out the palpable fact that the whole of India is parcelled out into estates of villages. Even so early an observer as Megasthenes[3] seems to have been struck by the same fact when he says that "in India the husbandmen with their wives and children live in the country, and entirely avoid going into town." What Colonel Sleeman was the first to point out was that all the native virtues of the Hindus are intimately connected with their village-life.

---

1. H. M. Elliot, "Supplement to the Glossary of Indian Terms," p. 151.
2. I see from Dr. Hunter's latest statistical tables that the whole number of towns and villages in British India amounts to 493,429. Out of this number 448,320 have less than 1000 inhabitants, and may be called villages. In Bengal, where the growth of towns has been most encouraged through Government establishments, the total number of homesteads is 117,042, and more than half of these contain less than 200 inhabitants. Only 10,077 towns in Bengal have more than 1000 inhabitants, that is, no more than about a seventeenth part of all the settlements are anything but what we should call substantial villages. In the North-Western Provinces the last census gives us 105,124 villages, against 297 towns. See London *Times*, 14th Aug. 1882.
3. "Ancient India as described by Megasthenes and Arrian," by McCrindle, p. 42.

That village-life, however, is naturally the least known to English officials, nay, the very presence of an English official is often said to be sufficient to drive away those native virtues which distinguish both the private life and the public administration of justice and equity in an Indian village.[1] Take a man out of his village-community, and you remove him from all the restraints of society. He is out of his element, and, under temptation, is more likely to go wrong than to remain true to the traditions of his home-life. Even between village and village the usual restraints of public morality are not always recognized. What would be called theft or robbery at home is called a successful raid or conquest if directed against distant villages; and what would be falsehood or trickery in private life is honored by the name of policy and diplomacy if successful against strangers. On the other hand, the rules of hospitality applied only to people of other villages, and a man of the same village could never claim the right of an *Atithi*, or guest.[2]

Let us here now what Colonel Sleeman tells us about the moral character of the members of these village-communities,[3] and let us

---

1. "Perjury seems to be committed by the meanest and encouraged by some of the better sort among the Hindus and Mussulmans, with as little remorse as if it were a proof of ingenuity, or even a merit."—Sir W. Jones, Address to Grand Jury at Calcutta, in Mill's "History of India," vol. i., p. 324. "The longer we possess a province, the more common and grave does perjury become."—Sir G. Campbell, quoted by Rev. Samuel Johnson, "Oriental Religions, India," p. 288.

2. Vasishtha, translated by Bühler, VIII. 8.

3. Mr. J. D. Baldwin, author of "Prehistoric Nations," declares that this system of village-communities existed in India long before the Aryan conquest. He attributes it to Cushite or Æthiopic influence, and with great plausibility. Nevertheless, the same system flourished in prehistoric Greece, even till the Roman conquests. Mr. Palgrave observed it existing in Arabia. "Oman is less a kingdom than an aggregation of municipalities," he remarks; "each town, each village has its separate existence and corporation, while towns and villages, in their turn, are subjected to one or other of the ancestral chiefs." The Ionian and Phœnician cities existed by a similar tenure, as did also the Free Cities of Europe. It appears, indeed, to have been the earlier form of rule. Megasthenes

not forget that the Commissioner for the suppression of Thuggee had ample opportunities of seeing the dark as well as the bright side of the Indian character.

He assures us that falsehood or lying between members of the same village is almost unknown. Speaking of some of the most savage tribes, the Gonds, for instance, he maintains that nothing would induce them to tell a lie, though they would think nothing of lifting a herd of cattle from a neighboring plain.

Of these men it might perhaps be said that they have not yet learned the value of a lie; yet even such blissful ignorance ought to count in a nation's character. But I am not pleading here for Gonds, or Bhils, or Santhals, and other non-Aryan tribes. I am speaking of the Aryan and more or less civilized inhabitants of India. Now among them, where rights, duties, and interests begin to clash in one and the same village, public opinion, in its limited sphere, seems strong enough to deter even an evil-disposed person from telling a falsehood. The fear of the gods also has not yet lost its power.[1] In most villages there is a sacred tree, a pipal-tree (Ficus Indica), and the gods are supposed to delight to sit among its leaves, and listen to the music of their rustling. The deponent takes one of these leaves in his hand, and invokes the god, who sits above him, to crush him, or those dear to him, as he crushes the leaf in his hand, if he speaks anything but the truth. He then plucks and crushes the leaf, and states what he has to say.

The pipal-tree is generally supposed to be occupied by one of the Hindu deities, while the large cotton-tree, particularly among

---

noticed it in India. "The village-communities," says Sir Charles Metcalf, "are little republics, having everything they want within themselves, and almost independent of any foreign relations. They seem to last where nothing else lasts." These villages usually consist of the holders of the land, those who farm and cultivate it, the established village-servants, priest, blacksmith, carpenter, accountant, washerman, potter, barber, watchman, shoemaker, etc. The tenure and law of inheritance varies with the different native races, but tenantship for a specific period seems to be the most common.—A. W.

1. "Sleeman," vol. ii., p. 111.

the wilder tribes, is supposed to be the abode of local gods, all the more terrible because entrusted with the police of a small settlement only. In their puncháyets, Sleeman tells us, men adhere habitually and religiously to the truth, and "I have had before me hundreds of cases," he says, "in which a man's property, liberty, and life has depended upon his telling a lie, and he has refused to tell it."

Could many an English judge say the same?

In their own tribunals under the pipal-tree or cotton-tree, imagination commonly did what the deities, who were supposed to preside, had the credit of doing. If the deponent told a lie, he believed that the god who sat on his sylvan throne above him, and searched the heart of man, must know it; and from that moment he knew no rest, he was always in dread of his vengeance. If any accident happened to him, or to those dear to him, it was attributed to this offended deity; and if no accident happened, some evil was brought about by his own disordered imagination.[1] It was an excellent superstition, inculcated in the ancient law-books, that the ancestors watched the answer of a witness, because, according as it was true or false, they themselves would go to heaven or to hell.[2]

Allow me to read you the abstract of a conversation between an English official and a native law-officer as reported by Colonel Sleeman. The native lawyer was asked what he thought would be the effect of an act to dispense with oaths on the Koran and Ganges-water, and to substitute a solemn declaration made in the name of God, and under the same penal liabilities as if the Koran or Ganges-water had been in the deponent's hand.

"I have practiced in the courts," the native said, "for thirty years, and during that time I have found only three kinds of witnesses — two of whom would, by such an act, be left precisely where they were, while the third would be released by it from a very salutary check."

---

1. Sleeman, "Rambles," vol. ii., p. 116.
2. Vasishtha XVI. 32.

"And, pray, what are the three classes into which you divide the witnesses in our courts?"

"First, Sir, are those who will always tell the truth, whether they are required to state what they know in the form of an oath or not."

"Do you think this a large class?"

"Yes, I think it is; and I have found among them many whom nothing on earth could make to swerve from the truth. Do what you please, you could never frighten or bribe them into a deliberate falsehood.

"The second are those who will not hesitate to tell a lie when they have a motive for it, and are not restrained by an oath. In taking an oath, they are afraid of two things, the anger of God and the odium of men.

"Only three days ago," he continued, "I required a power of attorney from a lady of rank, to enable me to act for her in a case pending before the court in this town. It was given to me by her brother, and two witnesses came to declare that she had given it. 'Now,' said I, 'this lady is known to live under the curtain, and you will be asked by the judge whether you saw her give this paper: what will you say?' They both replied: 'If the judge asks us the question without an oath, we will say "*Yes*;" it will save much trouble, and we know that she *did* give the paper, though we did not really *see* her give it; but if he puts the Koran into our hands, we must say "*No*," for we should otherwise be pointed at by all the town as perjured wretches – our enemies would soon tell everybody that we had taken a false oath.'

"Now," the native lawyer went on, "the form of an oath is a great check on this sort of persons.

"The third class consists of men who will tell lies whenever they have a sufficient motive, whether they have the Koran or Ganges-water in their hand or not. Nothing will ever prevent their doing so; and the declaration which you propose would be just as well as any other for them."

"Which class do you consider the most numerous of the three?"

"I consider the second the most numerous, and wish the oath to be retained for them."

"That is, of all the men you see examined in our courts, you think the most come under the class of those who will, under the influence of strong motives, tell lies, if they have not the Koran or Ganges-water in their hands?"

"Yes."

"But do not a great many of those whom you consider to be included among the second class come from the village-communities – the peasantry of the country?"

"Yes."

"And do you not think that the greatest part of those men who will tell lies in the court, under the influence of strong motives, unless they have the Koran or Ganges-water in their hands, would refuse to tell lies, if questioned before the people of their villages, among the circle in which they live?"

"Of course I do; three-fourths of those who do not scruple to lie in the courts, would be ashamed to lie before their neighbors, or the elders of their village."

"You think that the people of the village-communities are more ashamed to tell lies before their neighbors than the people of towns?"

"Much more – there is no comparison."

"And the people of towns and cities bear in India but a small proportion to the people of the village-communities?"

"I should think a very small proportion indeed."

"Then you think that in the mass of the population of India, *out of our courts*, the first class, or those who speak truth, whether they have the Koran or Ganges-water in their hands or not, would be found more numerous than the other two?"

"Certainly I do; if they were always to be questioned before their neighbors or elders, so that they could feel that their neighbors and elders could know what they say."

It was from a simple sense of justice that I felt bound to quote this testimony of Colonel Sleeman as to the truthful character of the natives of India, when *left to themselves*. My interest lies altogether with the people of India, *when left to themselves*, and historically I should like to draw a line after the year one thousand after Christ. When you read the atrocities committed by the Mohammedan conquerors of India from that time to the time when England stepped in and, whatever may be said by her envious critics, made, at all events, the broad principles of our common humanity respected once more in India, the wonder, to my mind, is how any nation could have survived such an *Inferno* without being turned into devils themselves.

Now, it is quite true that during the two thousand years which precede the time of Mahmud of Gazni, India has had but few foreign visitors, and few foreign critics; still it is surely extremely strange that whenever, either in Greek, or in Chinese, or in Persian, or in Arab writings, we meet with any attempts at describing the distinguishing features in the national character of the Indians, regard for truth and justice should always be mentioned first.

Ktesias, the famous Greek physician of Artaxerxes Mnemon (present at the battle of Cunaxa, 404 B.C.), the first Greek writer who tells us anything about the character of the Indians, such as he heard it described at the Persian court, has a special chapter "On the Justice of the Indians."[1]

Megasthenes,[2] the ambassador of Seleucus Nicator at the court of Sandrocottus in Palibothra (*Pâtaliputra*, the modern Patna), states that thefts were extremely rare, and that they honored truth and virtue.[3]

---

1. Ktesiæ Fragmenta (ed. Didot), p. 81.
2. See "Indian Antiquary," 1876, p. 333.
3. Megasthenis Fragmenta (ed. Didot) in "Fragm. Histor. Graec." vol. ii., p. 426
   b: Ἀλήθειάν τε ὑμοίως καὶἀρετὴν ἀποδεχονται.

Arrian (in the second century, the pupil of Epictetus), when speaking of the public overseers or superintendents in India, says:[1] "They oversee what goes on in the country or towns, and report everything to the king, where the people have a king, and to the magistrates, where the people are self-governed, and it is against use and wont for these to give in a false report; *but indeed no Indian is accused of lying.*"[2]

The Chinese, who come next in order of time, bear the same, I believe, unanimous testimony in favor of the honesty and veracity of the Hindus. [The earliest witness is Su-we, a relative of Fan-chen, King of Siam, who between 222 and 227 A.D. sailed round the whole of India, till he reached the mouth of the Indus, and then explored the country. After his return to Sinto, he received four Yueh-chi horses, sent by a king of India as a present to the King of Siam and his ambassador. At the time when these horses arrived in Siam (it took them four years to travel there), there was staying at the court of Siam an ambassador of the Emperor of China, Khang-thai, and this is the account which he received of the kingdom of India: "It is a kingdom in which the religion of Buddha flourishes. The inhabitants are straightforward and honest, and the soil is very fertile. The king is called Meu-lun, and his capital is surrounded by walls," etc. This was in about 231 A.D. In 605 we hear again of the Emperor Yang-ti sending an ambassador, Fei-tu, to India, and this is what among other things he points out as peculiar to the Hindus: "They believe in solemn oaths."][3] Let me quote Hiouen-thsang, the most famous of the Chinese Buddhist pilgrims, who visited India in the seventh century. "Though the Indians," he writes, "are of a light temperament, they are distinguished by the straightforwardness and honesty of their character. With regard to riches, they never take anything unjustly; with regard to justice, they make even

1. Indica, cap. xii. 6.
2. See McCrindle in. "Indian Antiquary," 1876, p. 92.
3. See Stanislas Julien, *Journal Asiatique*, 1847, Août, pp. 98, 105.

excessive concessions... Straightforwardness is the distinguishing feature of their administration."

If we turn to the accounts given by the Mohammedan conquerors of India, we find Idrisi, in his Geography (written in the eleventh century), summing up their opinion of the Indians in the following words:[1]

> "The Indians are naturally inclined to justice, and never depart from it in their actions. Their good faith, honesty, and fidelity to their engagements are well known, and they are so famous for these qualities that people flock to their country from every side."

Again, in the thirteenth century, Shems-ed-din Abu Abdullah quotes the following judgment of Bedi ezr Zenân: "The Indians are innumerable, like grains of sand, free from all deceit and violence. They fear neither death nor life."[2]

In the thirteenth century we have the testimony of Marco Polo,[3] who thus speaks of the *Abraiaman*, a name by which he seems to mean the Brahmans who, though, not traders by profession, might well have been employed for great commercial transactions by the king. This was particularly the case during times which the Brahmans would call times of distress, when many things were allowed which at other times were forbidden by the laws. "You must know," Marco Polo says, "that these Abraiaman are the best merchants in the world, and the most truthful, for they would not tell a lie for anything on earth."

In the fourteenth century we have Friar Jordanus, who goes out of his way to tell us that the people of Lesser India (South and Western India) are true in speech and eminent in justice.[4]

---

1. Elliot, "History of India," vol. i., p. 88.
2. See Mehren: "Manuel de la Cosmographie du moyen âge, traduction de l'ouvrage de Shems-ed-din Abou Abdallah de Damas." Paris: Leroux, 1874, p. 371.
3. "Marco Polo," ed. H. Yule, vol. ii., p. 350.
4. "Marco Polo," vol. ii., p. 354.

In the fifteenth century, Kamal-eddin Abd-errazak Samarkandi (1413-1482), who went as ambassador of the Khakan to the prince of Kalikut and to the King of Vidyânagara (about 1440-1445), bears testimony to the perfect security which merchants enjoy in that country.[1]

In the sixteenth century, Abu Fazl, the minister of the Emperor Akbar, says in his Ayin Akbari: "The Hindus are religious, affable, cheerful, lovers of justice, given to retirement, able in business, admirers of truth, grateful and of unbounded fidelity; and their soldiers know not what it is to fly from the field of battle."[2]

And even in quite modern times the Mohammedans seem willing to admit that the Hindus, at all events in their dealings with Hindus, are more straightforward than Mohammedans in their dealings with Mohammedans.

Thus Meer Sulamut Ali, a venerable old Mussulman, and, as Colonel Sleeman says, a most valuable public servant, was obliged to admit that "a Hindu may feel himself authorized to take in a Mussulman, and might even think it meritorious to do so; but he would never think it meritorious to take in one of his own religion. There are no less than seventy-two sects of Mohammedans; and every one of these sects would not only take in the followers of every other religion on earth, but every member of every one of the other seventy-one sects; and the nearer that sect is to his own, the greater the merit of taking in its members."[3]

So I could go on quoting from book after book, and again and again we should see how it was love of truth that struck all the people who came in contact with India, as the prominent feature in the national character of its inhabitants. No one ever accused them of falsehood. There must surely be some ground for this, for it is not

---

1. "Notices des Manuscrits," tom. xiv., p. 436. He seems to have been one of the first to state that the Persian text of the Kalilah and Dimna was derived from the wise people of India.

2. Samuel Johnson, "India," p. 294.

3. Sleeman, "Rambles," vol. i., p. 63.

a remark that is frequently made by travellers in foreign countries, even in our time, that their inhabitants invariably speak the truth. Read the accounts of English travellers in France, and you will find very little said about French honesty and veracity, while French accounts of England are seldom without a fling at *Perfide Albion*!

But if all this is true, how is it, you may well ask, that public opinion in England is so decidedly unfriendly to the people of India; at the utmost tolerates and patronizes them, but will never trust them, never treat them on terms of equality?

I have already hinted at some of the reasons. Public opinion with regard to India is made up in England chiefly by those who have spent their lives in Calcutta, Bombay, Madras, or some other of the principal towns in India. The native element in such towns contains mostly the most unfavorable specimens of the Indian population. An insight into the domestic life of the more respectable classes, even in towns, is difficult to obtain; and, when it is obtained, it is extremely difficult to judge of their manners according to our standard of what is proper, respectable, or gentlemanlike. The misunderstandings are frequent and often most grotesque; and such, we must confess, is human nature, that when we hear the different and often most conflicting accounts of the character of the Hindus, we are naturally skeptical with regard to unsuspected virtues among them, while we are quite disposed to accept unfavorable accounts of their character.

Lest I should seem to be pleading too much on the native side of the question, and to exaggerate the difficulty of forming a correct estimate of the character of the Hindus, let me appeal to one of the most distinguished, learned, and judicious members of the Indian Civil Service, the author of the "History of India," Mountstuart Elphinstone. "Englishmen in India,"[1] he says, "have less opportunity than might be expected of forming opinions of the native character. Even in England, few know much of the people beyond their own class, and what they do know, they learn from newspapers

---

1. Elphinstone's "History of India," ed. Cowell, p. 213.

and publications of a description which does not exist in India. In that country also, religion and manners put bars to our intimacy with the natives, and limit the number of transactions as well as the free communication of opinions. We know nothing of the interior of families but by report, and have no share in those numerous occurrences of life in which the amiable parts of character are most exhibited." "Missionaries of a different religion,[1] judges, police-magistrates, officers of revenue or customs, and even diplomatists, do not see the most virtuous portion of a nation, nor any portion, unless when influenced by passion, or occupied by some personal interest. What we *do* see we judge by our own standard. We conclude that a man who cries like a child on slight occasions must always be incapable of acting or suffering with dignity; and that one who allows himself to be called a liar would not be ashamed of any baseness. Our writers also confound the distinctions of time and place; they combine in one character the Maratta and the Bengalese, and tax the present generation with the crimes of the heroes of the Mahâbhârata. It might be argued, in opposition to many unfavorable testimonies, that those who have known the Indians longest have always the best opinion of them; but this is rather a compliment to human nature than to them, since it is true of every other people. It is more in point, that all persons who have retired from India think better of the people they have left, after comparing them with others, even of the most justly-admired nations."

But what is still more extraordinary than the ready acceptance of judgments unfavorable to the character of the Hindus, is the determined way in which public opinion, swayed by the statements of certain unfavorable critics, has persistently ignored the evidence which members of the Civil Service, officers and statesmen – men

---

1. This statement may well be doubted. The missionary staff in India is very large and has been for years past. There is no reason to doubt that many of its members are well informed respecting Hindoo character in all grades of society.—AM. PUBS.

of the highest authority – have given again and again, in direct opposition to these unfavorable opinions.

Here, too, I must ask to be allowed to quote at least a few of these witnesses on the other side.

Warren Hastings thus speaks of the Hindus in general: "They are gentle and benevolent, more susceptible of gratitude for kindness shown them, and less prompted to vengeance for wrongs inflicted than any people on the face of the earth; faithful, affectionate, submissive to legal authority."

Bishop Heber said: "The Hindus are brave, courteous, intelligent, most eager for knowledge and improvement; sober, industrious, dutiful to parents, affectionate to their children, uniformly gentle and patient, and more easily affected by kindness and attention to their wants and feelings than any people I ever met with."[1]

Elphinstone states: "No set of people among the Hindus are so depraved as the dregs of our own great towns. The villagers are everywhere amiable, affectionate to their families, kind to their neighbors, and toward all but the government honest and sincere. Including the Thugs and Dacoits, the mass of crime is less in India than in England. The Thugs are almost a separate nation, and the Dacoits are desperate ruffians in gangs. The Hindus are mild and gentle people, more merciful to prisoners than any other Asiatics. Their freedom from gross debauchery is the point in which they appear to most advantage; and their superiority in purity of manners is not flattering to our self-esteem."[2]

Yet Elphinstone can be most severe on the real faults of the people of India. He states that, at present, want of veracity is one of their prominent vices, but he adds "that such deceit is most common in people connected with government, a class which spreads far in India, as, from the nature of the land-revenue, the lowest villager is often obliged to resist force by fraud."[3]

1. Samuel Johnson, "India," p. 293.
2. See "History of India," pp. 375-381.
3. "History of India," p. 218.

Sir John Malcolm writes:[1] "I have hardly ever known where a person did understand the language, or where a calm communication was made to a native of India, through a well-informed and trustworthy medium, that the result did not prove, that what had at first been stated as falsehood had either proceeded from fear or from misapprehension. I by no means wish to state that our Indian subjects are more free from this vice than other nations that occupy a nearly equal position in society, but I am positive that they are not more addicted to untruth."

Sir Thomas Munro bears even stronger testimony. He writes: "If a good system of agriculture, unrivalled manufacturing skill, a capacity to produce whatever can contribute to either convenience or luxury, schools established in every village for teaching reading, writing, and arithmetic,[2] the general practice of hospitality and charity among each other, and, above all, a treatment of the female sex full of confidence, respect, and delicacy, are among the signs which denote a civilized people – then the Hindus are not inferior to the nations of Europe – and if civilization is to become an article of trade between England and India, I am convinced that England will gain by the import cargo."

My own experience with regard to the native character has been, of course, very limited. Those Hindus whom I have had the pleasure

---

1. Mill's "History of India," ed. Wilson, vol. i., p. 370.
2. Sir Thomas Munro estimated the children educated at public schools in the Madras presidency as less than one in three. But low as it was, it was, as he justly remarked, a higher rate than existed till very lately in most countries of Europe.—Elphinstone, "Hist. of India," p. 205.

   In Bengal there existed no less than 80,000 native schools, though, doubtless, for the most part, of a poor quality. According to a Government Report of 1835, there was a village-school for every 400 persons.—"Missionary Intelligencer," IX. 183-193.

   Ludlow ("British India," I. 62) writes: "In every Hindu village which has retained its old form I am assured that the children generally are able to read, write, and cipher; but where we have swept away the village-system, as in Bengal, there the village-school has also disappeared."

to know personally in Europe may be looked upon as exceptional, as the best specimens, it may be, that India could produce. Also, my intercourse with them has naturally been such that it could hardly have brought out the darker sides of human nature. During the last twenty years, however, I have had some excellent opportunities of watching a number of native scholars under circumstances where it is not difficult to detect a man's true character – I mean in literary work and, more particularly, in literary controversy. I have watched them carrying on such controversies both among themselves and with certain European scholars, and I feel bound to say that, with hardly one exception, they have displayed a far greater respect for truth and a far more manly and generous spirit than we are accustomed to even in Europe and America. They have shown strength, but no rudeness; nay, I know that nothing has surprised them so much as the coarse invective to which certain Sanskrit scholars have condescended, rudeness of speech being, according to their view of human nature, a safe sign not only of bad breeding, but of want of knowledge. When they were wrong, they have readily admitted their mistakes; when they were right, they have never sneered at their European adversaries. There has been, with few exceptions, no quibbling, no special pleading, no untruthfulness on their part, and certainly none of that low cunning of the scholar who writes down and publishes what he knows perfectly well to be false, and snaps his fingers at those who still value truth and self-respect more highly than victory or applause at any price. Here, too, we might possibly gain by the import cargo.

Let me add that I have been repeatedly told by English merchants that commercial honor stands higher in India than in any other country, and that a dishonored bill is hardly known there.

I have left to the last the witnesses who might otherwise have been suspected – I mean the Hindus themselves. The whole of their literature from one end to the other is pervaded by expressions of love and reverence for truth. Their very word for truth is full of meaning. It is *sat* or *satya*, sat being the participle of the verb *as*, to be.

True, therefore, was with them simply *that which is*. The English *sooth* is connected with sat, also the Greek ὄν for ἔσον, and the Latin *sens*, in *præsens*.

We are all very apt to consider truth to be what is trowed by others, or believed in by large majorities. That kind of truth is easy to accept. But whoever has once stood alone, surrounded by noisy assertions, and overwhelmed by the clamor of those who ought to know better, or perhaps who did know better – call him Galileo or Darwin, Colenso or Stanley, or any other name – he knows what a real delight it is to feel in his heart of hearts, this is true – this is – this is *sat* – whatever daily, weekly, or quarterly papers, whatever bishops, archbishops, or popes, may say to the contrary.

Another name for truth is the Sanskrit *rita*, which originally seems to have meant *straight, direct*, while an *rita* is untrue, false.

Now one of the highest praises bestowed upon the gods in the Veda is that they are satya, true, truthful, trustworthy;[1] and it is well known that both in modern and ancient times, men always ascribe to God or to their gods those qualities which they value most in themselves.

Other words applied to the gods as truthful beings are, adrogha, lit. not deceiving.[2] Adrogha-vâk means, he whose word is never broken. Thus Indra, the Vedic Jupiter, is said to have been praised by the fathers[3] "as reaching the enemy, overcoming him, standing on the summit, *true of speech*, most powerful in thought."

Droghavâk,[4] on the contrary, is used for deceitful men. Thus Vasishtha, one of the great Vedic poets, says: "If I had worshipped false gods, or if I believed in the gods vainly – but why art thou angry with us, O Gâtavedas? May liars go to destruction!"

Satyam, as a neuter, is often used as an abstract, and is then rightly translated by truth. But it also means that which is, the true,

---

1. Rig-Veda I. 87, 4; 145, 5; 174, 1; V. 23, 2.
2. Rig-Veda III. 32, 9; VI. 5, 1.
3. Rig-Veda VI. 22, 2.
4. Rig-Veda III. 14, 6.

the real; and there are several passages in the Rig-Veda where, instead of *truth*, I think we ought simply to translate *satyam* by the true, that is, the real, τὸὄντως ὄν.[1] It sounds, no doubt, very well to translate Satyena uttabhitâ bhûmih by "the earth is founded on truth;" and I believe every translator has taken satya in that sense here. Ludwig translates, "Von der Wahrheit ist die Erde gestützt." But such an idea, if it conveys any tangible meaning at all, is far too abstract for those early poets and philosophers. They meant to say "the earth, such as we see it, is held up, that is, rests on something real, though we may not see it, on something which they called the Real,[2] and to which, in course of time, they gave many more names, such as Rita, the right, Brahman," etc.

Of course where there is that strong reverence for truth, there must also be the sense of guilt arising from untruth. And thus we hear one poet pray that the waters may wash him clean, and carry off all his sins and all untruth:

"Carry away, ye waters,[3] whatever evil there is in me, wherever I may have deceived, or may have cursed, and also all untruth (an ritam)."[4]

Or again, in the Atharva-Veda IV. 16:

1. This is the favorite expression of Plato for the Divine, which Cary, Davis, and others render "Real Being."—A. W.

2. Sometimes they trace even this Satya or Rita, the Real or Right, to a still higher cause, and say (Rig-Veda X. 190, 1):
   "The Right and Real was born from the Lighted Heat; from thence was born Night, and thence the billowy sea. From the sea was born Samvatsara, the year, he who ordereth day and night, the Lord of all that moves (winks). The Maker (*dhâtri*) shaped Sun and Moon in order; he shaped the sky, the earth, the welkin, and the highest heaven."

3. Rig-Veda I. 23, 22.

4. Or it may mean, "Wherever I may have deceived, or sworn false."

"May all thy fatal snares, which stand spread out seven by seven and threefold, catch the man who tells a lie, may they pass by him who tells the truth!"

From the Brâhmanas, or theological treatises of the Brahmans, I shall quote a few passages only:

"Whosoever[1] speaks the truth, makes the fire on his own altar blaze up, as if he poured butter into the lighted fire. His own light grows larger, and from to-morrow to to-morrow he becomes better. But whosoever speaks untruth, he quenches the fire on his altar, as if he poured water into the lighted fire; his own light grows smaller and smaller, and from to-morrow to to-morrow he becomes more wicked. Let man therefore speak truth only."[2]

And again:[3] "A man becomes impure by uttering falsehood."

And again:[4] "As a man who steps on the edge of a sword placed over a pit cries out, I shall slip, I shall slip into the pit, so let a man guard himself from falsehood (or sin)."

In later times we see the respect for truth carried to such an extreme, that even a promise, unwittingly made, is considered to be binding.

In the Katha-Upanishad, for instance, a father is introduced offering what is called an All-sacrifice, where everything is supposed to be given up. His son, who is standing by, taunts his father with not having altogether fulfilled his vow, because he has not sacrificed his son. Upon this, the father, though angry and against his will, is obliged to sacrifice his son. Again, when the son arrives in the lower world, he is allowed by the Judge of the Dead to ask for three favors. He then asks to be restored to life, to be taught some

---

1. Satapatha Brâhmana II. 2, 3, 19.
2. Cf. Muir, "Metrical Translations," p. 268.
3. Sat. Br. III. 1, 2, 10.
4. Taitt. Âranyaka X. 9.

sacrificial mysteries, and, as the third boon, he asks to know what becomes of man after he is dead. Yama, the lord of the Departed, tries in vain to be let off from answering this last question. But he, too, is bound by his promise, and then follows a discourse on life after death, or immortal life, which forms one of the most beautiful chapters in the ancient literature of India.

The whole plot of one of the great epic poems, the Râmâyana, rests on a rash promise given by Dasaratha, king of Ayodhyâ, to his second wife, Kaikeyî, that he would grant her two boons. In order to secure the succession to her own son, she asks that Râma, the eldest son by the king's other wife, should be banished for fourteen years. Much as the king repents his promise, Râma, his eldest son, would on no account let his father break his word, and he leaves his kingdom to wander in the forest with his wife Sitâ and his brother Lakshmana. After the father's death, the son of the second wife declines the throne, and comes to Râma to persuade him to accept the kingdom of his father. But all in vain. Râma will keep his exile for fourteen years, and never disown his father's promise. Here follows a curious dialogue between a Brâhman Gâbâli and Prince Râma, of which I shall give some extracts:[1]

> "The Brâhman, who is a priest and courtier, says, 'Well, descendant of Raghu, do not thou, so noble in sentiments, and austere in character, entertain, like a common man, this useless thought. What man is a kinsman of any other? What relationship has any one with another? A man is born alone and dies alone. Hence he who is attached to any one as his father or his mother, is to be regarded as if he were insane, for no one belongs to another. Thou oughtest not to abandon thy father's kingdom and stay here in a sad and miserable abode, attended with many trials. Let thyself be inaugurated king in the wealthy Ayodhyâ. Dasaratha, thy father is nothing to thee, or thou to him; the king is one,

1. Muir, "Metrical Translations," p. 218.

and thou another, do therefore what is said... Then offer oblations to the departed spirits (of thy forefathers) on prescribed days; but see what a waste of food! For what can a dead man eat? If what is eaten by one here enters into the body of another (viz., of the departed), let Srâddhas be offered to those who are travelling; they need not then get food to eat on their journey. These books (the Vedas), (which enjoin men to) sacrifice, give, consecrate themselves, practise austerities, and forsake the world, are composed by clever men to induce others to bestow gifts. Authoritative words do not fall from heaven. Let me, and others like yourselves, embrace whatever assertion is supported by reason. Adhere to what is apparent to the senses, and reject what is invisible... _This world is the next world_; do thou therefore enjoy pleasure, for every virtuous man does not gain it. Virtuous men are greatly distressed, while the unrighteous are seen to be happy.'"

These positivist sentiments sound strange, particularly from the mouth of a Brâhman. But the poet evidently wishes to represent a Brâhman living at court, who has an argument ready for anything and everything that is likely to please his king.

But what does Râma answer? "The words," he says, "which you have addressed to me, though they recommend what _seems_ to be right and salutary, advise, in fact, the contrary. The sinful transgressor, who lives according to the rules of heretical systems, obtains no esteem from good men. It is good conduct that marks a man to be noble or ignoble, heroic or a pretender to manliness, pure or impure. Truth and mercy are immemorial characteristics of a king's conduct. Hence royal rule is in its essence _truth_. On truth the word is based. Both sages and gods have esteemed truth. The man who speaks truth in this world attains the highest imperishable state. Men shrink with fear and horror from a liar as from a serpent. In this world the chief element in virtue is truth; it is called the basis of everything. Truth is lord in the world; virtue always rests on truth.

All things are founded on truth; nothing is higher than it. Why, then, should I not be true to my promise, and faithfully observe the truthful injunction given by my father? Neither through covetousness, nor delusion, nor ignorance, will I, overpowered by darkness, break through the barrier of truth, but remain true to my promise to my father. How shall I, having promised to him that I would thus reside in the forests, transgress his injunction, and do what Bharata recommends?"

The other epic poem too, the Mahâbhârata, is full of episodes showing a profound regard for truth and an almost slavish submission to a pledge once given. The death of Bhîshma, one of the most important events in the story of the Mahâbhârata, is due to his vow never to hurt a woman. He is thus killed by Sikhandin, whom he takes to be a woman.[1]

Were I to quote from all the law-books, and from still later works, everywhere you would hear the same key-note of truthfulness vibrating through them all.

We must not, however, suppress the fact that, under certain circumstances, a lie was allowed, or, at all events, excused by Indian lawgivers. Thus Gautama says: "An untruth spoken by people under the influence of anger, excessive joy, fear, pain, or grief, by infants, by very old men, by persons laboring under a delusion, being under the influence of drink, or by madmen, does not cause the speaker to fall, or, as we should say, is a venial, not a mortal sin."[2]

---

1. Holtzmann, "Das alte indische Epos," p. 21, note 83.
2. This permission to prevaricate was still further extended. The following five untruths are enumerated by various writers as not constituting mortal sins— namely, at the time of marriage, during dalliance, when life is in danger, when the loss of property is threatened, and for the sake of a Brahmana. Again, another writer cites the declaration that an untruth is venial if it is spoken at the time of marriage, during dalliance, in jest, or while suffering great pain. It is evident that Venus laughed at lovers' oaths in India as well as elsewhere; and that false testimony extracted by torture was excused. Manu declared that in some cases the giver of false evidence from a pious motive would not lose his seat in heaven; indeed, that whenever the death of a man of any of the four

This is a large admission, yet even in that open admission there is a certain amount of honesty. Again and again in the Mahâbhârata is this excuse pleaded. Nay, there is in the Mahâbhârata[1] the well-known story of Kausika, called Satyavâdin, the Truth-speaker, who goes to hell for having spoken the truth. He once saw men flying into the forest before robbers (dasyu). The robbers came up soon after them, and asked Kausika, which way the fugitives had taken. He told them the truth, and the men were caught by the robbers and killed. But Kausika, we are told, went to hell for having spoken the truth.

The Hindus may seem to have been a priest-ridden race, and their devotion to sacrifice and ceremonial is well known. Yet this is what the poet of the Mahâbhârata dares to say:

"Let a thousand sacrifices (of a horse) and truth be weighed in the balance – truth will exceed the thousand sacrifices."[2]

These are words addressed by Sakuntalâ, the deserted wife, to King Dushyanta, when he declined to recognize her and his son. And when he refuses to listen to her appeal, what does she appeal to as the highest authority?—*The voice of conscience.*

"If you think I am alone," she says to the king, "you do not know that wise man within your heart. He knows of your evil deed – in *his* sight you commit sin. A man who has committed sin may think that no one knows it. The gods know it and the old man within."[3]

---

castes would be occasioned by true evidence, falsehood was even better than truth. He gives as the primeval rule, to say what is true and what is pleasant, but not what is true and unpleasant, or what is pleasant and not true. The *Vishnu-purana* gives like counsel, adding the following aphorism: "A considerate man will always cultivate, in fact, thought, and speech, that which is good for living beings, both in this world and in the next." About the same license appears to be used in this country and winked at.—A. W.

1. Mahâbhârata VIII. 3448.
2. Muir, l. c. p. 268; Mahâbhârata I. 3095.
3. Mahâbhârata I. 3015-16.

This must suffice. I say once more that I do not wish to represent the people of India as two hundred and fifty-three millions of angels, but I do wish it to be understood and to be accepted as a fact, that the damaging charge of untruthfulness brought against that people is utterly unfounded with regard to ancient times. It is not only not true, but the very opposite of the truth. As to modern times, and I date them from about 1000 after Christ, I can only say that, after reading the accounts of the terrors and horrors of Mohammedan rule, my wonder is that so much of native virtue and truthfulness should have survived. You might as well expect a mouse to speak the truth before a cat, as a Hindu before a Mohammedan judge.[1] If you frighten a child, that child will tell a lie; if you terrorize millions, you must not be surprised if they try to escape from your fangs. Truthfulness is a luxury, perhaps the greatest, and let me assure you, the most expensive luxury in our life – and happy the man who has been able to enjoy it from his very childhood. It may be easy enough in our days and in a free country, like England, never to tell a lie – but the older we grow, the harder we find it to be always true, to speak the truth, the whole truth, and nothing but the truth. The Hindus too had made that discovery. They too knew how hard, nay how impossible it is, always to speak the truth, the whole truth, and nothing but the truth. There is a short story in the Satapatha Brâhmana, to my mind full of deep meaning, and pervaded by the real sense of truth, the real sense of the difficulty of truth. His kinsman said to Aruna Aupavesi, "Thou art advanced in years, establish thou the sacrificial fires." He replied: "Thereby you tell me henceforth to keep silence. For he who has established the fires must not speak an untruth, and only by not speaking at all, one speaks no untruth. To that extent the service of the sacrificial fires consists in truth."[2]

---

1. This explains satisfactorily how the Hindoos became liars, and of course admits that they did become so.—AM. PUBS.
2. Satapatha Brâhmana, translated by Eggeling, "Sacred Books of the East," vol. xii., p. 313, § 20.

I doubt whether in any other of the ancient literatures of the world you will find traces of that extreme sensitiveness of conscience which despairs of our ever speaking the truth, and which declares silence gold, and speech silver, though, in a much higher sense than our proverb.

What I should wish to impress on those who will soon find themselves the rulers of millions of human beings in India, is the duty to shake off national prejudices, which are apt to degenerate into a kind of madness. I have known people with a brown skin whom I could look up to as my betters. Look for them in India, and you will find them, and if you meet with disappointments, as no doubt you will, think of the people with white skins whom you have trusted, and whom you can trust no more. We are all apt to be Pharisees in international judgments. I read only a few days ago in a pamphlet written by an enlightened politician, the following words:

> "Experience only can teach that nothing is so truly astonishing to a morally depraved people as the phenomenon of a race of men in whose word perfect confidence may be placed[1]... The natives are conscious of their inferiority in nothing so much as in this. They require to be taught rectitude of conduct much more than literature and science."

If you approach the Hindus with such feelings, you will teach them neither rectitude, nor science, nor literature. Nay, they might appeal to their own literature, even to their law-books, to teach us at least one lesson of truthfulness, truthfulness to ourselves, or, in other words, humility.

What does Yâgñavalkya say?

"It is not our hermitage," he says – our religion we might say – "still less the color of our skin, that produces virtue; virtue must

---

1. Sir Charles Trevelyan, "Christianity and Hinduism," p. 81.

be practiced. Therefore let no one do to others what he would not have done to himself."

And the laws of the Mânavas, which were so much abused by Mill, what do they teach?

"Evil-doers think indeed that no one sees them; but the gods see them, and the old man within."

"Self is the witness of Self, Self is the refuge of Self. Do not despise thy own Self, the highest witness of men."

"If, friend, thou thinkest thou art self-alone, remember there is the silent thinker (the Highest Self) always within thy heart, and *he* sees what is good and what is evil."

"O friend, whatever good thou mayest have done from thy very birth, all will go to the dogs, if thou speak an untruth."

Or in Vasishtha, XXX. 1:

"Practice righteousness, not unrighteousness; speak truth, not untruth; look far, not near; look up toward the highest, not toward anything low."

No doubt there is moral depravity in India, and where is there no moral depravity in this world? But to appeal to international statistics would be, I believe, a dangerous game. Nor must we forget that our standards of morality differ, and, on some points, differ considerably from those recognized in India; and we must not wonder if sons do not at once condemn as criminal what their fathers and grandfathers considered right. Let us hold by all means to *our* sense of what is right and what is wrong; but in judging others, whether in public or in private life, whether as historians or politicians, let us not forget that a kindly spirit will never do any harm. Certainly I can imagine nothing more mischievous, more dangerous, more fatal to the permanence of English rule in India, than for the young civil servants to go to that country with the idea that it is a sink of moral depravity, an ants' nest of lies; for no one is so sure to go wrong, whether in public or in private life, as he who says in his haste: "All men are liars."

Lecture 3

Human Interest of Sanskrit Literature

My first lecture was intended to remove the prejudice that India is and always must be a strange country to us, and that those who have to live there will find themselves stranded, and far away from that living stream of thoughts and interests which carries us along in England and in other countries of Europe.

My second lecture was directed against another prejudice, namely, that the people of India with whom the young civil servants will have to pass the best years of their life are a race so depraved morally, and more particularly so devoid of any regard for truth, that they *must* always remain strangers to us, and that any real fellowship or friendship with them is quite out of the question.

To-day I shall have to grapple with a third prejudice, namely, that the literature of India, and more especially the classical Sanskrit literature, whatever may be its interest to the scholar and the anti-quarian, has little to teach us which we cannot learn better from other sources, and that at all events it is of little practical use to young civilians. If only they learn to express themselves in Hindustani or

81

Tamil, that is considered quite enough; nay, as they have to deal with men and with the ordinary affairs of life, and as, before everything else, they are to be men of the world and men of business, it is even supposed to be dangerous, if they allowed themselves to become absorbed in questions of abstruse scholarship or in researches on ancient religion, mythology, and philosophy.

I take the very opposite opinion, and I should advise every young man who wishes to enjoy his life in India, and to spend his years there with profit to himself and to others, to learn Sanskrit, and to learn it well.

I know it will be said, what can be the use of Sanskrit at the present day? Is not Sanskrit a dead language? And are not the Hindus themselves ashamed of their ancient literature? Do they not learn English, and do they not prefer Locke, and Hume, and Mill to their ancient poets and philosophers?

No doubt Sanskrit, in one sense, is a dead language. It was, I believe, a dead language more than two thousand years ago. Buddha, about 500 B.C., commanded his disciples to preach in the dialects of the people; and King Asoka, in the third century B.C., when he put up his Edicts, which were intended to be read, or at least to be understood by the people, had them engraved on rocks and pillars in the various local dialects from Cabul[1] in the north to Ballabhi in the south, from the sources of the Ganges and the Jumnah to Allahabad and Patna, nay even down to Orissa. These various dialects are as different from Sanskrit as Italian is from Latin, and we have therefore good reason to suppose that, in the third century B.C., if not earlier, Sanskrit had ceased to be the spoken language of the people at large.

There is an interesting passage in the Kullavagga, where we are told that, even during Buddha's lifetime, some of his pupils, who were Brâhmans by birth, complained that people spoiled the words of Buddha by everyone repeating them in his own dialect (nirutti). They proposed to translate his words into Sanskrit; but he declined,

---

1. See Cunningham, "Corpus Inscriptionum Indicarum," vol. i., 1877.

and commanded that each man should learn his doctrine in his own language.[1]

And there is another passage, quoted by Hardy in his Manual of Buddhism, p. 186, where we read that at the time of Buddha's first preaching each of the countless listeners thought that the sage was looking toward him, and was speaking to him in his own tongue, though the language used was Mâgadhi.[2]

Sanskrit, therefore, as a language spoken by the people at large, had ceased to exist in the third century B.C.

Yet such is the marvellous continuity between the past and the present in India, that in spite of repeated social convulsions, religious reforms, and foreign invasions, Sanskrit may be said to be still the only language that is spoken over the whole extent of that vast country.

Though the Buddhist sovereigns published their edicts in the vernaculars, public inscriptions and private official documents continued to be composed in Sanskrit during the last two thousand years. And though the language of the sacred writings of Buddhists and Gainas was borrowed from the vulgar dialects, the literature of India never ceased to be written in Pâninean Sanskrit, while the few exceptions, as, for instance, the use of Prâkrit by women and inferior characters in the plays of Kâlidâsa and others, are themselves not without an important historical significance.

Even at the present moment, after a century of English rule and English teaching, I believe that Sanskrit is more widely understood in India than Latin was in Europe at the time of Dante.

Whenever I receive a letter from a learned man in India, it is written in Sanskrit. Whenever there is a controversy on questions of law and religion, the pamphlets published in India are written in Sanskrit. There are journals written in Sanskrit which must entirely depend for their support on readers who prefer that classical language to the vulgar dialects. There is *The Pandit*, published at Benares,

---

1. Kulavagga V. 33, 1. The expression used is Khandaso âropemấti.
2. See Rhys Davids, Buddhist Suttas, "Sacred Books of the East," vol. xi., p. 142.

containing not only editions of ancient texts, but treatises on modern subjects, reviews of books published in England, and controversial articles, all in Sanskrit.

Another paper of the same kind is the *Pratna-Kamra-nandinî*, "the Delight of lovers of old things," published likewise at Benares, and full of valuable materials.

There is also the *Vidyodaya*, "the Rise of Knowledge," a Sanskrit journal published at Calcutta, which sometimes contains important articles. There are probably others, which I do not know.

There is a monthly serial published at Bombay, by M. Moreshwar Kunte, called the *Shad-darshana-Chintanikâ*, or "Studies in Indian Philosophy," giving the text of the ancient systems of philosophy, with commentaries and treatises, written in Sanskrit, though in this case accompanied by a Marathi and an English translation.

Of the Rig-Veda, the most ancient of Sanskrit books, two editions are now coming out in monthly numbers, the one published at Bombay, by what may be called the liberal party, the other at Prayâga (Allahabad) by Dayânanda Sarasvatî, the representative of Indian orthodoxy. The former gives a paraphrase in Sanskrit, and a Marathi and an English translation; the latter a full explanation in Sanskrit, followed by a vernacular commentary. These books are published by subscription, and the list of subscribers among the natives of India is very considerable.

There are other journals, which are chiefly written in the spoken dialects, such as Bengali, Marathi, or Hindi; but they contain occasional articles in Sanskrit, as, for instance, the Hariskandrakandrikâ, published at Benares, the *Tattvabodhinî*, published at Calcutta, and several more.

It was only the other day that I saw in the *Liberal*, the journal of Keshub Chunder Sen's party,[1] an account of a meeting between Brahmavrata Samadhyayi, a Vedic scholar of Nuddea, and Kashinath Trimbak Telang, a M.A. of the University of Bombay. The one

1. The Brahmo-Samaj, a theistic school.—A. W.

came from the east, the other from the west, yet both could converse fluently in Sanskrit.[1]

Still more extraordinary is the number of Sanskrit texts, issuing from native presses, for which there seems to be a large demand, for if we write for copies to be sent to England, we often find that, after a year or two, all the copies have been bought up in India itself. That would not be the case with Anglo-Saxon texts in England, or with Latin texts in Italy!

But more than this, we are told that the ancient epic poems of the Mahâbhârata and Râmâyana are still recited in the temples for the benefit of visitors, and that in the villages large crowds assemble around the Kâthaka, the reader of these ancient Sanskrit poems, often interrupting his recitations with tears and sighs, when the hero of the poem is sent into banishment, while when he returns to his kingdom, the houses of the village are adorned with lamps and garlands. Such a recitation of the whole of the Mahâbhârata is said to occupy ninety days, or sometimes half a year.[2] The people at large require, no doubt, that the Brahman narrator (Kâthaka) should interpret the old poem, but there must be some few people present who understand, or imagine they understand, the old poetry of Vyâsa and Vâlmîki.

There are thousands of Brahmans[3] even now, when so little inducement exists for Vedic studies, who know the whole of the Rig-Veda by heart and can repeat it; and what applies to the Rig-Veda applies to many other books.

But even if Sanskrit were more of a dead language than it really is, all the living languages of India, both Aryan and Dravidian,

---

1. The *Liberal*, March 12, 1882.
2. See R. G. Bhandarkar, Consideration of the date of the Mahâbhârata, *Journal of the R. A. S. of Bombay*, 1872; Talboys Wheeler, "History of India," ii. 365, 572; Holtzmann, "Über das alte indische Epos," 1881, p. 1; Phear, "The Aryan Village in India and Ceylon," p. 19. That the Mahâbhârata was publicly read in the seventh century A.D., we learn from Bâna; see *Journal of the Royal Asiatic Society*, Bombay, vol. x., p. 87, note.—A. W.
3. "Hibbert Lectures," p. 157.

draw their very life and soul from Sanskrit.[1] On this point, and on the great help that even a limited knowledge of Sanskrit would render in the acquisition of the vernaculars, I, and others better qualified than I am, have spoken so often, though without any practical effect, that I need not speak again. Any candidate who knows but the elements of Sanskrit grammar will well understand what I mean, whether his special vernacular may be Bengali, Hindustani, or even Tamil. To a classical scholar I can only say that between a civil servant who knows Sanskrit and Hindustani, and another who knows Hindustani only, there is about the same difference in their power of forming an intelligent appreciation of India and its inhabitants, as there is between a traveller who visits Italy with a knowledge of Latin, and a party personally conducted to Rome by Messrs. Cook & Co.

Let us examine, however, the objection that Sanskrit literature is a dead or an artificial literature, a little more carefully, in order to see whether there is not some kind of truth in it. Some people hold that the literary works which we possess in Sanskrit never had any real life at all, that they were altogether scholastic productions, and that therefore they can teach us nothing of what we really care for, namely, the historical growth of the Hindu mind. Others maintain that at the present moment, at all events, and after a century of English rule, Sanskrit literature has ceased to be a motive power in India, and that it can teach us nothing of what is passing now through the Hindu mind and influencing it for good or for evil.

Let us look at the facts. Sanskrit literature is a wide and a vague term. If the Vedas, such as we now have them, were composed about

1. "Every person acquainted with the spoken speech of India knows perfectly well that its elevation to the dignity and usefulness of written speech has depended, and must still depend, upon its borrowing largely from its parent or kindred source; that no man who is ignorant of Arabic or Sanskrit can write Hindustani or Bengali with elegance, or purity, or precision, and that the condemnation of the classical languages to oblivion would consign the dialects to utter helplessness and irretrievable barbarism."—H. H. Wilson, *Asiatic Journal*, Jan., 1836; vol xix., p. 15.

1500 B.C., and if it is a fact that considerable works continue to be written in Sanskrit even now, we have before us a stream of literary activity extending over three thousand four hundred years. With the exception of China there is nothing like this in the whole world.

It is difficult to give an idea of the enormous extent and variety of that literature. We are only gradually becoming acquainted with the untold treasures which still exist in manuscripts, and with the titles of that still larger number of works which must have existed formerly, some of them being still quoted by writers of the last three or four centuries.[1]

The Indian Government has of late years ordered a kind of bibliographical survey of India to be made, and has sent some learned Sanskrit scholars, both European and native, to places where collections of Sanskrit MSS. are known to exist, in order to examine and catalogue them. Some of these catalogues have been published, and we learn from them that the number of separate works in Sanskrit, of which MSS. are still in existence, amounts to about 10,000.[2] This is more, I believe, than the whole classical literature of Greece and Italy put together. Much of it, no doubt, will be called mere rubbish; but then you know that even in our days the writings of a very eminent philosopher have been called "mere rubbish." What I wish you to see is this, that there runs through the whole history of India, through its three or four thousand years, a high road, or, it is perhaps more accurate to say, a high mountain-path of literature. It may be remote from the turmoil of the plain, hardly visible perhaps to the millions of human beings in their daily struggle of life. It may have been trodden by a few solitary wanderers only. But to the historian of the human race, to the student of the development of the human mind, those few solitary wanderers are after all the true representatives of India from age to age. Do not let us be deceived.

---

1. It would be a most useful work for any young scholar to draw up a list of Sanskrit books which are quoted by later writers, but have not yet been met with in Indian libraries.
2. "Hibbert Lectures," p. 133.

The true history of the world must always be the history of the few; and as we measure the Himâlaya by the height of Mount Everest, we must take the true measure of India from the poets of the Veda, the sages of the Upanishads, the founders of the Vedânta and Sânkhya philosophies, and the authors of the oldest law-books, and not from the millions who are born and die in their villages, and who have never for one moment been roused out of their drowsy dream of life.

To large multitudes in India, no doubt, Sanskrit literature was not merely a dead literature, it was simply non-existent; but the same might be said of almost every literature, and more particularly of the literatures of the ancient world.

Still, even beyond this, I am quite prepared to acknowledge to a certain extent the truth of the statement, that a great portion of Sanskrit literature has never been living and national, in the same sense in which the Greek and Roman literatures reflected at times the life of a whole nation; and it is quite true besides, that the Sanskrit books which are best known to the public at large, belong to what might correctly be called the Renaissance period of Indian literature, when those who wrote Sanskrit had themselves to learn the language, as we learn Latin, and were conscious that they were writing for a learned and cultivated public only, and not for the people at large.

This will require a fuller explanation.

We may divide the whole of Sanskrit literature, beginning with the Rig-Veda and ending with Dayânanda's Introduction to his edition of the Rig-Veda, his by no means uninteresting Rig-Veda-bhûmikâ, into two great periods: that preceding the great Turanian invasion, and that following it.

The former comprises the Vedic literature and the ancient literature of Buddhism, the latter all the rest.

If I call the invasion which is generally called the invasion of the Sakas, or the Scythians, or Indo-Scythians, or Turushkas, the *Turanian*[1] *invasion*, it is simply because I do not as yet wish to commit myself more than I can help as to the nationality of the tribes who took possession of India, or, at least, of the government of India, from about the first century B.C. to the third century A.D.

They are best known by the name of *Yueh-chi*, this being the name by which they are called in Chinese chronicles. These Chinese chronicles form the principal source from which we derive our knowledge of these tribes, both before and after their invasion of India. Many theories have been started as to their relationship with other races. They are described as of pink and white complexion and as shooting from horseback; and as there was some similarity between their Chinese name *Yueh-chi* and the *Gothi* or *Goths*, they were identified by Remusat[2] with those German tribes, and by others with the *Getae*, the neighbors of the Goths. Tod went even a step farther, and traced the Gâts in India and the Rajputs back to the *Yueh-chi* and *Getæ*.[3] Some light may come in time out of all this darkness, but for the present we must be satisfied with the fact that, between the first century before and the third century after our era, the greatest political revolution took place in India owing to the repeated inroads of Turanian, or, to use a still less objectionable term, of Northern tribes. Their presence in India, recorded by Chinese historians, is fully confirmed by coins, by inscriptions, and by the traditional history of the country, such as it is; but to my mind nothing attests the presence of these foreign invaders more clearly than the break, or, I could almost say, the blank in the Brahmanical

1. This vague term, *Turanian*, so much used in the Parsi Scriptures, is used here in the sense of unclassified ethnically.—A. W.
2. "Recherches sur les langues Tartares," 1820, vol. i., p. 327; "Lassen," I. A., vol. ii., p. 359.
3. Lassen, who at first rejected the identification of Gâts and Yueh-chi, was afterward inclined to accept it.

literature of India from the first century before to the third century after our era.[1]

If we consider the political and social state of that country, we can easily understand what would happen in a case of invasion and conquest by a warlike race. The invaders would take possession of the strongholds or castles, and either remove the old Rajahs, or make them their vassals and agents. Everything else would then go on exactly as before. The rents would be paid, the taxes collected, and the life of the villagers, that is, of the great majority of the people of India, would go on almost undisturbed by the change of government. The only people who might suffer would be, or, at all events, might be the priestly caste, unless they should come to terms with the new conquerors. The priestly caste, however, was also to a great extent the literary caste, and the absence of their old patrons, the native Rajahs, might well produce for a time a complete cessation of literary activity. The rise of Buddhism and its formal adoption by King Asoka had already considerably shaken the power and influence of the old Brahmanic hierarchy. The Northern conquerors, whatever their religion may have been, were certainly not believers in the Veda. They seem to have made a kind of compromise with Buddhism, and it is probably due to that compromise, or to an amalgamation of Saka legends with Buddhist doctrines, that we owe the so-called Mahâyâna form of Buddhism

---

1. The Yueh-chi appear to have begun their invasion about 130 B.C. At this period the Grecian kingdom of Bactria, after a brilliant existence of a century, had fallen before the Tochari, a Scythian people. The new invaders, called Ἐφθαλῖται by the Greeks, had been driven out of their old abodes and now occupied the country lying between Parthia at the west, the Oxus and Surkhâb, and extending into Little Thibet. They were herdsmen and nomads. At this time India was governed by the descendants of Asoka, the great propagandist of Buddhism. About twenty years before the Christian era, or probably earlier, the Yueh-chi, under Karranos, crossed the Indus and conquered the country, which remained subject to them for three centuries. The Chinese historians Sze-ma Tsien and Han-yo, give these accounts, which are however confirmed by numismatic and other evidence.—A. W.

– and more particularly the Amitâbha worship – which was finally settled at the Council under Kanishka, one of the Turanian rulers of India in the first century A.D.

If then we divide the whole of Sanskrit literature into these two periods, the one anterior to the great Turanian invasion, the other posterior to it, we may call the literature of the former period *ancient* and *natural*, that of the latter *modern* and *artificial*.

Of the former period we possess, *first*, what has been called the *Veda*, *i.e.*, Knowledge, in the widest sense of the word – a considerable mass of literature, yet evidently a wreck only, saved out of a general deluge; *secondly*, the works collected in the Buddhist Tripitaka, now known to us chiefly in what is called the Pâli dialect, the Gâthâ dialects, and Sanskrit, and probably much added to in later times.

The second period of Sanskrit literature comprehends everything else. Both periods may be subdivided again, but this does not concern us at present.

Now I am quite willing to admit that the literature of the second period, the modern Sanskrit literature, never was a living or national literature. It here and there contains remnants of earlier times, adapted to the literary, religious, and moral tastes of a later period; and whenever we are able to disentangle those ancient elements, they may serve to throw light on the past, and, to a certain extent, supplement what has been lost in the literature of the Vedic times. The metrical Law-books, for instance, contain old materials which existed during the Vedic period, partly in prose, as Sûtras, partly in more ancient metres, as Gâthâs. The Epic poems, the Mahâbhârata and Râmâyana, have taken the place of the old Itihâsas and Âkhyânas. The Purânas, even, may contain materials, though much altered, of what was called in Vedic literature the Purâna.[1]

But the great mass of that later literature is artificial or scholastic, full of interesting compositions, and by no means devoid of

---

1. "Hibbert Lectures," p. 154, note.

originality and occasional beauty; yet with all that, curious only, and appealing to the interests of the Oriental scholar far more than the broad human sympathies of the historian and the philosopher.

It is different with the ancient literature of India, the literature dominated by the Vedic and the Buddhistic religions. That literature opens to us a chapter in what has been called the Education of the Human Race, to which we can find no parallel anywhere else. Whoever cares for the historical growth of our language, that is, of our thoughts; whoever cares for the first intelligible development of religion and mythology; whoever cares for the first foundation of what in later times we call the sciences of astronomy, metronomy, grammar, and etymology; whoever cares for the first intimations of philosophical thought, for the first attempts at regulating family life, village life, and state life, as founded on religion, ceremonial, tradition and contract (samaya)—must in future pay the same attention to the literature of the Vedic period as to the literatures of Greece and Rome and Germany.

As to the lessons which the early literature of Buddhism may teach us, I need not dwell on them at present. If I may judge from the numerous questions that are addressed to me with regard to that religion and its striking coincidences with Christianity, Buddhism has already become a subject of general interest, and will and ought to become so more and more.[1] On that whole class of literature,

1. In June, 1882, a Conference on Buddhism was held at Sion College, to discuss the real or apparent coincidences between the religions of Buddha and Christ. Professor Müller addressed two letters to the secretary, which were afterward published, declaring such a discussion in general terms almost an impossibility. "The name of Buddhism," he says, "is applied to religious opinions, not only of the most varying, but of a decidedly opposite character, held by people on the highest and lowest stages of civilization, divided into endless sects, nay, founded on two distinct codes of canonical writings." Two Buddhist priests who were reading Sanskrit with him would hardly recognize the Buddhism now practiced in Ceylon as their own religion.

He also acknowledged the startling coincidences between Buddhism and Christianity, and that Buddhism existed at least 400 years before Christianity.

however, it is not my intention to dwell in this short course of Lectures, which can hardly suffice even for a general survey of Vedic literature, and for an elucidation of the principal lessons which, I think, we may learn from the Hymns, the Brâhmanas, the Upanishads, and the Sûtras.

It was a real misfortune that Sanskrit literature became first known to the learned public in Europe through specimens belonging to the second, or, what I called, the Renaissance period. The Bhagavadgîtâ, the plays of Kâlidâsa, such as Sakuntalâ or Urvasî, a few episodes from the Mahâbhârata and Râmâyana, such as those

---

He would go farther, and feel extremely grateful if anybody would point out to him the historical channels through which Buddhism had influenced early Christianity. "I have been looking for such channels all my life," says he, "but hitherto I have found none. What I have found is that for some of the most startling coincidences there are historical antecedents on both sides; and if we knew these antecedents, the coincidences become far less startling. If I do find in certain Buddhist works doctrines identically the same as in Christianity, so far from being frightened, I feel delighted, for surely truth is not the less true because it is believed by the majority of the human race.

"I believe we have made some progress during the last thirty years. I still remember the time when all heathen religions were looked upon as the work of the devil. (A1) We know now that they are stages in a growth, and in a growth not determined by an accidental environment only, but by an original purpose, a purpose to be realized in the history of the human race as a whole. Even missionaries have begun to approach the heathen in a new and better spirit. They look for what may safely be preserved in the religion of their pupils, and on that common ground they try to erect a purer faith and a better worship, instead of attempting to destroy the sacred foundations of religion, which, I believe, exist, or at least, existed, in every human heart."

He also states that the publishing of the "Rig-Veda and Commentary," his life-work, had produced a complete revolution both in our views of ancient religions and in the religious life of the Hindus themselves; and this not so much on the surface as in its deepest foundations.—A. W.

A1: We have no knowledge of such a belief. The common Christian theory is that Christianity is as old as the garden of Eden, and that truth in other religions is the result of contact, somewhere, at some time, with Christianity.—AM. PUBS.

of Nala and the Yagñadattabadha, the fables of the Hitopadesa, and
the sentences of Bhartrihari are, no doubt, extremely curious; and
as, at the time when they first became known in Europe, they were
represented to be of extreme antiquity, and the work of a people
formerly supposed to be quite incapable of high literary efforts,
they naturally attracted the attention of men such as Sir William
Jones in England, Herder and Goethe in Germany, who were
pleased to speak of them in terms of highest admiration. It was the
fashion at that time to speak of Kâlidâsa, as, for instance, Alexander
von Humboldt did even in so recent a work as his Kosmos, as "the
great contemporary of Virgil and Horace, who lived at the splendid
court of Vikramâditya," this Vikramâditya being supposed to be
the founder of the Samvat era, 56 B.C. But all this is now changed.
Whoever the Vikramâditya was who is supposed to have defeated
the Sakas, and to have founded another era, the Samvat era, 56
B.C., he certainly did not live in the first century B.C. Nor are
the Indians looked upon any longer as an illiterate race, and their
poetry as popular and artless. On the contrary, they are judged now
by the same standards as Persians and Arabs, Italians or French;
and, measured by that standard, such works as Kâlidâsa's plays are
not superior to many plays that have long been allowed to rest in
dust and peace on the shelves of our libraries. Their antiquity is
no longer believed in by any critical Sanskrit scholar. Kâlidâsa is
mentioned with Bhâravi as a famous poet in an inscription[1] dated
A.D. 585-6 (507 Saka era), and for the present I see no reason to
place him much earlier. As to the Laws of Manu, which used to
be assigned to a fabulous antiquity,[2] and are so still sometimes by
those who write at random or at second-hand, I doubt whether, in
their present form, they can be older than the fourth century of
our era, nay I am quite prepared to see an even later date assigned

1. Published by Fleet in the "Indian Antiquary," 1876, pp. 68-73, and first
   mentioned by Dr. Bhao Daji, Journal Asiatic Society, Bombay Branch, vol. ix.
2. Sir William Jones fixed their date at 1280 B.C.; Elphinstone as 900 B.C. It
   has recently been stated that they could not reasonably be placed later than
   the fifth century B.C.

to them. I know this will seem heresy to many Sanskrit scholars, but we must try to be honest to ourselves. Is there any evidence to constrain us to assign the Mânava-dharma-sâstra, such as we now possess it, written in continuous Slokas, to any date anterior to 300 A.D.? And if there is not, why should we not openly state it, challenge opposition, and feel grateful if our doubts can be removed?

That Manu was a name of high legal authority before that time, and that Manu and the Mânavam are frequently quoted in the ancient legal Sûtras, is quite true; but this serves only to confirm the conviction that the literature which succeeded the Turanian invasion is full of wrecks saved from the intervening deluge. If what we call the *Laws of Manu* had really existed as a code of laws, like the Code of Justinian, during previous centuries, is it likely that it should nowhere have been quoted and appealed to?

Varâhamihira (who died 587 A.D.) refers to Manu several times, but not to a Mânava-dharma-sâstra; and the only time where he seems actually to quote a number of verses from Manu, these verses are not to be met with in our text.[1]

---

1 A very useful indication of the age of the Dharma-sûtras, as compared with the metrical Dharma-sâstras or Samhitâs, is to be found in the presence or absence in them of any reference to written documents. Such written documents, if they existed, could hardly be passed over in silence in law-books, particularly when the nature of witnesses is discussed in support of loans, pledges, etc. Now, we see that in treating of the law of debt and debtors, (A1) the Dharma-sûtras of Gautama, Baudhâyana, and Âpastamba never mention evidence in writing. Vasishtha only refers to written evidence, but in a passage which may be interpolated, (A2) considering that in other respects his treatment of the law of debt is very crude. Manu's metrical code shows here again its usual character. It is evidently based on ancient originals, and when it simply reproduces them, gives us the impression of great antiquity. But it freely admits more modern ingredients, and does so in our case. It speaks of witnesses, fixes their minimum number at three, and discusses very minutely their qualifications and disqualifications, without saying a word about written documents. But in one place (VIII. 168) it speaks of the valuelessness of written agreements obtained by force, thus recognizing the practical employment of writing for commercial transactions. Professor Jolly, (A3) it is true, suggests

I believe it will be found that the century in which Varâhamihara
lived and wrote was the age of the literary Renaissance in India.[1]

---

that this verse may be a later addition, particularly as it occurs *totidem verbis*
in Nârada (IV. 55); but the final composition of Manu's Samhitâ, such as
we possess it, can hardly be referred to a period when writing was not yet
used, at all events for commercial purposes. Manu's "Law-book" is older than
Yâgñavalkya's, in which writing has become a familiar subject. Vishnu often
agrees literally with Yâgñavalkya, while Nârada, as showing the fullest development of the law of debt, is most likely the latest. (A4)

See Brihatsamhitâ, ed. Kern, pref., p. 43; *Journal of the R. A. S.*, 1875, p.
106.

A1: "Über das Indische Schuldrecht von J. Jolly," p. 291.

A2: Jolly, l. c., p. 322.

A3: L. c., p. 290.

A4: Jolly, l. c., p. 322. He places Kâtyâyana and Brihaspati after Nârada,
possibly Vyâsa and Hârîta also. See also Stenzler, Z. d D. M. G. ix. 664.

1. Professor Müller rejects the theory of the Samvat era and the Renaissance of
Sanskrit literature in the first century. Instead, he acknowledges the existence
of a Saka era, bearing date with the coronation of Kanishka, 78 A.D. Although
this monarch was a patron of the Buddhists, and the third collection of their
sacred books was made under his auspices, our author considers the period of
Saka or Yuen-chi domination from 24 B.C. till 178 A.D. as a literary interreg-
num. He is not willing to suggest any date for the Mahâbhârata or Râmâyana,
which appear to have been then extant. He exonerates Indian epic poetry,
however, from any imputation of Greek influence. Not so with astronomy.
Âryabhata, the elder, who described the motion of the earth very accurately,
he considers to have had no predecessors; and also cites other Indian authors
who described the twelve signs of the zodiac with Greek names or their equiv-
alents, and assigned each to a region in the body of the Creator, as we now see
it marked out in our almanacs. In this matter he is certainly plausible.

The period of the Renaissance and the reign and proper era of Vikramâditya are set down at about 550 A.D. He follows Dr. Bhao Daji, and is sustained
by Mr. Fergusson, author of "Tree and Serpent Worship," and other works on
religious architecture. It was the period of learned and literary men, as well as
of active religious controversy. "Believers in Buddha and believers in the Veda
lived together at this time," he remarks, "very much as Protestants and Roman
Catholics do at the present day—fighting when there is an opportunity or
necessity for it, but otherwise sharing the same air as fellow-creatures." Among

That Kâlidâsa and Bhâravi were famous at that time, we know from

a crowd of others we may instance Dignâga, a Buddhist, Kâlidâsa, a Siva worshipper, and Mânatunga, a Gaina, as frequenting the royal court. Vasubandhu, to whom the revival of Buddhist literature was largely due, was the son of a Brahman and a student of the Nyâya philosophy; as, indeed, Hiouenthsang, the Chinese traveller, also studied logic under a Brahmana teacher. Vikramâditya oscillated between all parties. Having quarrelled with the King of Kasmira and Manorhita, the great Buddhist teacher at the convent near Peshawer, he called an assembly of Sâstrikas and Sramanas, at which the latter were denounced. He also placed Matrigupta (Kalidasa?) over that country. At his death, however, the regal authority was surrendered to the legitimate king, who in his turn reinstated Silâditya, the successor of Vikrama, on the throne. This king also called an assembly of divines, and the Buddhists were restored to their former position. As they seem to have constituted the principal men of learning, I am disposed to believe that they were the actual restorers of the golden period to India. The "Nine Gems," Professor Müller is very confident, belong to this period. He declares that the philosophical Sûtras have no ascertained date prior to 300 A.D.

According to him, we need not refer many famous authors to a period anterior to the fifth century. Kalidasa, from being the contemporary of Augustus, becomes the contemporary of Justinian, and the very books which were most admired by Sanskrit students as specimens of ancient Indian poetry and wisdom find their rightful place in the period of literary renaissance, coinciding with an age of renewed literary activity in Persia, soon to be followed there, as later in India, by the great Mohammedan conquests. It appears to me that he is altogether too iconoclastic. It is more than probable that the apparent lateness of date is due to the destruction of books when the Buddhists were driven out of India. It would be as logical, it seems to me, to assign a post-Christian date to the *Vendidad* and *Yasna* because they had been lost and were collected anew under the auspices of a Sassanid king. We are told in the second book of the Maccabees that Antiochus Epiphanes burned the Hebrew Scriptures, and that Judas Makkabæus made a new collection; yet nobody pretends that they ought to be assigned to the second century B.C. In fact, we must in due sincerity give some room to faith.

Astronomy was also studied. Âryabhatta the elder had described the earth as making a revolution which produced the daily rising and setting of the sun. Professor Müller thinks he had no predecessors. Varâhamihira wrote during the reign of Vikramâditya, and employs the Yuga in opposition to the Saka era. It is apparent, however, that the Greek zodiac was employed.

the evidence of inscriptions. We also know that during that century the fame of Indian literature had reached Persia, and that the King of Persia, Khosru Nushirvan, sent his physician, Barzôî, to India, in order to translate the fables of the Pañkatantra, or rather their original, from Sanskrit into Pahlavi. The famous "Nine Gems," or "the nine classics," as we should say, have been referred, at least in part, to the same age,[1] and I doubt whether we shall be able to assign a much earlier date to anything we possess of Sanskrit literature, excepting always the Vedic and Buddhistic writings.

Although the specimens of this modern Sanskrit literature, when they first became known, served to arouse a general interest, and serve even now to keep alive a certain superficial sympathy for Indian literature, more serious students had soon disposed of these compositions, and while gladly admitting their claim to be called pretty and attractive, could not think of allowing to Sanskrit literature a place among the world-literatures, a place by the side of Greek and Latin, Italian, French, English, or German.

There was indeed a time when people began to imagine that all that was worth knowing about Indian literature was known, and that the only ground on which Sanskrit could claim a place among the recognized branches of learning in a university was its usefulness for the study of the Science of Language.

At that very time, however, now about forty years ago, a new start was made, which has given to Sanskrit scholarship an entirely new character. The chief author of that movement was Burnouf,

---

Bâdarâyana describes the pictorial representations of the Twelve Signs and their relation to the body of Brahman or the Creator:

"The Ram is the head; the face of the Creator is the Bull; the breast would be the Man-pair; the heart, the Crab; the Lion, the stomach; the Maid, the hip; the Balance-bearer, the belly; the eighth (Scorpion), the membrum; the Archer, his pair of thighs; the Makara, his pair of knees; the Pot, his pair of legs; the Fish-pair, his two feet." Another writer gives them in like series as the members of Kala or Time. Other evidence seems even more conclusive; Varâhamihira giving the actual Greek names in a Sanskrit dress.—A. W.

1. Kern, Preface to "Brihatsamâhitâ," p. 20.

then professor at the *Collège de France* in Paris, an excellent scholar, but at the same time a man of wide views and true historical instincts, and the last man to waste his life on mere Nalas and *Sakuntalâs*. Being brought up in the old traditions of the classical school in France (his father was the author of the well-known Greek Grammar), then for a time a promising young barrister, with influential friends such as Guizot, Thiers, Mignet, Villemain, at his side, and with a brilliant future before him, he was not likely to spend his life on pretty Sanskrit ditties. What he wanted when he threw himself on Sanskrit was history, human history, world-history, and with an unerring grasp he laid hold of Vedic literature and Buddhist literature, as the two stepping-stones in the slough of Indian literature. He died young, and has left a few arches only of the building he wished to rear. But his spirit lived on in his pupils and his friends, and few would deny that the first impulse, directly or indirectly, to all that has been accomplished since by the students of Vedic and Buddhist literature, was given by Burnouf and his lectures at the *Collège de France*.

What then, you may ask, do we find in that ancient Sanskrit literature and cannot find anywhere else? My answer is: We find there the Aryan man, whom we know in his various characters, as Greek, Roman, German, Celt, and Slave, in an entirely new character. Whereas in his migrations northward his active and political energies are called out and brought to their highest perfection, we find the other side of the human character, the passive and meditative, carried to its fullest growth in India. In some of the hymns of the Rig-Veda we can still watch an earlier phase. We see the Aryan tribes taking possession of the land, and under the guidance of such warlike gods as Indra and the Maruts, defending their new homes against the assaults of the black-skinned aborigines as well as against the inroads of later Aryan colonists. But that period of war soon came to an end, and when the great mass of the people had once settled down in their homesteads, the military and political duties seem to have been monopolized by what we call a *caste*,[1] that is by a small aristocracy, while the great majority of the people were satisfied with spending their days within the narrow spheres of their villages, little concerned about the outside world, and content with the gifts that nature bestowed on them, without much labor. We read in the Mahâbhârata (XIII. 22):

> "There is fruit on the trees in every forest, which everyone who likes may pluck without trouble. There is cool and sweet water in the pure rivers here and there. There is a soft bed made of the twigs of beautiful creepers. And yet wretched people suffer pain at the door of the rich!"

At first sight we may feel inclined to call this quiet enjoyment of life, this mere looking on, a degeneracy rather than a growth. It seems so different from what *we* think life ought to be. Yet, from a higher point of view it may appear that those Southern Aryans have chosen the good part, or at least the part good for them, while we, Northern Aryans, have been careful and troubled about many things.

It is at all events a problem worth considering whether, as there is in nature a South and a North, there are not two hemispheres also in human nature, both worth developing – the active, combative, and political on one side, the passive, meditative, and philosophical

---

1. During times of conquest and migration, such as are represented to us in the hymns of the Rig-Veda, the system of castes, as it is described, for instance, in the Laws of Manu, would have been a simple impossibility. It is doubtful whether such a system was ever more than a social ideal, but even for such an ideal the materials would have been wanting during the period when the Aryas were first taking possession of the land of the Seven Rivers. On the other hand, even during that early period, there must have been a division of labor, and hence we expect to find and do find in the grâmas of the Five Nations, *warriors*, sometimes called nobles, leaders, kings; *counsellors*, sometimes called priests, prophets, judges; and *working men*, whether ploughers, or builders, or road-makers. These three divisions we can clearly perceive even in the early hymns of the Rig-Veda.

on the other; and for the solution of that problem no literature furnishes such ample materials as that of the Veda, beginning with the Hymns and ending with the Upanishads. We enter into a new world – not always an attractive one, least of all to us; but it possesses one charm, it is real, it is of natural growth, and like everything of natural growth, I believe it had a hidden purpose, and was intended to teach us some kind of lesson that is worth learning, and that certainly we could learn nowhere else. We are not called upon either to admire or to despise that ancient Vedic literature; we have simply to study and to try to understand it.

There have been silly persons who have represented the development of the Indian mind as superior to any other, nay, who would make us go back to the Veda or to the sacred writings of the Buddhists in order to find there a truer religion, a purer morality, and a more sublime philosophy than our own. I shall not even mention the names of these writers or the titles of their works. But I feel equally impatient when I see other scholars criticising the ancient literature of India as if it were the work of the nineteenth century, as if it represented an enemy that must be defeated, and that can claim no mercy at our hands. That the Veda is full of childish, silly, even to our minds monstrous conceptions, who would deny? But even these monstrosities are interesting and instructive; nay, many of them, if we can but make allowance for different ways of thought and language, contain germs of truth and rays of light, all the more striking because breaking upon us through the veil of the darkest night.

Here lies the general, the truly human interest which the *ancient* literature of India possesses, and which gives it a claim on the attention, not only of Oriental scholars or of students of ancient history, but of every educated man and woman.

There are problems which we may put aside for a time, ay, which we must put aside while engaged each in our own hard struggle for life, but which will recur for all that, and which, whenever they do recur, will stir us more deeply than we like to confess to others, or even to ourselves. It is true that with us one day only out of seven is set apart for rest and meditation, and for the consideration of what the Greeks called τὰ μέγιστα—"the greatest things." It is true that that seventh day also is passed by many of us either in mere church-going routine or in thoughtless rest. But whether on week-days or on Sundays, whether in youth or in old age, there are moments, rare though they be, yet for all that the most critical moments of our life, when the old simple questions of humanity return to us in all their intensity, and we ask ourselves, What are we? What is this life on earth meant for? Are we to have no rest here, but to be always toiling and building up our own happiness out of the ruins of the happiness of our neighbors? And when we have made our home on earth as comfortable as it can be made with steam and gas and electricity, are we really so much happier than the Hindu in his primitive homestead?

With us, as I said just now, in these Northern climates, where life is and always must be a struggle, and a hard struggle too, and where accumulation of wealth has become almost a necessity to guard against the uncertainties of old age or the accidents inevitable in our complicated social life – with us, I say, and in our society, hours of rest and meditation are but few and far between. It was the same as long as we know the history of the Teutonic races; it was the same even with Romans and Greeks. The European climate, with its long cold winters, in many places also the difficulty of cultivating the soil, the conflict of interests between small communities, has developed the instinct of self-preservation (not to say self-indulgence) to such an extent that most of the virtues and most of the vices of European society can be traced back to that source. Our own character was formed under these influences, by inheritance, by education, by necessity. We all lead a fighting-life; our highest ideal of life is a fighting-life. We work till we can work no longer, and are proud, like old horses, to die in harness. We point with inward satisfaction to what we and our ancestors have achieved by hard work, in founding a family or a business, a town or a state. We point to the marvels of what we call civilization – our splendid cities, our high-roads and bridges, our ships, our railways, our telegraphs, our electric light, our pictures, our statues, our music, our theatres. We imagine we have made life on earth quite perfect – in some cases so perfect that we are almost sorry to leave it again. But the lesson which both Brahmans and Buddhists are never tired of teaching is that this life is but a journey from one village to another, and not a resting-place. Thus we read:[1]

> "As a man journeying to another village may enjoy a night's rest in the open air, but, after leaving his resting-place, proceeds again on his journey the next day, thus father, mother, wife, and wealth are all but like a night's rest to us – wise people do not cling to them forever."

Instead of simply despising this Indian view of life, might we not pause for a moment and consider whether their philosophy of life is entirely wrong, and ours entirely right; whether this earth was really meant for work only (for with us pleasure also has been changed into work), for constant hurry and flurry; or whether we, sturdy Northern Aryans, might not have been satisfied with a little less of work, and a little less of so-called pleasure, but with a little more of thought and a little more of rest. For, short as our life is, we are not mere may-flies, that are born in the morning to die at night. We have a past to look back to and a future to look forward to, and it may be that some of the riddles of the future find their solution in the wisdom of the past.

Then why should we always fix our eyes on the present only? Why should we always be racing, whether for wealth or for power or for fame? Why should we never rest and be thankful?

I do not deny that the manly vigor, the silent endurance, the public spirit, and the private virtues too, of the citizens of European states represent one side, it may be a very important side, of the destiny which man has to fulfil on earth.

---

1. Boehtlingk, Sprüche, 5101.

But there is surely another side of our nature, and possibly another destiny open to man in his journey across this life, which should not be entirely ignored. If we turn our eyes to the East, and particularly to India, where life is, or at all events was, no very severe struggle, where the climate was mild, the soil fertile, where vegetable food in small quantities sufficed to keep the body in health and strength, where the simplest hut or cave in a forest was all the shelter required, and where social life never assumed the gigantic, ay monstrous proportions of a London or Paris, but fulfilled itself within the narrow boundaries of village-communities – was it not, I say, natural there, or, if you like, was it not *intended* there, that another side of human nature should be developed – not the active, the combative, and acquisitive, but the passive, the meditative, and reflective? Can we wonder that the Aryans, who stepped as strangers into some of the happy fields and valleys along the Indus or the Ganges, should have looked upon life as a perpetual Sunday or holiday, or a kind of long vacation, delightful so long as it lasts, but which must come to an end sooner or later? Why should they have accumulated wealth? why should they have built palaces? why should they have toiled day and night? After having provided from day to day for the small necessities of the body, they thought they had the right, it may be the duty, to look round upon this strange exile, to look inward upon themselves, upward to something not themselves, and to see whether they could not understand a little of the true purport of that mystery which we call life on earth.

Of course *we* should call such notions of life dreamy, unreal, unpractical, but may not *they* look upon our notions of life as short-sighted, fussy, and, in the end, most unpractical, because involving a sacrifice of life for the sake of life?

No doubt these are both extreme views, and they have hardly ever been held or realized in that extreme form by any nation, whether in the East or in the West. We are not always plodding – we sometimes allow ourselves an hour of rest and peace and thought – nor were the ancient people of India always dreaming and meditating on τὰ μέγιστα, on the great problems of life, but, when called upon, we know that they too could fight like heroes, and that, without machinery, they could by patient toil raise even the meanest handiwork into a work of art, a real joy to the maker and to the buyer.

All then that I wish to put clearly before you is this, that the Aryan man, who had to fulfil his mission in India, might naturally be deficient in many of the practical and fighting virtues, which were developed in the Northern Aryans by the very struggle without which they could not have survived, but that his life on earth had not therefore been entirely wasted. His very view of life, though we cannot adopt it in this Northern climate, may yet act as a lesson and a warning to us, not, for the sake of life, to sacrifice the highest objects of life.

The greatest conqueror of antiquity stood in silent wonderment before the Indian Gymnosophists, regretting that he could not communicate with them in their own language, and that their wisdom could not reach him except through the contaminating channels of sundry interpreters.

That need not be so at present. Sanskrit is no longer a difficult language, and I can assure every young Indian civil servant that if he will but go to the fountain-head of Indian wisdom, he will find there, among much that is strange and useless, some lessons of life which are worth learning, and which we in our haste are too apt to forget or to despise.

Let me read you a few sayings only, which you may still hear repeated in India when, after the heat of the day, the old and the young assemble together under the shadow of their village tree – sayings which to them seem truth; to us, I fear, mere truism!

"As all have to sleep together laid low in the earth, why do foolish people wish to injure one another?"[1]

---

1. Mahâbh. XI. 121.

"A man seeking for eternal happiness (moksha) might obtain it by a hundredth part of the sufferings which a foolish man endures in the pursuit of riches.[1]

"Poor men eat more excellent bread than the rich: for hunger gives it sweetness.[2]

"Our body is like the foam of the sea, our life like a bird, our company with those whom we love does not last forever; why then sleepest thou, my son?

"As two logs of wood meet upon the ocean and then separate again, thus do living creatures meet.

"Our meeting with wives, relations, and friends occurs on our journey. Let a man therefore see clearly where he is, whither he will go, what he is, why tarrying here, and why grieving for anything.

"Family, wife, children, our very body and our wealth, they all pass away. They do not belong to us. What then is ours? Our good and our evil deeds.

"When thou goest away from here, no one will follow thee. Only thy good and thy evil deeds, they will follow thee wherever thou goest.

"Whatever act, good or bad, a man performs, of that by necessity he receives the recompense.

"According to the Vedathe soul (life) is eternal, but the body of all creatures is perishable. When the body is destroyed, the soul departs elsewhere, fettered by the bonds of our works.

"If I know that my own body is not mine, and yet that the whole earth is mine, and again that it is both mine and thine, no harm can happen then.[3]

---

1. Pañkat. II. 127 (117).
2. Mahâbh. V. 1144.
3. Kâm. Nîtis, 1, 23 (Boehtlingk, 918).

"As a man puts on new garments in this world, throwing aside those which he formerly wore, even so the Self[1] of man puts on new bodies which are in accordance with his acts.[2]

"No weapons will hurt the Self of man, no fire will burn it, no water moisten it, no wind will dry it up.

"It is not to be hurt, not to be burnt, not to be moistened, not to be dried up. It is imperishable, unchanging, immovable, without beginning.

"It is said to be immaterial, passing all understanding, and unchangeable. If you know the Self of man to be all this, grieve not.

"There is nothing higher than the attainment of the knowledge of the Self.[3]

"All living creatures are the dwelling of the Self who lies enveloped in matter, who is immortal, and spotless. Those who worship the Self, the immovable, living in a movable dwelling, become immortal.

"Despising everything else, a wise man should strive after the knowledge of the Self."

We shall have to return to this subject again, for this knowledge of the Self is really the *Vedânta*, that is, the end, the highest goal of the Veda. The highest wisdom of Greece was "to know ourselves;" the highest wisdom of India is "to know our Self."

If I were asked to indicate by one word the distinguishing feature of the Indian character, as I have here tried to sketch it, I should say it was *transcendent*, using that word, not in its strict technical sense, as fixed by Kant, but in its more general acceptation, as denoting a mind bent on transcending the limits of empirical knowledge. There are minds perfectly satisfied with empirical knowledge,

1. *Âtman,* see Lecture VII.—A. W.
2. Vishnu-sûtras XX. 50-53.
3. Âpastamba Dharma-sûtras I. 8, 22.

a knowledge of facts, well ascertained, well classified, and well labelled. Such knowledge may assume very vast proportions, and, if knowledge is power, it may impart great power, real intellectual power to the man who can wield and utilize it. Our own age is proud of that kind of knowledge, and to be content with it, and never to attempt to look beyond it, is, I believe, one of the happiest states of mind to be in.[1]

But, for all that, there is a Beyond, and he who has once caught a glance of it, is like a man who has gazed at the sun – wherever he looks, everywhere he sees the image of the sun. Speak to him of finite things, and he will tell you that the Finite is impossible and meaningless without the Infinite. Speak to him of death, and he will call it birth; speak to him of time, and he will call it the mere shadow of eternity. To us the senses seem to be the organs, the tools, the most powerful engines of knowledge; to him they are, if not actually deceivers, at all events heavy fetters, checking the flight of the spirit. To us this earth, this life, all that we see, and hear, and touch is certain. Here, we feel, is our home, here lie our duties, here our pleasures. To him this earth is a thing that once was not, and that again will cease to be; this life is a short dream from which we shall soon awake. Of nothing he professes greater ignorance than of what to others seems to be most certain, namely what we see, and hear, and touch; and as to our home, wherever that may be, he knows that certainly it is not here.

Do not suppose that such men are mere dreamers. Far from it! And if we can only bring ourselves to be quite honest to ourselves, we shall have to confess that at times we all have been visited by these transcendental aspirations, and have been able to understand what Wordsworth meant when he spoke of those

---

1. Can a state be justly regarded as one of happiness, in which the essential being is overlooked and not regarded; whereas that subtler essence is the reality which gives life, energy, and purity to all our motives? Is to be "of the earth, earthy," a greater felicity than to acknowledge that which is from heaven? I trow not.—A. W.

"Obstinate questionings
Of sense and outward things,
Fallings from us, vanishings;
Blank misgivings of a creature
Moving about in worlds not realized."

The transcendent temperament acquired no doubt a more complete supremacy in the Indian character than anywhere else; but no nation, and no individual, is entirely without that "yearning beyond;" indeed we all know it under a more familiar name – namely, *Religion*.

It is necessary, however, to distinguish between religion and *a* religion, quite as much as in another branch of philosophy we have to distinguish between language and *a* language or many languages. A man may accept *a* religion, he may be converted to the Christian religion, and he may change his own particular religion from time to time, just as he may speak different languages. But in order to have *a* religion, a man must have religion. He must once *at least* in his life have looked beyond the horizon of this world, and carried away in his mind an impression of the Infinite, which will never leave him again. A being satisfied with the world of sense, unconscious of its finite nature, undisturbed by the limited or negative character of all perceptions of the senses, would be incapable of any religious concepts. Only when the finite character of all human knowledge has been received is it possible for the human mind to conceive that which is beyond the Finite, call it what you like, the Beyond, the Unseen, the Infinite, the Supernatural, or the Divine. That step must have been taken before religion of any kind becomes possible. What kind of religion it will be, depends on the character of the race which elaborates it, its surroundings in nature, and its experience in history.

Now we may seem to know a great many religions – I speak here, of course, of ancient religions only, of what are sometimes called national or autochthonous religions – not of those founded in later times by individual prophets or reformers.

Yet, among those ancient religions we seldom know, what after all is the most important point, their origin and their gradual growth. The Jewish religion is represented to us as perfect and complete from the very first, and it is with great difficulty that we can discover its real beginnings and its historical growth. And take the Greek and the Roman religions, take the religions of the Teutonic, Slavonic, or Celtic tribes, and you will find that their period of growth has always passed, long before we know them, and that from the time we know them, all their changes are purely *metamorphic* – changes in form of substances ready at hand. Now let us look to the ancient inhabitants of India. With them, first of all, religion was not only *one* interest by the side of many. It was the all-absorbing interest; it embraced not only worship and prayer, but what we call philosophy, morality, law, and government – all was pervaded by religion. Their whole life was to them a religion – everything else was, as it were, a mere concession made to the ephemeral requirements of this life.

What then can we learn from the ancient religious literature of India, or from the Veda?

It requires no very profound knowledge of Greek religion and Greek language to discover in the Greek deities the original outlines of certain physical phenomena. Every schoolboy knows that in *Zeus* there is something of the sky, in *Poseidon* of the sea, in *Hades* of the lower world, in *Apollo* of the sun, in *Artemis* of the moon, in *Hephæstos* of the fire. But for all that, there is, from a Greek point of view, a very considerable difference between *Zeus* and the sky, between *Poseidon* and the sea, between *Apollo* and the sun, between *Artemis* and the moon.

Now what do we find in the Veda? No doubt here and there a few philosophical hymns which have been quoted so often that people have begun to imagine that the Veda is a kind of collection of Orphic hymns. We also find some purely mythological hymns, in which the Devas or gods have assumed nearly as much dramatic personality as in the Homeric hymns.

But the great majority of Vedic hymns consists in simple invocations of the fire, the water, the sky, the sun, and the storms, often under the same names which afterward became the proper names of Hindu deities, but as yet nearly free from all that can be called irrational or mythological. There is nothing irrational, nothing I mean we cannot enter into or sympathize with, in people imploring the storms to cease, or the sky to rain, or the sun to shine. I say there is nothing irrational in it, though perhaps it might be more accurate to say that there is nothing in it that would surprise anybody who is acquainted with the growth of human reason, or at all events, of childish reason. It does not matter how we call the tendency of the childish mind to confound the manifestation with that which manifests itself, effect with cause, act with agent. Call it Animism, Personification, Metaphor, or Poetry, we all know what is meant by it, in the most general sense of all these names; we all know that it exists, and the youngest child who beats the chair against which he has fallen, or who scolds his dog, or who sings: "Rain, rain, go to Spain," can teach us that, however irrational all this may seem to us, it is perfectly rational, natural, ay inevitable in the first periods, or the childish age of the human mind.

Now it is exactly this period in the growth of ancient religion, which was always presupposed or postulated, but was absent everywhere else, that is clearly put before us in the hymns of the Rig-Veda. It is this ancient chapter in the history of the human mind which has been preserved to us in Indian literature, while we look for it in vain in Greece or Rome or elsewhere.

It has been a favorite idea of those who call themselves "students of man," or anthropologists, that in order to know the earliest or so-called prehistoric phases in the growth of man, we should study the life of savage nations, as we may watch it still in some parts of Asia, Africa, Polynesia, and America.

There is much truth in this, and nothing can be more useful than the observations which we find collected in the works of such students as Waitz, Tylor, Lubbock, and many others. But let us be honest, and confess, first of all, that the materials on which we have here to depend are often extremely untrustworthy.

Nor is this all. What do we know of savage tribes beyond the last chapter of their history? Do we ever get an insight into their antecedents? Can we understand, what after all is everywhere the most important and the most instructive lesson to learn, how they have come to be what they are? There is indeed their language, and in it we see traces of growth that point to distant ages, quite as much as the Greek of Homer or the Sanskrit of the Vedas. Their language proves indeed that these so-called heathens, with their complicated systems of mythology, their artificial customs, their unintelligible whims and savageries, are not the creatures of to-day or yesterday. Unless we admit a special creation for these savages, they must be as old as the Hindus, the Greeks and Romans, as old as we ourselves. We may assume, of course, if we like, that their life has been stationary, and that they are to-day what the Hindus were no longer 3000 years ago. But that is a mere guess, and is contradicted by the facts of their language. They may have passed through ever so many vicissitudes, and what we consider as primitive may be, for all we know, a relapse into savagery, or a corruption of something that was more rational and intelligible in former stages. Think only of the rules that determine marriage among the lowest of savage tribes. Their complication passes all understanding, all seems a chaos of prejudice, superstition, pride, vanity, and stupidity. And yet we catch a glimpse here and there that there was some reason in most of that unreason; we see how sense dwindled away into nonsense, custom into ceremony, ceremony into farce. Why then should this surface of savage life represent to us the lowest stratum of human life, the very beginnings of civilization, simply because we cannot dig beyond that surface?

Now, I do not wish to be misunderstood. I do not claim for the ancient Indian literature any more than I should willingly concede to the fables and traditions and songs of savage nations, such as we can study at present in what we call a state of nature. Both are important documents to the student of the Science of Man. I simply say that in the Veda we have a nearer approach to a beginning, and an intelligible beginning, than in the wild invocations of Hottentots or Bushmen. But when I speak of a beginning, I do not mean an absolute beginning, a beginning of all things. Again and again the question has been asked whether we could bring ourselves to believe that man, as soon as he could stand on his legs, instead of crawling on all fours, as he is supposed to have done, burst forth into singing Vedic hymns? But who has ever maintained this? Surely whoever has eyes to see can see in every Vedic hymn, ay, in every Vedic word, as many rings within rings as are in the oldest tree that was ever hewn down in the forest.

I shall say even more, and I have said it before, namely, that supposing that the Vedic hymns were composed between 1500 and 1000 B.C., we can hardly understand how, at so early a date, the Indians had developed ideas which to us sound decidedly modern. I should give anything if I could escape from the conclusion that the collection of the Vedic Hymns, a collection in ten books, existed at least 1000 B.C., that is, about 500 years before the rise of Buddhism. I do not mean to say that something may not be discovered hereafter to enable us to refer that collection to a later date. All I say is that, so far as we know *at present*, so far as all honest Sanskrit scholars know *at present*, we cannot well bring our pre-Buddhistic literature into narrower limits than five hundred years.

What then is to be done? We must simply keep our preconceived notions of what people call primitive humanity in abeyance for a time, and if we find that people three thousand years ago were familiar with ideas that seem novel and nineteenth-century-like to us, well, we must somewhat modify our conceptions of the primitive savage, and remember that things hid from the wise and prudent have sometimes been revealed to babes.

I maintain then that for a study of man, or, if you like, for a study of Aryan humanity, there is nothing in the world equal in importance with the Veda. I maintain that to everybody who cares for himself, for his ancestors, for his history, or for his intellectual development, a study of Vedic literature is indispensable; and that, as an element of liberal education, it is far more important and far more improving than the reigns of Babylonian and Persian kings.

It is curious to observe the reluctance with which these facts are accepted, particularly by those to whom they ought to be most welcome, I mean the students of anthropology. Instead of devoting all their energy to the study of these documents, which have come upon us like a miracle, they seem only bent on inventing excuses why they need not be studied. Let it not be supposed that, because there are several translations of the Rig-Veda in English, French and German, therefore all that the Veda can teach us has been learned. Far from it. Every one of these translations has been put forward as tentative only. I myself, though during the last thirty years I have given translations of a number of the more important hymns, have only ventured to publish a specimen of what I think a translation of the Veda ought to be; and that translation, that *traduction raisonnée* as I ventured to call it, of twelve hymns only, fills a whole volume. We are still on the mere surface of Vedic literature, and yet our critics are ready with ever so many arguments why the Veda can teach us nothing as to a primitive state of man. If they mean by primitive that which came absolutely first, then they ask for something which they will never get, not even if they discovered the private correspondence of Adam and Eve, or of the first *Homo* and *Femina sapiens*. We mean by primitive the earliest state of many of which, from the nature of the case, we can hope to gain any knowledge; and here, next to the archives hidden away in the secret drawers of language, in the treasury of words common to all the Aryan tribes, and in the radical elements of which each word is compounded, there is no literary relic more full of lessons to the true anthropologist, to the true student of mankind, than the Rig-Veda.

Lecture 4

Objections

It may be quite true that controversy often does more harm than good, that it encourages the worst of all talents, that of plausibility, not to say dishonesty, and generally leaves the world at large worse confounded than it was before. It has been said that no clever lawyer would shrink from taking a brief to prove that the earth forms the centre of the world, and, with all respect for English juries, it is not impossible that even in our days he might gain a verdict against Galileo. Nor do I deny that there is a power and vitality in truth which in the end overcomes and survives all opposition, as shown by the very doctrine of Galileo which at present is held by hundreds and thousands who would find it extremely difficult to advance one single argument in its support. I am ready to admit also that those who have done the best work, and have contributed most largely toward the advancement of knowledge and the progress of truth, have seldom wasted their time in controversy, but have marched on straight, little concerned either about applause on the right or abuse on the left. All this is true, perfectly true, and yet I feel that I cannot escape from devoting the whole of a lecture to the answering of certain objections which have been raised against the views which I have put forward with regard to the character and the historical importance of Vedic literature. We must not forget that the whole subject is new, the number of competent judges small, and mistakes not only possible, but almost inevitable. Besides, there are mistakes and mistakes, and the errors of able men are often instructive, nay one might say sometimes almost indispensable for the discovery of truth. There are criticisms which may be safely ignored, criticisms for the sake of criticism, if not inspired by meaner motives. But there are doubts and difficulties which suggest themselves naturally, objections which have a right to be heard, and the very removal of which forms the best approach to the stronghold of truth. Nowhere has this principle been so fully recognized and been acted on as in Indian literature. Whatever subject is started, the rule is that the argument should begin with the pûrvapaksha, with all that can be said against a certain opinion. Every possible objection is welcome, if only it is not altogether frivolous and absurd, and then only follows the uttarapaksha, with all that can be said against these objections and in support of the original opinion. Only when this process has been fully gone through is it allowed to represent an opinion as siddhânta, or established.

Therefore, before opening the pages of the Veda, and giving you a description of the poetry, the religion, and philosophy of the ancient inhabitants of India, I thought it right and necessary to establish, first of all, certain points without which it would be impossible to form a right appreciation of the historical value of the Vedic hymns, and of their importance even to us who live at so great a distance from those early poets.

The *first* point was purely preliminary, namely that the Hindus in ancient, and in modern times also, are a nation deserving of our interest and sympathy, worthy also of our confidence, and by no means guilty of the charge so recklessly brought against them – the charge of an habitual disregard of truth.

Secondly, that the ancient literature of India is not to be considered simply as a curiosity and to be handed over to the good pleasure of Oriental scholars, but that, both by its language, the Sanskrit, and by its most ancient literary documents, the Vedas, it can teach us lessons which nothing else can teach, as to the origin of our own language, the first formation of our own concepts, and the true natural germs of all that is comprehended under the name of civilization, at least the civilization of the Aryan race, that race to which we and all the greatest nations of the world – the Hindus, the Persians, the Greeks and Romans, the Slaves, the Celts, and last, not least, the Teutons, belong. A man may be a good and useful ploughman without being a geologist, without knowing the stratum on which he takes his stand, or the strata beneath that give support to the soil on which he lives and works, and from which he draws his nourishment. And a man may be a good and useful citizen, without being an historian, without knowing how the world in which he lives came about, and how many phases mankind had to pass through in language, religion, and philosophy, before it could supply him with that intellectual soil on which he lives and works, and from which he draws his best nourishment.

But there must always be an aristocracy of those who know, and who can trace back the best which we possess, not merely to a Norman count, or a Scandinavian viking, or a Saxon earl, but to far older ancestors and benefactors, who thousands of years ago were toiling for us in the sweat of their face, and without whom we should never be what we are – the ancestors of the whole Aryan race, the first framers of our words, the first poets of our thoughts, the first givers of our laws, the first prophets of our gods, and of Him who is God above all gods.

That aristocracy of those who know – *di color che sanno* – or try to know, is open to all who are willing to enter, to all who have a feeling for the past, an interest in the genealogy of our thoughts, and a reverence for the ancestry of our intellect, who are in fact historians in the true sense of the word, *i.e.* inquirers into that which is past, but not lost.

Thirdly, having explained to you why the ancient literature of India, the really ancient literature of that country, I mean that of the Vedic period, deserves the careful attention, not of Oriental scholars only, but of every educated man and woman who wishes to know how we, even we here in England and in this nineteenth century of ours, came to be what we are, I tried to explain to you the difference, and the natural and inevitable difference, between the development of the human character in such different climates as those of India and Europe. And while admitting that the Hindus were deficient in many of those manly virtues and practical achievements which we value most, I wished to point out that there was another sphere of intellectual activity in which the Hindus excelled – the meditative and transcendent – and that here we might learn from them some lessons of life which we ourselves are but too apt to ignore or to despise.

Fourthly, fearing that I might have raised too high expectations of the ancient wisdom, the religion and philosophy of the Vedic Indians, I felt it my duty to state that, though primitive in one sense, we must not expect the Vedic religion to be primitive in the anthropological sense of the word, as containing the utterances of beings who had just broken their shells, and were wonderingly looking out for the first time upon this strange world. The Veda may be called primitive, because there is no other literary document more primitive than it; but the language, the mythology, the religion and philosophy that meet us in the Veda open vistas of the past which no one would venture to measure in years. Nay, they contain, by the side of simple, natural, childish thoughts, many ideas which to us sound modern, or secondary and tertiary, as I called them, but which nevertheless are older than any other literary document, and give us trustworthy information of a period in the history of human thought of which we knew absolutely nothing before the discovery of the Vedas.[1]

---

1. If we applied the name of literature to the cylinders of Babylon and the papyri of Egypt, we should have to admit that some of these documents are more ancient than any date we dare as yet assign to the hymns collected in the ten books of the Rig-Veda.

But even thus our path is not yet clear. Other objections have been raised against the Veda as an historical document. Some of them are important; and I have at times shared them myself. Others are at least instructive, and will give us an opportunity of testing the foundation on which we stand.

The first objection then against our treating the Veda as an historical document is that it is not truly national in its character, and does not represent the thoughts of the whole of the population of India, but only of a small minority, namely of the Brahmans, and not even of the whole class of Brahmans, but only of a small minority of them, namely of the professional priests.

Objections should not be based on demands which, from the nature of the case, are unreasonable. Have those who maintain that the Vedic hymns do not represent the whole of India, that is the whole of its ancient population, in the same manner as they say that the Bible represents the Jews or Homer the Greeks, considered what they are asking for? So far from denying that the Vedic hymns represent only a small and, it may be, a priestly minority of the ancient population of India, the true historian would probably feel inclined to urge the same cautions against the Old Testament and the Homeric poems also.

No doubt, after the books which compose the Old Testament had been collected as a Sacred Canon, they were known to the majority of the Jews. But when we speak of the primitive state of the Jews, of their moral, intellectual, and religious status while in Mesopotamia or Canaan or Egypt, we should find that the different books of the Old Testament teach us as little of the whole Jewish race, with all its local characteristics and social distinctions, as the Homeric poems do of all the Greek tribes, or the Vedic hymns of all the inhabitants of India. Surely, even when we speak of the history of the Greeks or the Romans, we know that we shall not find there a complete picture of the social, intellectual, and religious life of a whole nation. We know very little of the intellectual life of a whole nation, even during the Middle Ages, ay, even at the present day.

We may know something of the generals, of the commanders-in-chief, but of the privates, of the millions, we know next to nothing. And what we do know of kings or generals or ministers is mostly no more than what was thought of them by a few Greek poets or Jewish prophets, men who were one in a million among their contemporaries.

But it might be said that though the writers were few, the readers were many. Is that so? I believe you would be surprised to hear how small the number of readers is even in modern times, while in ancient times reading was restricted to the very smallest class of privileged persons. There may have been listeners at public and private festivals, at sacrifices, and later on in theatres, but readers, in our sense of the word, are a very modern invention.

There never has been so much reading, reading spread over so large an area, as in our times. But if you asked publishers as to the number of copies sold of books which are supposed to have been read by everybody, say Macaulay's History of England, the Life of the Prince Consort, or Darwin's Origin of Species, you would find that out of a population of thirty-two millions not one million has possessed itself of a copy of these works. The book which of late has probably had the largest sale is the Revised Version of the New Testament; and yet the whole number of copies sold among the eighty millions of English-speaking people is probably not more than four millions. Of ordinary books which are called books of the season, and which are supposed to have had a great success, an edition of three or four thousand copies is not considered unsatisfactory by publishers or authors in England. But if you look to other countries, such, for instance, as Russia, it would be very difficult indeed to name books that could be considered as representative of the whole nation, or as even known by more than a very small minority.

And if we turn our thoughts back to the ancient nations of Greece and Italy, or of Persia and Babylonia, what book is there, with the exception perhaps of the Homeric poems, of which we could say that it had been read or even heard of by more than a few thousand people? We think of Greeks and Romans as literary people, and so no doubt they were, but in a very different sense from what we mean by this. What we call Greeks and Romans are chiefly the citizens of Athens and Rome, and here again those who could produce or who could read such works as the Dialogues of Plato or the Epistles of Horace constituted a very small intellectual aristocracy indeed. What we call history – the memory of the past – has always been the work of minorities. Millions and millions pass away unheeded, and the few only to whom has been given the gift of fusing speech and thought into forms of beauty remain as witnesses of the past.

If then we speak of times so distant as those represented by the Rig-Veda, and of a country so disintegrated, or rather as yet so little integrated as India was three thousand years ago, surely it requires but little reflection to know that what we see in the Vedic poems are but a few snow-clad peaks, representing to us, from a far distance, the whole mountain-range of a nation, completely lost beyond the horizon of history. When we speak of the Vedic hymns as representing the religion, the thoughts and customs of India three thousand years ago, we cannot mean by India more than some unknown quantity of which the poets of the Veda are the only spokesmen left. When we now speak of India, we think of 250 millions, a sixth part of the whole human race, peopling the vast peninsula from the Himalayan mountains between the arms of the Indus and the Ganges, down to Cape Comorin and Ceylon, an extent of country nearly as large as Europe. In the Veda the stage on which the life of the ancient kings and poets is acted, is the valley of the Indus and the Punjab, as it is now called, the Sapta Sindhasah, the Seven Rivers of the Vedic poets. The land watered by the Ganges is hardly known, and the whole of the Dekkan seems not yet to have been discovered.

Then again, when these Vedic hymns are called the lucubrations of a few priests, not the outpourings of the genius of a whole nation, what does that mean? We may no doubt call these ancient Vedic poets priests, if we like, and no one would deny that their poetry is pervaded not only by religious, mythological, and philosophical, but likewise by sacrificial and ceremonial conceits. Still a priest, if we trace him back far enough, is only a *presbyteros* or an elder, and, as such, those Vedic poets had a perfect right to speak in the name of a whole class, or of the village community to which they belonged. Call Vasishtha a priest by all means, only do not let us imagine that he was therefore very like Cardinal Manning.

After we have made every possible concession to arguments, most of which are purely hypothetical, there remains this great fact that here, in the Rig-Veda, we have poems, composed in perfect language, in elaborate metre, telling us about gods and men, about sacrifices and battles, about the varying aspects of nature and the changing conditions of society, about duty and pleasure, philosophy and morality – articulate voices reaching us from a distance from which we never heard before the faintest whisper; and instead of thrilling with delight at this almost miraculous discovery, some critics stand aloof and can do nothing but find fault, because these songs do not represent to us primitive men exactly as they think they ought to have been; not like Papúas or Bushmen, with arboraceous habits and half-animal clicks, not as worshipping stocks or stones, or believing in fetiches, as according to Comte's inner consciousness they ought to have done, but rather, I must confess, as beings whom we can understand, with whom to a certain extent we can sympathize, and to whom, in the historical progress of the human intellect, we may assign a place not very far behind the ancient Jews and Greeks.

Once more then, if we mean by primitive, people who inhabited this earth as soon as the vanishing of the glacial period made this earth inhabitable, the Vedic poets were certainly not primitive. If we mean by primitive, people who were without a knowledge of fire, who used unpolished flints, and ate raw flesh, the Vedic poets were not primitive. If we mean by primitive, people who did not cultivate the soil, had no fixed abodes, no kings, no sacrifices, no laws, again, I say, the Vedic poets were not primitive. But if we mean by primitive the people who have been the first of the Aryan race to leave behind literary relics of their existence on earth, then I say the Vedic poets are primitive, the Vedic language is primitive, the Vedic religion is primitive, and, taken as a whole, more primitive than anything else that we are ever likely to recover in the whole history of our race.

When all these objections had failed, a last trump was played. The ancient Vedic poetry was said to be, if not of foreign origin, at least very much infected by foreign, and more particularly by Semitic influences. It had always been urged by Sanskrit scholars as one of the chief attractions of Vedic literature that it not only allowed us an insight into a very early phase of religious thought, but that the Vedic religion was the only one the development of which took place without any extraneous influences, and could be watched through a longer series of centuries than any other religion. Now with regard to the first point, we know how perplexing it is in the religion of ancient Rome to distinguish between Italian and Greek ingredients, to say nothing of Etruscan and Phœnician influences. We know the difficulty of finding out in the religion of the Greeks what is purely home-grown, and what is taken over from Egypt, Phœnicia, it may be from Scythia; or at all events, slightly colored by those foreign rays of thought. Even in the religion of the Hebrews, Babylonian, Phœnician, and at a later time Persian influences have been discovered, and the more we advance toward modern times, the more extensive becomes the mixture of thought, and the more difficult the task of assigning to each nation the share which it contributed to the common intellectual currency of the world. In India alone, and more particularly in Vedic India, we see a plant entirely grown on native soil, and entirely nurtured by native air. For this reason, because the religion of the Veda was so completely guarded from all strange infections, it is full of lessons which the student of religion could learn nowhere else.

Now what have the critics of the Veda to say against this? They say that the Vedic poems show clear traces of *Babylonian* influences. I must enter into some details, because, small as they seem, you can see that they involve very wide consequences.

There is one verse in the Rig-Veda, VIII. 78, 2,[1] which has been translated as follows: "Oh Indra, bring to us a brilliant jewel, a cow, a horse, an ornament, together with a golden Manâ."[2] Now what is a golden Manâ? The word does not occur again by itself, either in the Veda or anywhere else, and it has been identified by Vedic scholars with the Latin *mina*, the Greek μνᾶ, the Phœnician *manah* (הֲנֶמ), the well-known weight[3] which we actually possess now among the treasures brought from Babylon and Nineveh to the British Museum.[4]

If this were so, it would be irrefragable evidence of at all events a commercial intercourse between Babylon and India at a very early time, though it would in no way prove a real influence of Semitic on Indian thought. But is it so? If we translate sakâ manâ hiranyayâ by "with a mina of gold," we must take manâ hiranyayâ as instrumental cases. But sakâ never governs an instrumental case. This translation therefore is impossible, and although the passage is difficult, because manâ does not occur again in the Rig-Veda, I should think we might take manâ hiranyayâ for a dual, and translate, "Give us also two golden armlets." To suppose that the Vedic poets should

---

1. Ã nah bhara vyâṅganam gãm ásvam abhyâṅganam Sákâ manã hiranyáyâ.
2. Grassman translates, "Zugleich mit goldenem Geräth;" Ludwig, "Zusammt mit goldenem Zierrath;" Zimmer, "Und eine Manâ gold." The Petersburg Dictionary explains manâ by "ein bestimmtes Geräth oder Gewicht" (Gold).
3. According to Dr. Haupt, Die Sumerisch-akkadische Sprache, p. 272, mana is an Akkadian word.
4. According to the weights of the lions and ducks preserved in the British Museum, an Assyrian mina was = 7747 grains. The same difference is still preserved to the present day, as the *man* of Shiraz and Bagdâd is just double that of Tabraz and Bushir, the average of the former being 14.0 and that of the latter only 6.985. See Cunningham, "Journal of the Asiatic Society," Calcutta, 1881, p. 163.

have borrowed this one word and this one measure from the Babylonians, would be against all the rules of historical criticism. The word manâ never occurs again in the whole of Sanskrit literature, no other Babylonian weight occurs again in the whole of Sanskrit literature, and it is not likely that a poet who asks for a cow and a horse, would ask in the same breath for a foreign weight of gold, that is, for about sixty sovereigns.

But this is not the only loan that India has been supposed to have negotiated in Babylon. The twenty-seven Nakshatras, or the twenty-seven constellations, which were chosen in India as a kind of lunar Zodiac, were supposed to have come from Babylon. Now the Babylonian Zodiac was solar, and, in spite of repeated researches, no trace of a lunar Zodiac has been found, where so many things have been found, in the cuneiform inscriptions. But supposing even that a lunar Zodiac had been discovered in Babylon, no one acquainted with Vedic literature and with the ancient Vedic ceremonial would easily allow himself to be persuaded that the Hindus had borrowed that simple division of the sky from the Babylonians. It is well known that most of the Vedic sacrifices depend on the moon, far more than on the sun.[1] As the Psalmist says, "He appointed the moon for seasons; the sun knoweth his going down," we read in the Rig-Veda X. 85, 18, in a verse addressed to sun and moon, "They walk by their own power, one after the other (or from east to west), as playing children they go round the sacrifice. The one looks upon all the worlds, the other is born again and again, determining the seasons."

"He becomes new and new, when he is born; as the herald of the days, he goes before the dawns. By his approach he determines their share for the gods, the moon increases a long life."

The moon, then, determines the seasons, the ritus, the moon fixes the share, that is, the sacrificial oblation for all the gods. The seasons

---

1. Preface to the fourth volume of my edition of the Rig-Veda, p. li.

and the sacrifices were in fact so intimately connected together in the thoughts of the ancient Hindus, that one of the commonest names for priest was ritv-ig, literally, the season-sacrificer.

Besides the rites which have to be performed every day, such as the five Mahâyagñas, and the Agnihotra in the morning and the evening, the important sacrifices in Vedic times were the Full and New-moon sacrifices (darsapûrnamâsa); the Season-sacrifices (kâturmâsya), each season consisting of four months;[1] and the Half-yearly sacrifices, at the two solstices. There are other sacrifices (âgrayana, etc.) to be performed in autumn and summer, others in winter and spring, whenever rice and barley are ripening.[2]

The regulation of the seasons, as one of the fundamental conditions of an incipient society, seems in fact to have been so intimately connected with the worship of the gods, as the guardians of the seasons and the protectors of law and order, that it is sometimes difficult to say whether in their stated sacrifices the maintenance of the calendar or the maintenance of the worship of the gods was more prominent in the minds of the old Vedic priests.

The twenty-seven Nakshatras then were clearly suggested by the moon's passage.[3] Nothing was more natural for the sake of counting days, months, or seasons than to observe the twenty-seven places which the moon occupied in her passage from any point of the sky back to the same point. It was far easier than to determine the sun's position either from day to day, or from month to month; for the stars, being hardly visible at the actual rising and setting of the sun, the idea of the sun's conjunction with certain stars could not suggest itself to a listless observer. The moon, on the contrary, progressing from night to night, and coming successively in contact with certain stars, was like the finger of a clock, moving round a circle,

---

1. Vaisvadevam on the full-moon of Phalguna, Varunapraghâsâh on the full-moon of Ashâdha, Sâkamedhâh on the full-moon of Krittikâ, see Boehtlingk, Dictionary, s. v.
2. See Vishnu-smriti, ed. Jolly LIX. 4; Áryabhata, Introduction.
3. See Preface to vol. iv. of Rig-Veda, p. li. (1862).

and coming in contact with one figure after another on the dial-plate of the sky. Nor would the portion of about one third of a lunation in addition to the twenty-seven stars from new moon to new moon, create much confusion in the minds of the rough-and-ready reckoners of those early times. All they were concerned with were the twenty-seven celestial stations which, after being once traced out by the moon, were fixed, like so many mile-stones, for determining the course of all the celestial travellers that could be of any interest for signs and for seasons, and for days and for years. A circle divided into twenty-seven sections, or any twenty-seven poles planted in a circle at equal distances round a house, would answer the purpose of a primitive Vedic observatory. All that was wanted to be known was between which pair of poles the moon, or afterward the sun also, was visible at their rising or setting, the observer occupying the same central position on every day.

Our notions of astronomy cannot in fact be too crude and too imperfect if we wish to understand the first beginnings in the reckoning of days and seasons and years. We cannot expect in those days more than what any shepherd would know at present of the sun and moon, the stars and seasons. Nor can we expect any observations of heavenly phenomena unless they had some bearing on the practical wants of primitive society.

If then we can watch in India the natural, nay inevitable, growth of the division of the heaven into twenty-seven equal divisions, each division marked by stars, which may have been observed and named long before they were used for this new purpose – if, on the other hand, we could hardly understand the growth and development of the Indian ceremonial except as determined by a knowledge of the lunar asterisms, the lunar months, and the lunar seasons, surely it would be a senseless hypothesis to imagine that the Vedic shepherds or priests went to Babylonia in search of a knowledge which every shepherd might have acquired on the banks of the Indus, and that, after their return from that country only, where a language was spoken which no Hindu could understand, they set to work to compose their sacred hymns and arrange their simple ceremonial. We must never forget that what is natural in one place is natural in other places also, and we may sum up without fear of serious contradiction, that no case has been made out in favor of a foreign origin of the elementary astronomical notions of the Hindus as found or presupposed in the Vedic hymns.[1]

The Arabs, as is well known, have twenty-eight lunar stations, the *Manzil*, and I can see no reason why Mohammed and his Bedouins in the desert should not have made the same observation as the Vedic poets in India, though I must admit at the same time that Colebrooke has brought forward very cogent arguments to prove that, in their scientific employment at least, the Arabic Manzil were really borrowed from an Indian source.

The Chinese, too, have their famous lunar stations, *the Sieu*, originally twenty-four in number, and afterward raised to twenty-eight.[2] But here again there is no necessity whatever for admitting, with Biot, Lassen, and others, that the Hindus went to China to gain their simplest elementary notions of lunar chronomy. First of all, the Chinese began with twenty-four, and raised them to twenty-eight; the Hindus began with twenty-seven, and raised them to twenty-eight. Secondly, out of these twenty-eight asterisms, there are seventeen only which can really be identified with the Hindu stars (târâs). Now if a scientific system is borrowed, it is borrowed complete. But, in our case, I see really no possible channel through which Chinese astronomical knowledge could have been conducted to India so early as 1000 before our era. In Chinese literature India is never mentioned before the middle of the second century before Christ; and if the Kînas in the later Sanskrit literature are meant for Chinese, which is doubtful, it is important to observe that that name never occurs in Vedic literature.[3]

---

1. See Zimmer, Altindisches Leben, pp. 352-357.
2. See Zimmer, Altindisches Leben, p. xlvii.
3. In the Mahâbhârata and elsewhere the Kînas are mentioned among the Dasyus or non-Aryan races in the north and in the east of India. King Bhaga-

When therefore the impossibility of so early a communication between China and India had at last been recognized, a new theory was formed, namely, "that the knowledge of Chinese astronomy was not imported straight from China to India, but was carried, together with the Chinese system of division of the heavens into twenty-eight mansions, into Western Asia, at a period not much later than 1100 B.C., and was then adopted by some Western people, either Semitic or Iranian. In their hands it was supposed to have received a new form, such as adapted it to a ruder and less scientific method of observation, the limiting stars of the mansions being converted into zodiacal groups or constellations, and in some instances altered in position, so as to be brought nearer to the general planetary path of the ecliptic. In this changed form, having become a means of roughly determining and describing the places and movements of the planets, it was believed to have passed into the keeping of the Hindus, very probably along with

---

datta is said to have had an army of Kînas and Kirâtas, (B1) and the Pândavas are said to reach the town of the King of the Kulindas, after having passed through the countries of Kînas, Tukhâras, and Daradas. All this is as vague as ethnological indications generally are in the late epic poetry of India. The only possibly real element is that Kirâta and Kîna soldiers are called kâñkana, gold or yellow colored, (B2) and compared to a forest of Karnikâras, which were trees with yellow flowers. (B3) In Mahâbh. VI. 9, v. 373, vol. ii., p. 344, the Kînas occur in company with Kambogas and Yavanas, which again conveys nothing definite.

B1: Lassen, i. p. 1029; Mahâbh. III. 117, v. 12,350; vol. i. p. 619.

B2: Mahâbh. V. 18, v. 584; vol. ii. p. 106.

B3: See Vâkaspatya s. v.; Kaskit Karnikâragaurah.

Chinese scholars tell us that the name of China is of modern origin, and only dates from the Thsin dynasty or from the famous Emperor Shi hoang-ti, 247 B.C. But the name itself, though in a more restricted sense, occurs in earlier documents, and may, as Lassen thinks, (B4) have become known to the Western neighbors of China. It is certainly strange that the *Sinim* too, mentioned in Isaiah xlix. 12, have been taken by the old commentators for people of China, visiting Babylon as merchants and travellers.

B4: Lassen, vol. i. p. 1029, n. 2.

the first knowledge of the planets themselves, and entered upon an independent career of history in India. It still maintained itself in its old seat, leaving its traces later in the Bundahash; and made its way so far westward as finally to become known and adopted by the Arabs." With due respect for the astronomical knowledge of those who hold this view, all I can say is that this is a novel, and nothing but a novel, without any facts to support it, and that the few facts which are known to us do not enable a careful reasoner to go beyond the conclusions stated many years ago by Colebrooke, that the "Hindus had undoubtedly made some progress at an early period in the astronomy cultivated by them for the regulation of time. Their calendar, both civil and religious, was governed chiefly, not exclusively, by the moon and the sun; and the motions of these luminaries were carefully observed by them, and with such success that their determination of the moon's synodical revolution, which was what they were principally concerned with, is a much more correct one than the Greeks ever achieved. They had a division of the ecliptic into twenty-seven and twenty-eight parts, suggested evidently by the moon's period in days, and seemingly their own; it was certainly borrowed by the Arabians."

There is one more argument which has been adduced in support of a Babylonian, or, at all events, a Semitic influence to be discovered in Vedic literature which we must shortly examine. It refers to the story of the *Deluge*.

That story, as you know, has been traced in the traditions of many races, which could not well have borrowed it from one another; and it was rather a surprise that no allusion even to a local deluge should occur in any of the Vedic hymns, particularly as very elaborate accounts of different kinds of deluges are found in the later Epic poems, and in the still later Purânas, and form in fact a very familiar subject in the religious traditions of the people of India.

Three of the *Avatâras* or incarnations of Vishnu are connected with a deluge, that of the *Fish*, that of the *Tortoise*, and that of the *Boar*,

Vish*n*u in each case rescuing mankind from destruction by water, by assuming the form of a fish, or a tortoise, or a boar.

This being so, it seemed a very natural conclusion to make that, as there was no mention of a deluge in the most ancient literature of India, that legend had penetrated into India from without at a later time.

When, however, the Vedic literature became more generally known, stories of a deluge were discovered, if not in the hymns, at least in the prose writings, belonging to the second period, commonly called the Brâhmana period. Not only the story of Manu and the *Fish*, but the stories of the *Tortoise* and of the *Boar* also, were met with there in a more or less complete form, and with this discovery the idea of a foreign importation lost much of its plausibility. I shall read you at least one of these accounts of a Deluge which is found in the Satapatha Brâhmana, and you can then judge for yourselves whether the similarities between it and the account in Genesis are really such as to require, nay as to admit, the hypothesis that the Hindus borrowed their account of the Deluge from their nearest Semitic neighbors.

We read in the Satapatha Brâhmana I. 8, 1:

"In the morning they brought water to Manu for washing, as they bring it even now for washing our hands.

"While he was thus washing, a fish came into his hands.

"2. The fish spoke this word to Manu: 'Keep me, and I shall save thee.'

"Manu said: 'From what wilt thou save me?'

"The fish said: 'A flood will carry away all these creatures, and I shall save thee from it.'

"Manu said: 'How canst thou be kept?'

"3. The fish said: 'So long as we are small, there is much destruction for us, for fish swallows fish. Keep me therefore first in a jar. When I outgrow that, dig a hole and keep me in it. When I outgrow that, take me to the sea, and I shall then be beyond the reach of destruction.'

"4. He became soon a large fish (ghasha), for such a fish grows largest. The fish said: 'In such and such a year the flood will come. Therefore when thou hast built a ship, thou shalt meditate on me. And when the flood has risen, thou shalt enter into the ship, and I will save thee from the flood.'

"5. Having thus kept the fish, Manu took him to the sea. Then in the same year which the fish had pointed out, Manu, having built the ship, meditated on the fish. And when the flood had risen, Manu entered into the ship. Then the fish swam toward him, and Manu fastened the rope of the ship to the fish's horn, and he thus hastened toward[1] the Northern Mountain.

"6. The fish said: 'I have saved thee; bind the ship to a tree. May the water not cut thee off, while thou art on the mountain. As the water subsides, do thou gradually slide down with it.' Manu then slid down gradually with the water, and therefore this is called 'the Slope of Manu' on the Northern Mountain. Now the flood had carried away all these creatures, and thus Manu was left there alone.

"7. Then Manu went about singing praises and toiling, wishing for offspring. And he sacrificed there also with a Pâka-sacrifice. He poured clarified butter, thickened milk, whey, and curds in the water as a libation. In one year a woman arose from it. She came forth as if dripping, and clarified butter gathered on her step. Mitra and Varuna came to meet her.

"8. They said to her: 'Who art thou?' She said: 'The daughter of Manu.' They rejoined: 'Say that thou art ours.' 'No,' she said, 'he who has begotten me, his I am.'

---

1. I prefer now the reading of the Kânva-sâkhâ, abhidudrâva, instead of atidudrâva or adhidudrâva of the other MSS. See Weber, Ind. Streifen, i. p. 11.

"Then they wished her to be their sister, and she half agreed and half did not agree, but went away, and came to Manu.

"9. Manu said to her: 'Who art thou?' She said: 'I am thy daughter.' 'How, lady, art thou my daughter?' he asked.

"She replied: 'The libations which thou hast poured into the water, clarified butter, thickened milk, whey and curds, by them thou hast begotten me. I am a benediction – perform (me) this benediction at the sacrifices. If thou perform (me) it at the sacrifice, thou wilt be rich in offspring and cattle. And whatever blessing thou wilt ask by me, will always accrue to thee.' He therefore performed that benediction in the middle of the sacrifice, for the middle of the sacrifice is that which comes between the introductory and the final offerings.

"10. Then Manu went about with her, singing praises and toiling, wishing for offspring. And with her he begat that offspring which is called the offspring of Manu; and whatever blessing he asked with her, always accrued to him. She is indeed Idâ, and whosoever, knowing this, goes about (sacrifices) with Idâ, begets the same offspring which Manu begat, and whatever blessing he asks with her, always accrues to him."

This, no doubt, is the account of a deluge, and Manu acts in some respects the same part which is assigned to Noah in the Old Testament. But if there are similarities, think of the dissimilarities, and how they are to be explained. It is quite clear that, if this story was borrowed from a Semitic source, it was not borrowed from the Old Testament, for in that case it would really seem impossible to account for the differences between the two stories. That it may have been borrowed[1] from some unknown Semitic source cannot,

---

1. It is not necessary to establish literary borrowing; for on the theory of Bible inspiration and trustworthiness we must assume that the Aryans as well as the

of course, be disproved, because no tangible proof has ever been produced that would admit of being disproved. But if it were, it would be the only Semitic loan in ancient Sanskrit literature – and that alone ought to make us pause!

The story of the boar and the tortoise too, can be traced back to the Vedic literature. For we read in the Taittirîya Samhitâ:[1]

"At first this was water, fluid. Pragâpati, the lord of creatures, having become wind, moved on it. He saw this earth, and becoming a boar, he took it up. Becoming Visvakarman, the maker of all things, he cleaned it. It spread and became the widespread Earth, and this is why the Earth is called Prithivî, the widespread."

And we find in the Satapatha Brâhmana[2] the following slight allusion at least to the tortoise myth:

"Pragâpati, assuming the form of a tortoise (Kûrma), brought forth all creatures. In so far as he brought them forth, he made them (akarot), and because he made them he was (called) tortoise (Kûrma). A tortoise is (called) Kâsyapa, and therefore all creatures are called Kâsyapa, tortoise-like. He who was this tortoise (Kûrma) was really Âditya (the sun)."

One other allusion to something like a deluge,[3] important chiefly on account of the name of Manu occurring in it, has been pointed out in the Kâthaka (XI. 2), where this short sentence occurs: "The waters cleaned this, Manŭ alone remained."

All this shows that ideas of a deluge, that is, of a submersion of the earth by water and of its rescue through divine aid, were not

---

Semites were saved in the ark. The story of *a* flood supports the story of *the* flood to a certain extent.—AM. PUBS.

1. VII. 1, 5, 1 seq.; Muir, i. p. 52; Colebrooke, Essays, i. 75.
2. VII. 5, 1, 5; Muir, "Original Sanskrit Texts," i. p. 54.
3. Weber, "Indische Streifen," i. p. 11.

altogether unknown in the early traditions of India, while in later times they were embodied in several of the Avâtaras of Vishnu.

When we examine the numerous accounts of a deluge among different nations in almost every part of the world, we can easily perceive that they do not refer to one single historical event, but to a natural phenomenon repeated every year, namely, the deluge or flood of the rainy season or the winter.[1]

This, is nowhere clearer than in Babylon. Sir Henry Rawlinson was the first to point out that the twelve cantos of the poem of Izdubar or Nimrod refer to the twelve months of the year and the twelve representative signs of the Zodiac. Dr. Haupt afterward pointed out that Êabânî, the wise bull-man in the second canto, corresponds to the second month, Ijjar, April-May, represented in the Zodiac by the bull; that the union between Êabânî and Nimrod in the third canto corresponds to the third month, Sivan, May-June, represented in the Zodiac by the twins; that the sickness of Nimrod in the seventh canto corresponds to the seventh month, Tishri, September-October, when the sun begins to wane; and that the flood in the eleventh canto corresponds to the eleventh month, Shabatu, dedicated to the storm-god Rimmôn,[2] represented in the Zodiac by the waterman.[3]

If that is so, we have surely a right to claim the same natural origin for the story of the Deluge in India which we are bound to admit in other countries. And even if it could be proved that in the form in which these legends have reached us in India they show traces of foreign influences,[4] the fact would still remain that such influences have been perceived in comparatively modern treatises only, and not in the ancient hymns of the Rig-Veda.

---

1. See Lecture V. p. 172.
2. More accurately Ramanu, the Vul or storm-god of George Smith; and the god of the Mind and higher intellect at Babylon. His arcane name is said to have been Yav, וחי or Ἰάω.—A. W.
3. See Haupt, "Der Keilinschriftliche Sintfluthbericht, 1881," p. 10.
4. See M. M., "Genesis and Avesta" (German translation), i. p. 148.

Other conjectures have been made with even less foundation than that which would place the ancient poets of India under the influence of Babylon. China has been appealed to, nay even Persia, Parthia, and Bactria, countries beyond the reach of India at that early time of which we are here speaking, and probably not even then consolidated into independent nations or kingdoms. I only wonder that traces of the lost Jewish tribes have not been discovered in the Vedas, considering that Afghanistan has so often been pointed out as one of their favorite retreats.

After having thus carefully examined all the traces of supposed foreign influences that have been brought forward by various scholars, I think I may say that there really is no trace whatever of any foreign influence in the language, the religion, or the ceremonial of the ancient Vedic literature of India. As it stands before us now, so it has grown up, protected by the mountain ramparts in the north, the Indus and the Desert in the west, the Indus or what was called the sea in the south, and the Ganges in the east. It presents us with a home-grown poetry and a home-grown religion; and history has preserved to us at least this one relic, in order to teach us what the human mind can achieve if left to itself, surrounded by a scenery and by conditions of life that might have made man's life on earth a paradise, if man did not possess the strange art of turning even a paradise into a place of misery.[1]

---

1. No one is more competent than the learned author to give a verdict on all the evidence which has been gathered; but we are only at the beginning of research into the intercourse of mankind in remote times, and much that was once thought home-grown has already been traced to distant points. It is in the general line of progress in research that more evidence may be expected to connect Vedic thought with other cultures.—AM. PUBS.

Lecture 5

The Lessons of the Veda

Although there is hardly any department of learning which has not received new light and new life from the ancient literature of India, yet nowhere is the light that comes to us from India so important, so novel, and so rich as in the study of religion and mythology. It is to this subject therefore that I mean to devote the remaining lectures of this course. I do so, partly because I feel myself most at home in that ancient world of Vedic literature in which the germs of Aryan religion have to be studied, partly because I believe that for a proper understanding of the deepest convictions, or, if you like, the strongest prejudices of the modern Hindus, nothing is so useful as a knowledge of the Veda. It is perfectly true that nothing would give a false impression of the actual Brahmanical religion than the ancient Vedic literature, supposing we were to imagine that three thousand years could have passed over India without producing any change. Such a mistake would be nearly as absurd as to deny any difference between the Vedic Sanskrit and the spoken Bengali. But no one will gain a scholarlike knowledge or a true insight into the secret springs of Bengali who is ignorant of the grammar of Sanskrit; and no one will ever understand the present religious, philosophical, legal, and social opinions of the Hindus who is unable to trace them back to their true sources in the Veda.

I still remember how, many years ago, when I began to publish for the first time the text and the commentary of the Rig-Veda, it was argued by a certain, perhaps not quite disinterested party, that the Veda was perfectly useless; that no man in India, however learned, could read it, and that it was of no use either for missionaries or for anyone else who wished to study and to influence the native mind. It was said that we ought to study the later Sanskrit, the Laws of Manu, the epic poems, and, more particularly, the Purânas. The Veda might do very well for German students, but not for Englishmen.

There was no excuse for such ignorant assertions even thirty years ago, for in these very books, in the Laws of Manu, in the Mahâbhârata, and in the Purânas, the Veda is everywhere proclaimed as the highest authority in all matters of religion.[1] "A Brahman," says Manu, "unlearned in holy writ, is extinguished in an instant like dry grass on fire." "A twice-born man (that is, a Brâhmana, a Kshatriya, and a Vaisya) not having studied the Veda, soon falls, even when living, to the condition of a Sûdra, and his descendants after him."

How far this license of ignorant assertion may be carried is shown by the same authorities who denied the importance of the Veda for a historical study of Indian thought, boldly charging those wily priests, the Brahmans, with having withheld their sacred literature from any but their own caste. Now, so far from withholding it, the Brahmans have always been striving, and often striving in vain, to make the study of their sacred literature obligatory on all castes except the Sûdras, and the passages just quoted from Manu show what penalties were threatened if children of the second and third castes, the Kshatriyas and Vaisyas, were not instructed in the sacred literature of the Brahmans.

---

1. Wilson, Lectures, p. 9.

At present the Brahmans themselves have spoken, and the reception they have accorded to my edition of the Rig-Veda[1] and its native commentary, the zeal with which they have themselves taken up the study of Vedic literature, and the earnestness with which different sects are still discussing the proper use that should be made of their ancient religious writings, show abundantly that a Sanskrit scholar ignorant of, or, I should rather say, determined to ignore the Veda, would be not much better than a Hebrew scholar ignorant of the Old Testament.

I shall now proceed to give you some characteristic specimens of the religion and poetry of the Rig-Veda. They can only be few, and as there is nothing like system or unity of plan in that collection of 1017 hymns, which we call the Samhitâ of the Rig-Veda, I cannot promise that they will give you a complete panoramic view of that intellectual world in which our Vedic ancestors passed their life on earth.

I could not even answer the question, if you were to ask it whether the religion of the Veda was *polytheistic* or *monotheistic*. Monotheistic, in the usual sense of that word, it is decidedly not, though there are hymns that assert the unity of the Divine as fearlessly as any passage of the Old Testament, or the New Testament, or the Koran. Thus one poet says (Rig-Veda I. 164, 46): "That which

---

1. As it has been doubted, and even denied, that the publication of the Rig-Veda and its native commentary has had some important bearing on the resuscitation of the religious life of India, I feel bound to give at least one from the many testimonials which I have received from India. It comes from the Âdi Brahma Samâj, founded by Ram Mohun Roy, and now represented by its three branches, the Âdi Brahma Samâj, the Brahma Samâj of India, and the Sadhârano Brahma Samâj. "The Committee of the Âdi Brahma Samâj beg to offer you their hearty congratulations on the completion of the gigantic task which has occupied you for the last quarter of a century. By publishing the Rig-Veda at a time when Vedic learning has by some sad fatality become almost extinct in the land of its birth, you have conferred a boon upon us Hindus, for which we cannot but be eternally grateful."

is *one*, sages name it in various ways – they call it Agni, Yama, Mâtarisvan."

Another poet says: "The wise poets represent by their words Him who is one with beautiful wings, in many ways."[1]

And again we hear of a being called Hiranyagarbha, the golden germ (whatever the original of that name may have been), of whom the poet says:[2] "In the beginning there arose Hiranyagarbha; he was the one born lord of all this. He established the earth and this sky. Who is the god to whom we shall offer our sacrifice?" That Hiranyagarbha, the poet says, "is alone God above all gods" (yah deveshu adhi devah ekah âsît) – an assertion of the unity of the Divine which could hardly be exceeded in strength by any passage from the Old Testament.

But by the side of such passages, which are few in number, there are thousands in which ever so many divine beings are praised and prayed to. Even their number is sometimes given as "thrice eleven"[3] or thirty-three, and one poet assigns eleven gods to the sky, eleven to the earth, and eleven to the waters,[4] the waters here intended being those of the atmosphere and the clouds. These thirty-three gods have even wives apportioned to them,[5] though few of these only have as yet attained to the honor of a name.[6]

These thirty-three gods, however, by no means include all the Vedic gods, for such important deities as Agni, the fire, Soma, the rain, the Maruts or Storm-gods, the Asvins, the gods of Morning and Evening, the Waters, the Dawn, the Sun are mentioned separately;

---

1. Rig-Veda X. 114, 5.
2. Rig-Veda X. 121.
3. Muir, iv. 9.
4. Rig-Veda I. 139, 11.
5. Rig-Veda III. 6, 9.
6. The following names of Devapatnîs or wives of the gods are given in the Vaitâna Sûtra XV. 3 (ed. Garbe): Prithivî, the wife of Agni, Vâk of Vâta, Senâ of Indra, Dhenâ of Brihaspati, Pathyâ of Pûshan, Gâyatrî of Vasu, Trishtubh of Rudra, Gagati of Âditya, Anushtubh of Mitra, Virâg of Varuna, Pankti of Vishnu, Dîkshâ of Soma.

and there are not wanting passages in which the poet is carried away into exaggerations, till he proclaims the number of his gods to be, not only thirty-three, but three thousand three hundred and thirty-nine.[1]

If therefore there must be a name for the religion of the Rig-Veda, polytheism would seem at first sight the most appropriate. Polytheism, however, has assumed with us a meaning which renders it totally inapplicable to the Vedic religion.

Our ideas of polytheism being chiefly derived from Greece and Rome, we understand by it a certain more or less organized system of gods, different in power and rank, and all subordinate to a supreme God, a Zeus or Jupiter. The Vedic polytheism differs from the Greek and Roman polytheism, and, I may add, likewise from the polytheism of the Ural-Altaic, the Polynesian, the American, and most of the African races, in the same manner as a confederacy of village communities differs from a monarchy. There are traces of an earlier stage of village-community life to be discovered in the later republican and monarchical constitutions, and in the same manner nothing can be clearer, particularly in Greece, than that the monarchy of Zeus was preceded by what may be called the septarchy of several of the great gods of Greece. The same remark applies to the mythology of the Teutonic nations also.[2] In the Veda, however, the gods worshipped as supreme by each sept stand still side by side. No one is first always, no one is last always. Even gods of a decidedly inferior and limited character assume occasionally in the eyes of a devoted poet a supreme place above all other gods.[3]

---

1. Rig-Veda III. 9, 9.

2. Grimm showed that Thôrr is sometimes the supreme god, while at other times he is the son of Ôdinn. This, as Professor Zimmer truly remarks, need not be regarded as the result of a revolution, or even of gradual decay, as in the case of Dyaus and Týr, but simply as inherent in the character of a nascent polytheism. See Zeitschrift für D. A., vol. xii. p. 174.

3. "Among not yet civilized races prayers are addressed to a god with a special object, and to that god who is supposed to be most powerful in a special domain. He becomes for the moment the highest god to whom all others must

It was necessary, therefore, for the purpose of accurate reasoning, to have a name, different from *polytheism*, to signify this worship of single gods, each occupying for a time a supreme position, and I proposed for it the name of *Kathenotheism*, that is, a worship of one god after another, or of *Henotheism*, the worship of single gods. This shorter name of *Henotheism* has found more general acceptance, as conveying more definitely the opposition between *Monotheism*, the worship of one only God, and *Henotheism*, the worship of single gods; and, if but properly defined, it will answer its purpose very well. However, in researches of this kind we cannot be too much on our guard against technical terms. They are inevitable, I know; but they are almost always misleading. There is, for instance, a hymn addressed to the *Indus* and the rivers that fall into it, of which I hope to read you a translation, because it determines very accurately the geographical scene on which the poets of the Veda passed their life. Now native scholars call these rivers *devatâs* or deities, and European translators too speak of them as gods and goddesses. But in the language used by the poet with regard to the Indus and the other rivers, there is nothing to justify us in saying that he considered these rivers as *gods* and *goddesses*, unless we mean by *gods* and *goddesses* something very different from what the Greeks called River-gods and River-goddesses, Nymphs, Najades, or even Muses.

And what applies to these rivers applies more or less to all the objects of Vedic worship. They all are still oscillating between what is seen by the senses, what is created by fancy, and what is postulated by the understanding; they are things, persons, causes, according to the varying disposition of the poets; and if we call them gods or goddesses, we must remember the remark of an ancient native theologian, who reminds us that by *devatâ* or deity he means no more than the object celebrated in a hymn, while Rishi or seer means no more than the subject or the author of a hymn.

---

give place. He may be invoked as the highest and the only god, without any slight being intended for the other gods."—Zimmer, l. c. p. 175.

It is difficult to treat of the so-called gods celebrated in the Veda according to any system, for the simple reason that the concepts of these gods and the hymns addressed to them sprang up spontaneously and without any pre-established plan. It is best perhaps for our purpose to follow an ancient Brahmanical writer, who is supposed to have lived about 400 B.C. He tells us of students of the Veda, before his time, who admitted three deities only, viz., *Agni* or fire, whose place is on the earth; *Vâyu* or *Indra*, the wind and the god of the thunderstorm, whose place is in the air; and *Sûrya*, the sun, whose place is in the sky. These deities, they maintained, received severally many appellations, in consequence of their greatness, or of the diversity of their functions, just as a priest, according to the functions which he performs at various sacrifices, receives various names.

This is *one* view of the Vedic gods, and, though too narrow, it cannot be denied that there is some truth in it. A very useful division of the Vedic gods might be made, and has been made by Yâska, into *terrestrial, aërial,* and *celestial,* and if the old Hindu theologians meant no more than that all the manifestations of divine power in nature might be traced back to three centres of force, one in the sky, one in the air, and one on the earth, he deserves great credit for his sagacity.

But he himself perceived evidently that this generalization was not quite applicable to all the gods, and he goes on to say: "Or, it may be, these gods are all distinct beings, for the praises addressed to them are distinct, and their appellations also." This is quite right. It is the very object of most of these divine names to impart distinct individuality to the manifestations of the powers of nature; and though the philosopher or the inspired poet might perceive that these numerous names were but names, while that which was named was *one* and *one* only, this was certainly not the idea of most of the Vedic Rishis themselves, still less of the people who listened to their songs at fairs and festivals. It is the peculiar character of that phase of religious thought which we have to study in the Veda, that in it the Divine is conceived and represented as manifold, and that many functions are shared in common by various gods, no attempt having yet been made at organizing the whole body of the gods, sharply separating one from the other, and subordinating all of them to several or, in the end, to one supreme head.

Availing ourselves of the division of the Vedic gods into terrestrial, aërial, and celestial, as proposed by some of the earliest Indian theologians, we should have to begin with the gods connected with the earth.

Before we examine them, however, we have first to consider one of the earliest objects of worship and adoration, namely *Earth and Heaven*, or *Heaven and Earth*, conceived as a divine couple. Not only in India, but among many other nations, both savage, half-savage, or civilized, we meet with Heaven and Earth as one of the earliest objects, pondered on, transfigured, and animated by the early poets, and more or less clearly conceived by early philosophers. It is surprising that it should be so, for the conception of the Earth as an independent being, and of Heaven as an independent being, and then of both together as a divine couple embracing the whole universe, requires a considerable effort of abstraction, far more than the concepts of other divine powers, such as the Fire, the Rain, the Lightning, or the Sun.

Still so it is, and as it may help us to understand the ideas about Heaven and Earth, as we find them in the Veda, and show us at the same time the strong contrast between the mythology of the Aryans and that of real savages (a contrast of great importance, though I admit very difficult to explain), I shall read you first some extracts from a book, published by a friend of mine, the Rev. William Wyatt Gill, for many years an active and most successful missionary in Mangaia, one of those Polynesian islands that form a girdle round one quarter of our globe,[1] and all share in the same language, the same religion,

---

1. "Es handelt sich hier nicht um amerikanische oder afrikanische Zersplitterung, sondern eine überraschende Gleichartigkeit dehnt sich durch die Weite und Breite des Stillen Oceans, und wenn wir Oceanien in der vollen

the same mythology, and the same customs. The book is called "Myths and Songs from the South Pacific,"[1] and it is full of interest to the student of mythology and religion.

The story, as told him by the natives of Mangaia, runs as follows:

"The sky is built of solid blue stone. At one time it almost touched the earth; resting upon the stout broad leaves of the *teve* (which attains the height of about six feet) and the delicate indigenous arrow-root (whose slender stem rarely exceeds three feet)... In this narrow space between earth and sky the inhabitants of this world were pent up. Ru, whose usual residence was in Avaiki, or the shades, had come up for a time to this world of ours. Pitying the wretched confined residence of the inhabitants, he employed himself in endeavoring to raise the sky a little. For this purpose he cut a number of strong stakes of different kinds of trees, and firmly planted them in the ground at Rangimotia, the centre of the island, and with him the centre of the world. This was a considerable improvement, as mortals were thereby enabled to stand erect and to walk about without inconvenience. Hence Ru was named 'The sky-supporter.' Wherefore Teka sings (1794):

'Force up the sky, O Ru,
And let the space be clear!'

"One day when the old man was surveying his work, his grace-less son Mâui contemptuously asked him what he was doing there. Ru replied: 'Who told youngsters to talk? Take care of yourself, or I will hurl you out of existence.'

Auffassung nehmen mit Einschluss Mikro-und Mela-nesiens (bis Malaya), selbst weiter. Es lässt sich sagen, dass ein einheitlicher Gedankenbau, in etwa 120 Längen und 70 Breitegraden, ein Viertel unsers Erdglobus überwölbt."— Bastian, Die Heilige Sage der Polynesier, p. 57.
1. Henry S. King & Co., London, 1876.

"'Do it, then,' shouted Mâui.

"Ru was as good as his word, and forthwith seized Mâui, who was small of stature, and threw him to a great height. In falling Mâui assumed the form of a bird, and lightly touched the ground, perfectly unharmed. Mâui, now thirsting for revenge, in a moment resumed his natural form, but exaggerated to gigantic proportions, and ran to his father, saying:

'Ru, who supportest the many heavens,
The third, even to the highest, ascend!'

Inserting his head between the old man's legs, he exerted all his prodigious strength, and hurled poor Ru, sky and all, to a tremendous height – so high, indeed, that the blue sky could never get back again. Unluckily, however, for the sky-supporting Ru, his head and shoulders got entangled among the stars. He struggled hard, but fruitlessly, to extricate himself. Mâui walked off well pleased with having raised the sky to its present height, but left half his father's body and both his legs ingloriously suspended between heaven and earth. Thus perished Ru. His body rotted away, and his bones came tumbling down from time to time, and were shivered on the earth into countless fragments. These shivered bones of Ru are scattered over every hill and valley of Mangaia, to the very edge of the sea."

What the natives call "the bones of Ru" (*te ivio Ru*) are pieces of pumice-stone.

Now let us consider, first of all, whether this story, which with slight variations is told all over the Polynesian islands,[1] is pure nonsense, or whether there was originally some sense in it. My conviction is that nonsense is everywhere the child of sense, only that unfortunately many children, like that youngster Mâui, consider themselves much wiser than their fathers, and occasionally succeed in hurling them out of existence.

---

1. There is a second version of the story even in the small island of Mangaia; see "Myths and Songs," p. 71.

It is a peculiarity of many of the ancient myths that they represent events which happen every day, or every year, as having happened once upon a time. The daily battle between day and night, the yearly battle between winter and spring, are represented almost like historical events, and some of the episodes and touches belonging originally to these constant battles of nature, have certainly been transferred into and mixed up with battles that took place at a certain time, such as, for instance, the siege of Troy. When historical recollections failed, legendary accounts of the ancient battles between Night and Morning, Winter and Spring, were always at hand; and, as in modern times we constantly hear "good stories," which we have known from our childhood, told again and again of any man whom they seem to fit, in the same manner, in ancient times, any act of prowess, or daring, or mischief, originally told of the sun, "the orient Conqueror of gloomy Night," was readily transferred to and believed of any local hero who might seem to be a second Jupiter, or Mars, or Hercules.

I have little doubt therefore that as the accounts of a deluge, for instance, which we find almost everywhere, are originally recollections of the annual torrents of rain or snow that covered the little worlds within the ken of the ancient village-bards,[1] this tearing asunder of heaven and earth too was originally no more than a description of what might be seen every morning. During a dark night the sky seemed to cover the earth; the two seemed to be one, and could not be distinguished one from the other.[2] Then came the Dawn, which with its bright rays lifted the covering of the dark night to a certain point, till at last Mâui appeared, small in stature,

---

1. This explanation is considered altogether inadequate by many scholars. It is, of course, not altogether a question of learning, but also one of judgment.—AM. PUBS.

2. "The Sacred Books of the East," vol. i. p. 249: "The first half is the earth, the second half the heaven, their uniting the rain, the uniter Parganya." And so it is when it (Parganya) rains thus strongly—without ceasing, day and night together—then they say also, "Heaven and earth have come together."—From the Aitareya-Âranyaka, III. 2, 2.—A. W.

a mere child, that is, the sun of the morning – thrown up suddenly, as it were, when his first rays shot through the sky from beneath the horizon, then falling back to the earth, like a bird, and rising in gigantic form on the morning sky. The dawn now was hurled away, and the sky was seen lifted high above the earth; and Mâui, the sun, marched on well pleased with having raised the sky to its present height.

Why pumice-stone should be called the bones of Ru, we cannot tell, without knowing a great deal more of the language of Mangaia than we do at present. It is most likely an independent saying, and was afterward united with the story of Ru and Mâui.

Now I must quote at least a few extracts from a Maori legend as written down by Judge Manning:[1]

"This is the Genesis of the New Zealanders:

"The Heavens which are above us, and the Earth which lies beneath us, are the progenitors of men, and the origin of all things.

"Formerly the Heaven lay upon the Earth, and all was darkness...

"And the children of Heaven and Earth sought to discover the difference between light and darkness, between day and night...

"So the sons of Rangi (Heaven) and of Papa (Earth) consulted together, and said, 'Let us seek means whereby to destroy Heaven and Earth, or to separate them from each other.'

"Then said Tumatauenga (the God of War), 'Let us destroy them both.'

"Then said Tane-Mahuta (the Forest God), 'Not so; let them be separated. Let one of them go upward and become a stranger to us; let the other remain below and be a parent for us.'

---

1. Bastian, Heilige Sage der Polynesier, p. 36.

"Then four of the gods tried to separate Heaven and Earth, but did not succeed, while the fifth, Tane, succeeded.

"After Heaven and Earth had been separated, great storms arose, or, as the poet expresses it, one of their sons, Tawhiri-Matea, the god of the winds, tried to revenge the outrage committed on his parents by his brothers. Then follow dismal dusky days, and dripping chilly skies, and arid scorching blasts. All the gods fight, till at last Tu only remains, the god of war, who had devoured all his brothers, except the Storm. More fights follow, in which the greater part of the earth was overwhelmed by the waters, and but a small portion remained dry. After that, light continued to increase, and as the light increased, so also the people who had been hidden between Heaven and Earth increased... And so generation was added to generation down to the time of Mâui-Potiki, he who brought death into the world.

"Now in these latter days Heaven remains far removed from his wife, the Earth; but the love of the wife rises upward in sighs toward her husband. These are the mists which fly upward from the mountain-tops; and the tears of Heaven fall downward on his wife; behold the dew-drops!"

So far the Maori Genesis.

Let us now return to the Veda, and compare these crude and somewhat grotesque legends with the language of the ancient Aryan poets. In the hymns of the Rig-Veda the separating and keeping apart of Heaven and Earth is several times alluded to, and here too it is represented as the work of the most valiant gods. In I. 67, 3 it is Agni, fire, who holds the earth and supports the heaven; in X. 89, 4 it is Indra who keeps them apart; in IX. 101, 15 Soma is celebrated for the same deed, and in III. 31, 12 other gods too share the same honor.[1]

---

1. Bergaigne, "La Religion Védique," p. 240.

In the Aitareya Brâhmana we read:[1] "These two worlds (Heaven and Earth) were once joined together. They went asunder. Then it did not rain, nor did the sun shine. And the five tribes did not agree with one another. The gods then brought the two (Heaven and Earth) together, and when they came together they formed a wedding of the gods."

Here we have in a shorter form the same fundamental ideas: first, that formerly Heaven and Earth were together; that afterward they were separated; that when they were thus separated there was war throughout nature, and neither rain nor sunshine; that, lastly, Heaven and Earth were conciliated, and that then a great wedding took place.

Now I need hardly remind those who are acquainted with Greek and Roman literature, how familiar these and similar conceptions about a marriage between Heaven and earth were in Greece and Italy. They seem to possess there a more special reference to the annual reconciliation between Heaven and Earth, which takes place in spring, and to their former estrangement during winter. But the first cosmological separation of the two always points to the want of light and the impossibility of distinction during the night, and the gradual lifting up of the blue sky through the rising of the sun.[2]

In the Homeric hymns[3] the Earth is addressed as

"Mother of gods, the wife of the starry Heaven;"[4]

and the Heaven or Æther is often called the father. Their marriage too is described, as, for instance, by Euripides, when he says:

"There is the mighty Earth, Jove's Æther:
*   He (the Æther) is the creator of men and gods;*
The earth receiving the moist drops of rain,

1. Ait. Br. IV. 27; Muir, iv. p. 23.
2. See Muir, iv. p. 24.
3. Homer, Hymn xxx. 17.
4. Χαῖρε θεῶν μήτηρ, ἄλοχ᾽ Οὐρανοῦ ἀστερόεντος.

Bears mortals,
Bears food, and the tribes of animals.
Hence she is not unjustly regarded
As the mother of all."[1]

And what is more curious still is that we have evidence that
Euripides received this doctrine from his teacher, the philosopher
Anaxagoras. For Dionysius of Halicarnassus[2] tells us that Euripides
frequented the lectures of Anaxagoras. Now, it was the theory of that
philosopher that originally all things were in all things, but that afterward they became separated. Euripides later in life associated with
Sokrates, and became doubtful regarding that theory. He accord-
ingly propounds the ancient doctrine by the mouth of another,
namely Melanippê, who says:

"This saying (myth) is not mine, but came from my mother,
that formerly Heaven and Earth were one shape; but when
they were separated from each other, they gave birth and
brought all things into the light, trees, birds, beasts, and the
fishes whom the sea feeds, and the race of mortals."

Thus we have met with the same idea of the original union, of
a separation, and of a subsequent reunion of Heaven and Earth in
Greece, in India, and in the Polynesian islands.

Let us now see how the poets of the Veda address these two
beings, Heaven and Earth.

---

1. Euripides, Chrysippus, fragm. 6 (edit. Didot, p. 824):
    Γαῖα μεγίστη καὶ Διὸς αἰθήρ,
    ὁ μὲν ἀνθρώπων καὶ θεῶν γενέτωρ,
    ἡ δ' ὑγροβόλους σταγόνας νοτίους
    παραδεξαμένη τίκτει θνατούς,
    τίκτει δὲ βορὰν, φῦλά τε θηρῶν,
    ὅθεν οὐκ ἀδίκως
    μήτηρ πάντων νενόμισται.
2. Dionysius Halic., vol. v. p. 355; Muir, v. p. 27.

They are mostly addressed in the dual, as two beings forming but one concept. We meet, however, with verses which are
addressed to the Earth by herself, and which speak of her as "kind,
without thorns, and pleasant to dwell on,"[1] while there are clear
traces in some of the hymns that at one time Dyaus, the sky, was
the supreme deity.[2] When invoked together they are called Dyâvâ-
prithivyau, from *dyu*, the sky, and prithivî, the broad earth.

If we examine their epithets, we find that many of them reflect
simply the physical aspects of Heaven and Earth. Thus they are
called *uru*, wide; uruvyakas, widely expanded, *dûre-ante*, with limits
far apart, *gabhîra*, deep; *ghritavat*, giving fat; madhudugha, yielding
honey or dew; *payasvat*, full of milk; *bhûri-retas*, rich in seed.

Another class of epithets represents them already as endowed
with certain human and superhuman qualities, such as asaskat,
never tiring, agara, not decaying, which brings us very near to
immortal; adruh, not injuring, or not deceiving, praketas, provi-
dent, and then pitâ-mâta, father and mother, devaputra, having the
gods for their sons, rita-vridh and ritavat, protectors of the Rita, of
what is right, guardians of eternal laws.

Here you see what is so interesting in the Veda, the gradual
advance from the material to the spiritual, from the sensuous to the
supersensuous, from the human to the superhuman and the divine.
Heaven and Earth were seen, and, according to our notions, they
might simply be classed as visible and finite beings. But the ancient
poets were more honest to themselves. They could see Heaven and
Earth, but they never saw them in their entirety. They felt that there
was something beyond the purely finite aspect of these beings, and
therefore they thought of them, not as they would think of a stone,
or a tree, or a dog, but as something not-finite, not altogether visible or knowable, yet as something important to themselves, powerful, strong to bless, but also strong to hurt. Whatever was between
Heaven and Earth seemed to be theirs, their property, their realm,

---

1. Rig-Veda I. 22, 15.
2. See "Lectures on the Science of Language," vol. ii. p. 468.

their dominion. They held and embraced all; they seemed to have produced all. The Devas or bright beings, the sun, the dawn, the fire, the wind, the rain, were all theirs, and were called therefore the offspring of Heaven and Earth. Thus Heaven and Earth became the Universal Father and Mother.

Then we ask at once: "Were then these Heaven and Earth gods?" But gods in what sense? In our sense of God? Why, in our sense, God is altogether incapable of a plural. Then in the Greek sense of the word? No, certainly not; for what the Greeks called gods was the result of an intellectual growth totally independent of the Veda or of India. We must never forget that what we call gods in ancient mythologies are not substantial, living, individual beings, of whom we can predicate this or that. *Deva*, which we translate by god, is nothing but an adjective, expressive of a quality shared by heaven and earth, by the sun and the stars and the dawn and the sea, namely *brightness*; and the idea of god, at that early time, contains neither more nor less than what is shared in common by all these bright beings. That is to say, the idea of god is not an idea ready-made, which could be applied in its abstract purity to heaven and earth and other such like beings; but it is an idea, growing out of the concepts of heaven and earth and of the other bright beings, slowly separating itself from them, but never containing more than what was contained, though confusedly, in the objects to which it was successively applied.

Nor must it be supposed that heaven and earth, having once been raised to the rank of undecaying or immortal beings, of divine parents, of guardians of the laws, were thus permanently settled in the religious consciousness of the people. Far from it. When the ideas of other gods, and of more active and more distinctly personal gods had been elaborated, the Vedic Rishis asked without hesitation: Who then has made heaven and earth? not exactly Heaven and Earth, as conceived before, but heaven and earth as seen every day, as a part of what began to be called Nature or the Universe.

Thus one poet says:[1]

"He was indeed among the gods the cleverest workman who produced the two brilliant ones (heaven and earth), that gladden all things; he who measured out the two bright ones (heaven and earth) by his wisdom, and established them on everlasting supports."

And again: "He was a good workman who produced heaven and earth; the wise, who by his might brought together these two (heaven and earth), the wide, the deep, the well-fashioned in the bottomless space."

Very soon this great work of making heaven and earth was ascribed, like other mighty works, to the mightiest of their gods, to Indra. At first we read that Indra, originally only a kind of *Jupiter pluvius*, or god of rain, stretched out heaven and earth, like a hide; that he held them in his hand, that he upholds heaven and earth, and that he grants heaven and earth to his worshippers. But very soon Indra is praised for having made Heaven and Earth; and then, when the poet remembers that Heaven and Earth had been praised elsewhere as the parents of the gods, and more especially as the parents of Indra, he does not hesitate for a moment, but says: "What poets living before us have reached the end of all thy greatness? for thou hast indeed begotten thy father and thy mother together[2] from thy own body!"

That is a strong measure, and a god who once could do that, was no doubt capable of anything afterward. The same idea, namely that Indra is greater than heaven and earth, is expressed in a less outrageous way by another poet, who says[3] that Indra is greater than heaven and earth, and that both together are only a half of Indra. Or again: "The divine Dyaus bowed before Indra, before Indra the great Earth bowed with her wide spaces." "At the birth

---

1. Rig-Veda I. 160, 4.
2. Cf. IV. 17, 4, where Dyaus is the father of Indra; see however Muir, iv. 31, note.
3. Rig-Veda VI. 30, 1.

of thy splendor Dyaus trembled, the Earth trembled for fear of thy anger."

Thus, from one point of view, Heaven and Earth were the greatest gods, they were the parents of everything, and therefore of the gods also, such as Indra and others.

But, from another point of view, every god that was considered as supreme at one time or other, must necessarily have made heaven and earth, must at all events be greater than heaven and earth, and thus the child became greater than the father, ay, became the father of his father. Indra was not the only god that created heaven and earth. In one hymn that creation is ascribed to Soma and Pûshan, by no means very prominent characters; in another to Hiranyagarbha (the golden germ); in another again to a god who is simply called Dhatri, the Creator, or Visvakarman, the maker of all things. Other gods, such as Mitra and Savitri, names of the sun, are praised for upholding Heaven and Earth, and the same task is sometimes performed by the old god Varuna[1] also.

What I wish you to observe in all this is the perfect freedom with which these so-called gods or Devas are handled, and particularly the ease and naturalness with which now the one, now the other emerges as supreme out of this chaotic theogony. This is the peculiar character of the ancient Vedic religion, totally different both from the Polytheism and from the Monotheism as we see it in the Greek and the Jewish religions; and if the Veda had taught us nothing else but this *henotheistic* phase, which must everywhere have preceded the more highly-organized phase of Polytheism which we see in Greece, in Rome, and elsewhere, the study of the Veda would not have been in vain.

It may be quite true that the poetry of the Veda is neither beautiful, in our sense of the word, nor very profound; but it is instructive. When we see those two giant spectres of Heaven and Earth on the background of the Vedic religion, exerting their influence for a time, and then vanishing before the light of younger and more

---

1. Rig-Veda VI. 70, 1.

active gods, we learn a lesson which it is well to learn, and which we can hardly learn anywhere else – the lesson *how gods were made and unmade* – how the Beyond or the Infinite was named by different names in order to bring it near to the mind of man, to make it for a time comprehensible, until, when name after name had proved of no avail, a nameless God was felt to answer best the restless cravings of the human heart.

I shall next translate to you the hymn to which I referred before as addressed to the Rivers. If the Rivers are to be called deities at all, they belong to the class of terrestrial deities. But the reason why I single out this hymn is not so much because it throws new light on the theogonic process, but because it may help to impart some reality to the vague conceptions which we form to ourselves of the ancient Vedic poets and their surroundings. The rivers invoked are, as we shall see, the real rivers of the Punjâb, and the poem shows a much wider geographical horizon than we should expect from a mere village-bard.[1]

1. "Let the poet declare, O Waters, your exceeding greatness, here in the seat of Vivasvat.[2] By seven and seven they have come forth in three courses, but the Sindhu (the Indus) exceeds all the other wandering rivers by her strength.

2. "Varuna dug out paths for thee to walk on, when thou rannest to the race.[3] Thou proceedest on a precipitous ridge

---

1. Rig-Veda X. 75. See Hibbert Lectures, Lect. iv.

2. Vivasvat is a name of the sun, and the seat or home of Vivasvat can hardly be anything but the earth, as the home of the sun, or, in a more special sense, the place where a sacrifice is offered.

3. I formerly translated yát vāgân abhí ádravahtvám by "when thou rannest for the prizes." Grassman had translated similarly, "When thou, O Sindhu, rannest to the prize of the battle," while Ludwig wrote, "When thou, O Sindhu, wast flowing on to greater powers." Vâga, connected with vegeo, vigeo, vigil, wacker (see Curtius, Grundzüge, No. 159), is one of the many difficult words in the Veda the general meaning of which may be guessed, but in many places cannot yet be determined with certainty. Vâga occurs very frequently, both in the singular and the plural, and some of its meanings are clear enough.

of the earth, when thou art lord in the van of all the moving
streams.

3. "The sound rises up to heaven above the earth; she stirs
up with splendor her endless power.[1] As from a cloud, the
showers thunder forth, when the Sindhu comes, roaring
like a bull.

4. "To thee, O Sindhu, they (the other rivers) come as lowing
mother-cows (run) to their young with their milk.[2] Like
a king in battle thou leadest the two wings, when thou
reachest the front of these down-rushing rivers.

The Petersburg Dictionary gives the following list of them—swiftness, race,
prize of race, gain, treasure, race-horse, etc. Here we perceive at once the
difficulty of tracing all these meanings back to a common source, though it
might be possible to begin with the meanings of strength, strife, contest, race,
whether friendly or warlike, then to proceed to what is won in a race or in war,
viz. booty, treasure, and lastly to take vâgâh in the more general sense of acqui-
sitions, goods, even goods bestowed as gifts. We have a similar transition of
meaning in the Greek ἄθλος, contest, contest for a prize, and ἄθλον, the prize
of contest, reward, gift, while in the plural τάάθλα stands again for contest, or
even the place of combat. The Vedic vâgambhara may in fact be rendered by
ἀθλοφύρος, vâgasâti by ἀθλοσύνη.

The transition from fight to prize is seen in passages such as:

Rig-Veda VI. 45, 12, vâgân indrasravâyyân tváyâgeshna hitám dhánam,
"May we with thy help, O Indra, win the glorious fights, the offered prize" (cf.
ἀθλοθέτης).

Rig-Veda VIII. 19, 18, té it vâgebhih gigyuh mahát dhánam, "They won
great-wealth by battles."

What we want for a proper understanding of our verse, are passages
where we have, as here, a movement toward vâgas in the plural. Such passages
are few; for instance: X. 53, 8, átra gahâma yé asan ásevâh sivân vayám út
tarema abhí vâgân, "Let us leave here those who were unlucky (the dead), and
let us get up to lucky toils." No more is probably meant here when the Sindhu
is said to run toward her vâgas, that is, her struggles, her fights, her race across
the mountains with the other rivers.

1. On sushma, strength, see Rig-Veda, translation, vol. i. p. 105. We find subhrám
    sūshmam II. 11, 4; and iyarti with sūshmam IV. 17, 12.
2. See Muir, Santkrit Texts, v. p. 344.

5. "Accept, O Gangâ (Ganges), Yamunâ (Jumna), Sarasvatî (Sursûti), Sutudri (Sutlej), Parushnî (Irâvâtî, Ravi), my praise![1] With the Asiknî (Akesines) listen, O Marudvridhâ[2] and with the Vitastâ (Hydaspes, Behat); O Ârgîkîyâ,[3] listen with the Sushomâ.[4]

6. "First thou goest united with the Trishtamâ on thy journey, with the Susartu, the Rasâ (Râmhâ, Araxes?[5]), and the Svetî – O Sindhu, with the Kubhâ (Kophen, Cabul river) to the Gomatî (Gomal), with the Mehatnu to the Krumu (Kurum) – with whom thou proceedest together.

7. "Sparkling, bright, with mighty splendor she carries the waters across the plains – the unconquered Sindhu, the quickest of the quick, like a beautiful mare – a sight to see.

---

1. "O Marudvridhâ with Asiknî, Vitastâ; O Ârgîkîyâ, listen with the Sushomâ," *Ludwig.* "Asiknî and Vitastâ and Marudvridhâ, with the Sushomâ, hear us, O Ârgîkîyâ," *Grassman.*

2. Marudvridhâ, a general name for river. According to Roth the combined course of the Akesines and Hydaspes, *before* the junction with the Hydraotes; according to Ludwig, the river *after* the junction with Hydraotes. Zimmer (Altindisches Leben, p. 12) adopts Roth's, Kiepert in his maps follows Ludwig's opinion.

3. According to Yâska, the Ârgîkîyâ is the Vipâs. Vivien de Saint-Martin takes it for the country watered by the Suwan, the Soanos of Megasthenes.

4. According to Yâska the Sushomâ is the Indus. Vivien de Saint-Martin identifies it with the Suwan. Zimmer (l. c. p. 14) points out that in Arrian, Indica, iv. 12, there is a various reading Soamos for Soanos.

5. "Chips from a German Workshop," vol. i. p. 157.

8. "Rich in horses, in chariots, in garments, in gold, in booty,[1]
    in wool,[2] and in straw,[3] the Sindhu, handsome and young,
    clothes herself in sweet flowers.[4]

---

1   Vâginîvatî is by no means an easy word. Hence all translators vary, and none
    settles the meaning. Muir translates, "yielding nutriment;" Zimmer, "having
    plenty of quick horses;" Ludwig, "like a strong mare." Vagin, no doubt, means
    a strong horse, a racer, but vaginî never occurs in the Rig-Veda in the sense of
    a mare, and the text is not vaginîvat, but vaginîvatî. If vâginî meant mare, we
    might translate rich in mares, but that would be a mere repetition after svasvâ,
    possessed of good horses. Vaginîvatî is chiefly applied to Ushas, Sarasvatî, and
    here to the river Sindhu. It is joined with vagebhih, Rig-Veda I. 3, 10, which,
    if vâginî meant mare, would mean "rich in mares through horses." We also
    read, Rig-Veda I. 48, 16, sám (nah mimikshvá) vâgaih vâginîvati, which we
    can hardly translate by "give us horses, thou who art possessed of mares;" nor,
    Rig-Veda I. 92, 15, yúkshva hí vâginîvati ásvân, "harness the horses, thou who
    are rich in mares." In most of the passages where vâginîvatî occurs, the goddess
    thus addressed is represented as rich, and asked to bestow wealth, and I should
    therefore prefer to take vâgínî, as a collective abstract noun, like tretínî, in the
    sense of wealth, originally booty, and to translate vâginîvatî simply by rich, a
    meaning well adapted to every passage where the word occurs.

2. Urnâvatî, rich in wool, probably refers to the flocks of sheep for which the
    North-West of India was famous. See Rig-Veda I. 126, 7.

3. Sîlamâvatî does not occur again in the Rig-Veda. Muir translates, "rich in
    plants;" Zimmer, "rich in water;" Ludwig takes it as a proper name. Sâyana
    states that sîlamâ is a plant which is made into ropes. That the meaning of
    sîlamâvatî was forgotten at an early time we see by the Atharva-Veda III. 12,
    2, substituting sûnritâvatî, for sîlamâvatî, as preserved in the Sânkhâyana
    Grihya-sûtras, 3, 3. I think sîlamâ means straw, from whatever plant it may be
    taken, and this would be equally applicable to asâla, a house, a sthûna, a post,
    and to the river Indus. It may have been, as Ludwig conjectures, an old local
    name, and in that case it may possibly account for the name given in later times
    to the Suleiman range.

4. Madhuvridh is likewise a word which does not occur again in the Rig-Veda.
    Sâyana explains it by nirgundi and similar plants, but it is doubtful what plant
    is meant. Gunda is the name of a grass, madhuvridh therefore may have
    been a plant such as sugar-cane, that yielded a sweet juice, the Upper Indus
    being famous for sugar-cane; see Hiouen-thsang, II. p. 105. I take adhivaste
    with Roth in the sense "she dresses herself," as we might say "the river is

9. "The Sindhu has yoked her easy chariot with horses; may she conquer prizes for us in the race. The greatness of her chariot is praised as truly great – that chariot which is irresistible, which has its own glory, and abundant strength."[1]

This hymn does not sound perhaps very poetical, in our sense of the word; yet if you will try to realize the thoughts of the poet who composed it, you will perceive that it is not without some bold and powerful conceptions.

Take the modern peasants, living in their villages by the side of the Thames, and you must admit that he would be a remarkable man who could bring himself to look on the Thames as a kind of a general, riding at the head of many English rivers, and leading them on to a race or a battle. Yet it is easier to travel in England, and to gain a commanding view of the river-system of the country, than it was three thousand years ago to travel over India, even over that part of India which the poet of our hymn commands. He takes in at one swoop three great river-systems, or, as he calls them, three great armies of rivers – those flowing from the north-west into the Indus, those joining it from the north-east, and, in the distance, the Ganges and the Jumnah with their tributaries. Look on the map and you will see how well these three armies are determined; but our poet had no map – he had nothing but high mountains and sharp eyes to carry out his trigonometrical survey. Now I call a man, who for the first time could *see* those three marching armies of rivers, a poet.

The next thing that strikes one in that hymn – if hymn we must call it – is the fact that all these rivers, large and small, have their

dressed in heather." Muir translates, "she traverses a land yielding sweetness;" Zimmer, "she clothes herself in Madhuvridh;" Ludwig, "the Sîlamâvatî throws herself into the increaser of the honey-sweet dew." All this shows how little progress can be made in Vedic scholarship by merely translating either words or verses, without giving at the same time a full justification of the meaning assigned to every single word.

1. See Petersburg Dictionary, s. v. virapsin.

own proper names. That shows a considerable advance in civilized life, and it proves no small degree of coherence, or what the French call *solidarity*, between the tribes who had taken possession of Northern India. Most settlers call the river on whose banks they settle "*the river.*" Of course there are many names for river. It may be called the runner,[2] the fertilizer, the roarer – or, with a little poetical metaphor, the arrow, the horse, the cow, the father, the mother, the watchman, the child of the mountains. Many rivers had many names in different parts of their course, and it was only when communication between different settlements became more frequent, and a fixed terminology was felt to be a matter of necessity, that the rivers of a country were properly baptized and registered. All this had been gone through in India before our hymn became possible.

And now we have to consider another, to my mind most startling fact. We here have a number of names of the rivers of India, as they were known to one single poet, say about 1000 B.C. We then hear nothing of India till we come to the days of Alexander, and when we look at the names of the Indian rivers, represented as well as they could be by Alexander's companions, mere strangers in India, and by means of a strange language and a strange alphabet, we recognize, without much difficulty, nearly all of the old Vedic names.

In this respect the names of rivers have a great advantage over the names of towns in India. What we now call *Dilli* or *Delhi*[3] was in ancient times called Indraprastha, in later times *Shahjahânabâd*. *Oude* is Ayodhyâ, but the old name of Saketa is forgotten. The town of Pataliputra, known to the Greeks as *Palimbothra*, is now called *Patna*.[4]

---

2. "Among the Hottentots, the Kunene, Okavango, and Orange rivers, all have the name of Garib, *i.e.* the Runner."—Dr. Theoph. Hahn, *Cape Times*, July 11, 1882.
3. Dehli, not Del-high.—A. W.
4. Cunningham, "Archæological Survey of India," vol. xii. p. 113.

Now I can assure you this persistency of the Vedic river-names was to my mind something so startling that I often said to myself, This cannot be – there must be something wrong here. I do not wonder so much at the names of the *Indus* and the *Ganges* being the same. The Indus was known to early traders, whether by sea or by land. Skylax sailed from the country of the Paktys, *i.e.* the Pushtus, as the Afghans still call themselves, down to the mouth of the Indus. That was under Darius Hystaspes (521-486). Even before that time India and the Indians were known by their name, which was derived from *Sindhu*, the name of their frontier river. The neighboring tribes who spoke Iranic languages all pronounced, like the Persian, the *s* as an *h*.[1] Thus Sindhu became Hindhu (Hidhu), and, as h's were dropped even at that early time, Hindhu became Indu. Thus the river was called *Indos*, the people *Indoi* by the Greeks, who first heard of India from the Persians.

Sindhu probably meant originally the divider, keeper, and defender, from sidh, to keep off. It was a masculine, before it became a feminine. No more telling name could have been given to a broad river, which guarded peaceful settlers both against the inroads of hostile tribes and the attacks of wild animals. A common name for the ancient settlements of the Aryans in India was "the Seven Rivers," "Sapta Sindhavah." But though sindhu was used as an appellative noun for river in general (cf. Rig-Veda VI. 19, 5, samudré ná síndhavah yâdamânâh, "like rivers longing for the sea"), it remained throughout the whole history of India the name of its powerful guardian river, the Indus.

In some passages of the Rig-Veda it has been pointed out that sindhu might better be translated by "sea," a change of meaning, if so it can be called, fully explained by the geographical conditions of the country. There are places where people could swim across the Indus, there are others where no eye could tell whether the boundless expanse of water should be called river or sea. The two run

---

1. Pliny, Hist. Nat. vi. 20, 71: "Indus incolis Sindus appellatus."

into each other, as every sailor knows, and naturally the meaning of sindhu, river, runs into the meaning of sindhu, sea.

But besides the two great rivers, the Indus and the Ganges – in Sanskrit the Gangâ, literally the Go-go – we have the smaller rivers, and many of their names also agree with the names preserved to us by the companions of Alexander.[1]

The Yamunâ, the Jumna, was known to Ptolemy as $\Delta\iota\acute{\alpha}\mu o\upsilon\nu\alpha$,[2] to Pliny as Jomanes, to Arrian, somewhat corrupted, as Jôbares.[3]

The Sutudrî, or, as it was afterward called, Satadru, meaning "running in a hundred streams," was known to Ptolemy as $Z\alpha\delta\acute{\alpha}\rho\delta\eta\varsigma$ or $Z\acute{\alpha}\rho\alpha\delta o\varsigma$; Pliny called it Sydrus; and Megasthenes, too, was probably acquainted with it as $Z\alpha\delta\acute{\alpha}\rho\delta\eta\varsigma$. In the Veda[4] it formed with the Vipas the frontier of the Punjâb, and we hear of fierce battles fought at that time, it may be on the same spot where in 1846 the battle of the Sutledge was fought by Sir Hugh Gough and Sir Henry Hardinge. It was probably on the Vipâs (later Vipâsâ), a north-western tributary of the Sutledge, that Alexander's army turned back. The river was then called Hyphasis; Pliny calls it Hypasis,[5] a very fair approximation to the Vedic Vipâs, which means "unfettered." Its modern name is Bias or Bejah.

---

1. The history of these names has been treated by Professor Lassen, in his "Indische Alterthumskunde," and more lately by Professor Kaegi, in his very careful essay, "Der Rig-Veda," pp. 146, 147.
2. Ptol. vii. 1, 29.
3. Arrian, Indica, viii. 5.
4. Rig-Veda III. 33, 1: "From the lap of the mountains Vipâs and Sutudrî rush forth with their water like two lusty mares neighing, freed from their tethers, like two bright mother-cows licking (their calf).

    "Ordered by Indra and waiting his bidding you run toward the sea like two charioteers; running together, as your waters rise, the one goes into the other, you bright ones."
5. Other classical names are Hypanis, Bipasis, and Bibasis. Yâska identifies it with the Ârgîkîyâ.

The next river on the west is the Vedic Parushnî, better known as Irâvatî,[1] which Strabo calls Hyarotis, while Arrian gives it a more Greek appearance by calling it Hydraotes. It is the modern Rawi. It was this river which the Ten Kings when attacking the Tritsus under Sudâs tried to cross from the west by cutting off its water. But their stratagem failed, and they perished in the river (Rig-Veda VII. 18, 8-9).

We then come to the Asiknî, which means "black." That river had another name also, Kandrabhâga, which means "streak of the moon." The Greeks, however, pronounced that Σανδαροφάγος, and this had the unlucky meaning of "the devourer of Alexander." Hesychius tells us that in order to avert the bad omen Alexander changed the name of that river into Ακεσίνης, which would mean "the Healer;" but he does not tell, what the Veda tells us, that this name Ακεσίνης was a Greek adaptation of another name of the same river, namely Asiknî, which had evidently supplied to Alexander the idea of calling the Asiknî Ακεσίνης. It is the modern Chinâb.

Next to the Akesines we have the Vedic Vitastâ, the last of the rivers of the Punjâb, changed in Greek into Hydaspes. It was to this river that Alexander retired, before sending his fleet down the Indus and leading his army back to Babylon. It is the modern Behat or Jilam.

I could identify still more of these Vedic rivers, such as, for instance, the Kubhâ, the Greek Cophen, the modern Kabul river;[2]

---

1. Cf. Nirukta IX. 26.

2 "The first tributaries which join the Indus before its meeting with the Kubhâ or the Kabul river cannot be determined. All travellers in these northern countries complain of the continual changes in the names of the rivers, and we can hardly hope to find traces of the Vedic names in existence there after the lapse of three or four thousand years. The rivers intended may be the Shauyook, Ladak, Abba Seen, and Burrindu, and one of the four rivers, the Rasâ, has assumed an almost fabulous character in the Veda. After the Indus has joined the Kubhâ or the Kabul river, two names occur, the Gomatî and Krumu, which I believe I was the first to identify with the modern rivers

but the names which I have traced from the Veda to Alexander, and in many cases from Alexander again to our own time, seem to me sufficient to impress upon us the real and historical character of the Veda. Suppose the Veda were a forgery – suppose at least that it had been put together after the time of Alexander – how could we explain these names? They are names that have mostly a meaning in Sanskrit, they are names corresponding very closely to their Greek corruptions, as pronounced and written down by people who did not know Sanskrit. How is a forgery possible here?

I selected this hymn for two reasons. First, because it shows us the widest geographical horizon of the Vedic poets, confined by the snowy mountains in the north, the Indus and the range of the Suleiman mountains in the west, the Indus or the seas in the south, and the valley of the Jumna and Ganges in the east. Beyond that, the world, though open, was unknown to the Vedic poets. Secondly, because the same hymn gives us also a kind of historical background to the Vedic age. These rivers, as we may see them to-day, as they were seen by Alexander and his Macedonians, were seen also by the Vedic poets. Here we have an historical continuity – almost

---

the Gomal and Kurrum. (Roth, Nirukta, Erläuterungen, p. 43, Anm.) The Gomal falls into the Indus, between Dera Ismael Khan and Paharpore, and although Elphinstone calls it a river only during the rainy season, Klaproth (Foe-koue-ki, p. 23) describes its upper course as far more considerable, and adds: 'Un peu à l'est de Sirmágha, le Gomal traverse la chaîne de montagnes de Solimán, passe devant Raghzi, et fertilise le pays habité par les tribus de Dauletkhail et de Gandehpour. Il se dessèche au défilé de Pezou, et son lit ne se remplit plus d'eau que dans la saison des pluies; alors seulement il rejoint la droite de l'Indus, au sud-est de bourg de Paharpour.' The Kurrum falls into the Indus north of the Gomal, while, according to the poet, we should expect it south. It might be urged that poets are not bound by the same rules as geographers, as we see, for instance, in the verse immediately preceding. But if it should be taken as a serious objection, it will be better to give up the Gomatî than the Krumu, the latter being the larger of the two, and we might then take Gomatî, 'rich in cattle,' as an adjective belonging to Krumu."—From a review of General Cunningham's "Ancient Geography of India," in *Nature*, 1871, Sept. 14.

living witnesses, to tell us that the people whose songs have been so strangely, ay, you may almost say, so miraculously preserved to us, were real people, lairds with their clans, priests, or rather, servants of their gods, shepherds with their flocks, dotted about on the hills and valleys, with inclosures or palisades here and there, with a few strongholds, too, in case of need – living their short life on earth, as at that time life might be lived by men, without much pushing and crowding and trampling on each other – spring, summer, and winter leading them on from year to year, and the sun in his rising and setting lifting up their thoughts from their meadows and groves which they loved, to a world in the East, from which they had come, or to a world in the West, to which they were gladly hastening on. They had what I call religion, though it was very simple, and hardly reduced as yet to the form of a creed. "There is a Beyond," that was all they felt and knew, though they tried, as well as they could, to give names to that Beyond, and thus to change religion into *a* religion. They had not as yet a name for God – certainly not in our sense of the word – or even a general name for the gods; but they invented name after name to enable them to grasp and comprehend by some outward and visible tokens powers whose presence they felt in nature, though their true and full essence was to them, as it is to us, invisible and incomprehensible.

Lecture 6

Vedic Deities

The next important phenomenon of nature which was represented in the Veda as a terrestrial deity is Fire, in Sanskrit Agni, in Latin *ignis*. In the worship which is paid to the Fire and in the high praises bestowed on Agni we can clearly perceive the traces of a period in the history of man in which not only the most essential comforts of life, but life itself, depended on the knowledge of producing fire. To us fire has become so familiar that we can hardly form an idea of what life would be without it. But how did the ancient dwellers on earth get command and possession of fire? The Vedic poets tell us that fire first came to them from the sky, in the form of lightning, but that it disappeared again, and that then Mâtarisvan, a being to a certain extent like Prometheus, brought it back and confided it to the safe keeping of the clan of the Bhrigus (Phlegyas).[1]

In other poems we hear of the mystery of fire being produced by rubbing pieces of wood; and here it is a curious fact that the name of the wood thus used for rubbing is in Sanskrit Pramantha, a word which, as Kuhn has shown, would in Greek come very near to the name of Prometheus. The possession of fire, whether by

---

1. Muir, iv. p. 209

preserving it as sacred on the hearth, or by producing it at pleasure with the fire-drill, represents an enormous step in early civilization. It enabled people to cook their meat instead of eating it raw; it gave them the power of carrying on their work by night; and in colder climates it really preserved them from being frozen to death. No wonder, therefore, that the fire should have been praised and worshipped as the best and kindest of gods, the only god who had come down from heaven to live on earth, the friend of man, the messenger of the gods, the mediator between gods and men, the immortal among mortals. He, it is said, protects the settlements of the Aryans, and frightens away the black-skinned enemies.

Soon, however, fire was conceived by the Vedic poets under the more general character of light and warmth, and then the presence of Agni was perceived, not only on the hearth and the altar, but in the Dawn, in the Sun, and in the world beyond the Sun, while at the same time his power was recognized as ripening, or as they called it, as cooking, the fruits of the earth, and as supporting also the warmth and the life of the human body. From that point of view Agni, like other powers, rose to the rank of a Supreme God.[1] He is said to have stretched out heaven and earth – naturally, because without his light heaven and earth would have been invisible and undistinguishable. The next poet says that Agni held heaven aloft by his light, that he kept the two worlds asunder; and in the end Agni is said to be the progenitor and father of heaven and earth, and the maker of all that flies, or walks, or stands, or moves on earth.

Here we have once more the same process before our eyes. The human mind begins with being startled by a single or repeated event, such as the lightning striking a tree and devouring a whole forest, or a spark of fire breaking forth from wood being rubbed against wood, whether in a forest, or in the wheel of a carriage, or at last in a fire-drill, devised on purpose. Man then begins to wonder at what to him is a miracle, none the less so because it is a fact, a simple,

---

1. Muir, iv. p. 214.

natural fact. He sees the effects of a power, but he can only guess at its cause, and if he is to speak of it, he can only do so by speaking of it as an agent, or as something like a human agent, and, if in some respects not quite human, in others more than human or superhuman. Thus the concept of Fire grew; and while it became more and more generalized, it also became more sublime, more incomprehensible, more divine. Without Agni, without fire, light, and warmth, life would have been impossible. Hence he became the author and giver of life, of the life of plants and animals and of men; and his favor having once been implored for "light and life and all things," what wonder that in the minds of some poets, and in the traditions of this or that village-community he should have been raised to the rank of a supreme ruler, a god above all gods, their own true god!

* * *

We now proceed to consider the powers which the ancient poets might have discovered in the air, in the clouds, and, more particularly, in those meteoric conflicts which by thunder, lightning, darkness, storms, and showers of rain must have taught man that very important lesson that he was not alone in this world. Many philosophers, as you know, believe that all religion arose from fear or terror, and that without thunder and lightning to teach us, we should never have believed in any gods or god. This is a one-sided and exaggerated view. Thunderstorms, no doubt, had a large share in arousing feelings of awe and terror, and in making man conscious of his weakness and dependence. Even in the Veda, Indra is introduced as saying: "Yes, when I send thunder and lightning, then you believe in me." But what we call religion would never have sprung from fear and terror alone. *Religion is trust*, and that trust arose in the beginning from the impressions made on the mind and heart of man by the order and wisdom of nature, and more particularly by those regularly recurring events, the return of the sun, the revival of the moon, the order of the seasons, the law of cause and effect, gradually discovered in all things, and traced back in the end to a cause of all causes, by whatever name we choose to call it.

Still the meteoric phenomena had, no doubt, their important share in the production of ancient deities; and in the poems of the Vedic Rishis they naturally occupy a very prominent place. If we were asked who was the principal god of the Vedic period, we should probably, judging from the remains of that poetry which we possess, say it was Indra, the god of the blue sky, the Indian Zeus, the gatherer of the clouds, the giver of rain, the wielder of the thunder-bolt, the conqueror of darkness, and of all the powers of darkness, the bringer of light, the source of freshness, vigor, and life, the ruler and lord of the whole world. Indra is this, and much more in the Veda. He is supreme in the hymns of many poets, and may have been so in the prayers addressed to him by many of the ancient septs or village communities in India. Compared with him the other gods are said to be decrepit old men. Heaven, the old Heaven or Dyaus, formerly the father of all the gods, nay the father of Indra himself, bows before him, and the Earth trembles at his approach. Yet Indra never commanded the permanent allegiance of all the other gods, like Zeus and Jupiter; nay, we know from the Veda itself that there were skeptics, even at that early time, who denied that there was any such thing as Indra.[1]

By the side of Indra, and associated with him in his battles, and sometimes hardly distinguishable from him, we find the representatives of the wind, called Vâta or Vâyu, and the more terrible storm-gods, the Maruts, literally the Smashers.

When speaking of the Wind, a poet says: "Where was he born? Whence did he spring? the life of the gods, the germ of the world! That god moves about where he listeth, his voices are heard, but he is not to be seen."

The Maruts are more terrible than Vâta, the wind. They are clearly the representatives of such storms as are known in India, when the air is darkened by dust and clouds, when in a moment

---

1. Hibbert Lectures, p. 307.

the trees are stripped of their foliage, their branches shivered, their stems snapped, when the earth seems to reel and the mountains to shake, and the rivers are lashed into foam and fury. Then the poet sees the Maruts approaching with golden helmets, with spotted skins on their shoulders, brandishing golden spears, whirling their axes, shooting fiery arrows, and cracking their whips amid thunder and lightning. They are the comrades of Indra, sometimes, like Indra, the sons of Dyaus or the sky, but also the sons of another terrible god, called Rudra, or the Howler, a fighting god, to whom many hymns are addressed. In him a new character is evolved, that of a healer and saviour – a very natural transition in India, where nothing is so powerful for dispelling miasmas, restoring health, and imparting fresh vigor to man and beast, as a thunderstorm, following after weeks of heat and drought.

All these and several others, such as Parganya and the Ribhus, are the gods of mid-air, the most active and dramatic gods, ever present to the fancy of the ancient poets, and in several cases the prototypes of later heroes, celebrated in the epic poems of India. In battles, more particularly, these fighting gods of the sky were constantly invoked.[1] Indra is the leader in battles, the protector of the bright Aryans, the destroyer of the black aboriginal inhabitants of India. "He has thrown down fifty thousand black fellows," the poet says, "and their strongholds crumbled away like an old rag." Strange to say, Indra is praised for having saved his people from their enemies, much as Jehovah was praised by the Jewish prophets. Thus we read in one hymn that when Sudâs, the pious king of the Tritsus, was pressed hard in his battle with the ten kings, Indra changed the flood into an easy ford, and thus saved Sudâs.

In another hymn we read:[2] "Thou hast restrained the great river for the sake of Turvîtî Vâyya: the flood moved in obedience to thee, and thou madest the rivers easy to cross." This is not very different

---

1. See Kaegi, Rig-Veda, p. 61.
2. Rig-Veda II. 13, 12; IV. 19, 6.

from the Psalmist (78:13): "He divided the sea, and caused them to
pass through; and he made the waters to stand as an heap."

And there are other passages which have reminded some
students of the Veda of Joshua's battle,[1] when the sun stood still and
the moon stayed, until the people had avenged themselves upon
their enemies. For we read in the Veda also, as Professor Kaegi has
pointed out (l. c. p. 63), that "Indra lengthened the days into the
night," and that "the Sun unharnessed its chariot in the middle of
the day."[2]

In some of the hymns addressed to Indra his original connection with the sky and the thunderstorm seems quite forgotten.
He has become a spiritual god, the only king of all worlds and all
people, who sees and hears everything, nay, who inspires men with
their best thoughts. No one is equal to him, no one excels him.

The name of Indra is peculiar to India, and must have been
formed after the separation of the great Aryan family had taken
place, for we find it neither in Greek, nor in Latin, nor in German.
There are Vedic gods, as I mentioned before, whose names must
have been framed before that separation, and which occur therefore,
though greatly modified in character, sometimes in Greek, sometimes in Latin, sometimes in the Celtic, Teutonic, and Slavonic
dialects. *Dyaus*, for instance, is the same word as Zeus or Jupiter,
Ushasis Eos, *Naktâ* is Nyx, *Sûrya* is Helios, *Agni* is ignis, *Bhaga* is
Baga in Old Persian, Bogŭ in Old Slavonic, Varuna is Uranos, *Vâta*
is Wotan, Vâk is vox, and in the name of the *Maruts*, or the storm-
gods, the germs of the Italic god of war, Mars, have been discovered.
Besides these direct coincidences, some indirect relations have been
established between Hermes and *Sârameya*, Dionysos and Dyuni-
sya, Prometheus and *pramantha*, Orpheus and Ribhu, Erinnys and
Sâranyu, Pân and *Pavaṇa*.[3]

---

1. Joshua x. 13.

2. Rig-Veda IV. 30, 3; X. 138, 3.

3. I am very strongly inclined to regard these names as Kushite or Semitic;
   Hermes, from חרם, the sun; Dionysos, from *dyan*, the judge, and *nisi*, mankind;

But while the name of Indra as the god of the sky, also as the god of the thunderstorm, and the giver of rain, is unknown among the north-western members of the Aryan family, the name of another god who sometimes acts the part of Indra (Indrah Parganyâtmâ), but is much less prominent in the Veda, I mean Parganya, must have existed before that of Indra, because two at least of the Aryan languages have carried it, as we shall see, to Germany, and to the very shores of the Baltic.

Sometimes this Parganya stands in the place of Dyaus, the sky. Thus we read in the Atharva-Veda, XII. 1, 12:[1] "The Earth is the mother, and I am the son of the Earth. Parganya is the father; may he help us!"

In another place (XII. 1, 42) the Earth, instead of being the wife of Heaven or Dyaus, is called the wife of Parganya.

Now who or what is this Parganya? There have been long controversies about him,[2] as to whether he is the same as Dyaus, Heaven, or the same as Indra, the successor of Dyaus, whether he is the god of the sky, of the cloud, or of the rain.

To me it seems that this very expression, god of the sky, god of the cloud, is so entire an anachronism that we could not even translate it into Vedic Sanskrit without committing a solecism. It is true, no doubt, we must use our modern ways of speaking when we wish to represent the thoughts of the ancient world; but we cannot be too much on our guard against accepting the dictionary representative of an ancient word for its real counterpart. Deva, no doubt, means "gods" and "god," and Parganya means "cloud," but no one could say in Sanskrit parganyasya devah, "the god of the cloud." The god, or the divine, or transcendental element, does not come from without, to be added to the cloud or to the sky or to the earth,

---

Orpheus, from *Orfa*, the Arabic name of Edessa; Prometheus, from *pro* and *manthanô*, to learn.—A. W.

1. Muir, iv. p. 23.
2. Ibid. p. 142. An excellent paper on Parganya was published by Bühler in 1862, "Orient und Occident," vol. i. p. 214.

but it springs from the cloud and the sky and the earth, and is slowly elaborated into an independent concept. As many words in ancient languages have an undefined meaning, and lend themselves to various purposes according to the various intentions of the speakers, the names of the gods also share in this elastic and plastic character of ancient speech. There are passages where Parganya means cloud, there are passages where it means rain. There are passages where Parganya takes the place which elsewhere is filled by Dyaus, the sky, or by Indra, the active god of the atmosphere. This may seem very wrong and very unscientific to the scientific mythologist. But it cannot be helped. It is the nature of ancient thought and ancient language to be unscientific, and we must learn to master it as well as we can, instead of finding fault with it, and complaining that our forefathers did not reason exactly as we do.

There are passages in the Vedic hymns where Parganya appears as a supreme god. He is called father, like Dyaus, the sky. He is called *asura*, the living or life-giving god, a name peculiar to the oldest and the greatest gods. One poet says,[1] "He rules as god over the whole world; all creatures rest in him; he is the life (âtmâ) of all that moves and rests."

Surely it is difficult to say more of a supreme god than what is here said of Parganya. Yet in other hymns he is represented as performing his office, namely that of sending rain upon the earth, under the control of Mitra and Varun, who are then considered as the highest lords, the mightiest rulers of heaven and earth.[2]

There are other verses, again, where parganya occurs with hardly any traces of personality, but simply as a name of cloud or rain.

Thus we read: "Even by day the Maruts (the storm-gods) produce darkness with the cloud that carries water, when they moisten the earth." Here cloud is parganya, and it is evidently used as an appellative, and not as a proper name. The same word occurs

---

1. Rig-Veda VII. 101, 6.
2. Rig-Veda V. 63, 3-6.

in the plural also, and we read of many parganyas or clouds vivify-
ing the earth.

When Devapi prays for rain in favor of his brother, he says: "O
lord of my prayer (Brihaâpati), whether thou be Mitra or Varuna
or Pûshan, come to my sacrifice! Whether thou be together with
the Âdityas, the Vasus or the Maruts, let the cloud (parganya) rain
for Santanu."

And again: "Stir up the rainy cloud" (parganya).

In several places it makes no difference whether we translate
parganya by cloud or by rain, for those who pray for rain, pray for
the cloud, and whatever may be the benefits of the rain, they may
nearly all be called the benefits of the cloud. There is a curious
hymn, for instance, addressed to the frogs who, at the beginning
of the rains, come forth from the dry ponds, and embrace each
other and chatter together, and whom the poet compares to priests
singing at a sacrifice, a not very complimentary remark from a poet
who is himself supposed to have been a priest. Their voice is said to
have been revived by parganya, which we shall naturally translate
"by rain," though, no doubt, the poet may have meant, for all we
know, either a cloud, or even the god Parganya himself.

I shall try to translate one of the hymns addressed to Parganya,
when conceived as a god, or at least as so much of a god as it
was possible to be at that stage in the intellectual growth of the
human race.[1]

1. "Invoke the strong god with these songs! praise Parganya,
   worship him with veneration! for he, the roaring bull,
   scattering drops, gives seed-fruit to plants.

2. "He cuts the trees asunder, he kills evil spirits; the whole
   world trembles before his mighty weapon. Even the guiltless flees before the powerful, when Parganya thundering
   strikes down the evil-doers.

---

1. Rig-Veda V. 83. See Bühler, "Orient und Occident," vol. i. p. 214; Zimmer,
   "Altindisches Leben," p. 43.

3. "Like a charioteer, striking his horses with a whip, he puts forths his messenger of rain. From afar arise the roarings of the lion, when Parganya makes the sky full of rain.

4. "The winds blow, the lightnings[1] fly, plants spring up, the sky pours. Food is produced for the whole world, when Parganya blesses the earth with his seed.

5. "O Parganya, thou at whose work the earth bows down, thou at whose work hoofed animals are scattered, thou at whose work the plants assume all forms, grant thou to us thy great protection!

6. "O, Maruts, give us the rain of heaven, make the streams of the strong horse run down! And come thou hither with thy thunder, pouring out water, for thou (O Parganya) art the living god, thou art our father.

7. "Do thou roar, and thunder, and give fruitfulness! Fly around us with thy chariot full of water! Draw forth thy water-skin, when it has been opened and turned downward, and let the high and the low places become level!

8. "Draw up the large bucket, and pour it out; let the streams pour forth freely! Soak heaven and earth with fatness! and let there be a good draught for the cows!

9. "O Parganya, when roaring and thundering thou killest the evil-doers, then everything rejoices, whatever lives on earth.

10. "Thou hast sent rain, stop now! Thou hast made the deserts passable, thou hast made plants grow for food, and thou hast obtained praise from men."

This is a Vedic hymn, and a very fair specimen of what these ancient hymns are. There is nothing very grand and poetical about them, and yet, I say, take thousands and thousands of people living in our villages, and depending on rain for their very life,

---

1. Both Bühler ("Orient und Occident," vol. i, p. 224) and Zimmer (Z. f. D. A. vii. p. 169) say that the lightning is represented as the son of Parganya in Rig-Veda VII. 101, 1. This seems doubtful.

and not many of them will be able to compose such a prayer for rain, even though three thousand years have passed over our heads since Parganya was first invoked in India. Nor are these verses entirely without poetical conceptions and descriptions. Whoever has watched a real thunderstorm in a hot climate will recognize the truth of those quick sentences: "the winds blow, the lightnings fly, plants spring up, the hoofed cattle are scattered." Nor is the idea without a certain drastic reality, that Parganya draws a bucket of water from his well in heaven, and pours out skin after skin (in which water was then carried) down upon the earth.

There is even a moral sentiment perceptible in this hymn. "When the storms roar, and the lightnings flash and the rain pours down, even the guiltless trembles, and evil-doers are struck down." Here we clearly see that the poet did not look upon the storm simply as an outbreak of the violence of nature, but that he had a presentiment of a higher will and power which even the guiltless fears; for who, he seems to say, is entirely free from guilt?

If now we ask again, Who is Parganya? or What is Parganya? we can answer that parganya was meant originally for the cloud, so far as it gives rain; but as soon as the idea of a giver arose, the visible cloud became the outward appearance only, or the body of that giver, and the giver himself was somewhere else, we know not where. In some verses Parganya seems to step into the place of Dyaus, the sky, and Prithivî, the earth, is his wife. In other places,[1] however, he is the son of Dyaus or the sky, though no thought is given in that early stage to the fact that thus Parganya might seem to be the husband of his mother. We saw that even the idea of Indra being the father of his own father did not startle the ancient poets beyond an exclamation that it was a very wonderful thing indeed.

Sometimes Parganya does the work of Indra, the Jupiter Pluvius of the Veda; sometimes of Vâyu, the wind, sometimes of Soma, the giver of rain. Yet with all this he is not Dyaus, nor Indra, nor the Maruts, nor Vâyu, nor Soma. He stands by himself, a separate person,

---

1. Rig-Veda VII. 102, 1.

a separate god, as we should say – nay, one of the oldest of all the Aryan gods.

His name, parganya, is derived from a root parg, which, like its parallel forms pars and parsh, must (I think) have had the meaning of sprinkling, irrigating, moistening. An interchange between final g, s, and sh, may, no doubt, seem unusual, but it is not without parallel in Sanskrit. We have, for instance, the roots piñg, pingere; pish, to rub; pis, to adorn (as in pesas, ποικίλος, etc.); mrig, to rub, mrish, to rub out, to forget; mris, mulcere.

This very root mrig forms its participle as mrish-ta, like yag, ishta, and vis, vishta; nay there are roots, such as druh, which optionally take a final lingual or guttural, such as dhrut and dhruk.1

We may therefore compare pargin parganya with such words as prishata, prishatî, speckled, drop of water;2 also parsu, cloud, prisni, speckled, cloud, earth; and in Greek πρόξ(ω), περκνός, etc.3

If derived from parg, to sprinkle, Parganya would have meant originally "he who irrigates or gives rain."4

When the different members of the Aryan family dispersed, they might all of them, Hindus as well as Greeks and Celts, and Teutons and Slaves, have carried that name for cloud with them. But you know that it happened very often that out of the commonwealth of their ancient language, one and the same word was preserved, as the case might be, not by all, but by only six, or five, or four, or three, or two, or even by one only of the seven principal heirs; and yet, as we know that there was no historical contact between them, after they had once parted from each other, long before the beginning of

1. See Max Müller, Sanskrit Grammar, § 174, 10.
2. Cf. Gobh. Grihyà S. III. 3, 15, vidyut—stanayitnu—prishiteshu.
3. Uggvaladatta, in his commentary on the Unâdi-sûtras, iii. 103. admits the same transition of she into g in the verb prish, as the etymon of parganya.
4. For different etymologies, see Bühler, "Orient und Occident," i. p. 214; Muir, "Original Sanskrit Texts," v. p. 140; Grassmann, in his Dictionary to the Rig-Veda, s. v.; Zimmer, "Zeitscrift für Deutsches Alterthum, Neue Folge," vii. p. 164.

what we call history, the fact that two of the Aryan languages have preserved the same finished word with the same finished meaning, is proof sufficient that it belonged to the most ancient treasure of Aryan thought.

Now there is no trace, at least no very clear trace, of Parganya, in Greek, or Latin, or Celtic, or even in Teutonic. In Slavonic, too, we look in vain, till we come to that almost forgotten side-branch called the *Lettic*, comprising the spoken *Lituanian* and *Lettish*, and the now extinct *Old Prussian*. Lituania is no longer an independent state, but it was once, not more than six centuries ago, a Grand Duchy, independent both of Russia and Poland. Its first Grand Duke was Ringold, who ruled from 1235, and his successors made successful conquests against the Russians. In 1368 these grand dukes became kings of Poland, and in 1569 the two countries were united. When Poland was divided between Russia and Prussia, part of Lituania fell to the former, part to the latter. There are still about one million and a half of people who speak Lituanian in Russia and Prussia, while Lettish is spoken by about one million in Curland and Livonia.

The Lituanian language even as it is now spoken by the common people, contains some extremely primitive grammatical forms – in some cases almost identical with Sanskrit. These forms are all the more curious, because they are but few in number, and the rest of the language has suffered much from the wear and tear of centuries.

Now in that remote Lituanian language we find that our old friend Parganya has taken refuge. There he lives to the present day, while even in India he is almost forgotten, at least in the spoken languages; and there, in Lituania, not many centuries back might be heard among a Christianized or nearly Christianized people, prayers for rain, not very different from that which I translated to you from the Rig-Veda. In Lituanian the god of thunder was called *Perkúnas*,[1] and the same word is still used in the sense of thunder.

---

1. In order to identify Perkunas with Parganya, we must go another step backward, and look upon g or g, in the root parg, as a weakening of an original k

In Old Prussian, thunder was *percunos*, and in Lettish to the present
day *pérkons*is thunder, god of thunder.[1]

It was, I believe, Grimm who for the first time identified the
Vedic Parganya with the Old Slavonic Perûn, the Polish Piorun,
the Bohemian Peraun. These words had formerly been derived
by Dobrovsky and others from the root peru, I strike. Grimm
("Teutonic Mythology," Engl. transl., p. 171) showed that the fuller
forms Perkunas, Pehrkons, and Perkunos existed in Lituanian, Lettish, Old Prussian, and that even the Mordvinians had adopted the
name Porguini as that of their thunder-god.

Simon Grunau, who finished his chronicle in 1521, speaks of
three gods, as worshipped by the Old Prussians, Patollo, Patrimpo,
and Perkuno, and he states that Perkuno was invoked "for storm's
sake, that they might have rain and fair weather at the proper time,
and thunder and lightning should not injure them."[2]

The following Lituanian prayer has been preserved to us by
Lasitzki:[3]

"Check thyself, O Percuna, and do not send misfortune on
my field! and I shall give thee this flitch."

Among the neighbors of the Lets, the Esthonians, who, though
un-Aryan in language, have evidently learned much from their

in park. This, however, is a frequent phonetic process. See Bühler, in Benfey's
"Orient und Occident," ii. p. 717.

1. Lituanian perkun-kulke, thunder-bolt, perkuno gaisis, storm. See Voelkel,
"Die lettischen Sprachreste," 1879, p. 23.
2. "Perkuno, war der dritte Abgott und man ihn anruffte um's Gewitters willen,
damit sie Regen hätten und schön wetter zu seiner Zeit, und ihn der Donner
und blix kein schaden thett." Cf. "Gottesides bei den alten Preussen," Berlin,
1870, p. 23. The triad of the gods is called Triburti, Tryboze; l. c. p. 29.
3. Grimm, "Teutonic Mythology," p. 175; and Lasitzki (Lasicius) "Joannes De
Russorum, Moscovitarum et Tartarorum religione, sacrificiis, nuptiarum et
funerum ritu, Spiræ Nemetum," 1582; idem De Diis Samagitarun.

Aryan neighbors, the following prayer was heard,[1] addressed by an old peasant to their god *Picker* or *Picken*, the god of thunder and rain, as late as the seventeenth century.[2]

> "Dear Thunder (woda Picker), we offer to thee an ox that has two horns and four cloven hoofs; we would pray thee for our ploughing and sowing, that our straw be copper-red, our grain golden-yellow. Push elsewhere all the thick black clouds, over great fens, high forests, and wildernesses. But unto us, ploughers and sowers, give a fruitful season and sweet rain. Holy Thunder (pöha Picken), guard our seed-field, that it bear good straw below, good ears above, and good grain within."[3]

Now, I say again, I do not wish you to admire this primitive poetry, primitive, whether it is repeated in the Esthonian fens in the seventeenth century of our era, or sung in the valley of the Indus in the seventeenth century before our era. Let æsthetic critics say what they like about these uncouth poems. I only ask you, Is it not worth a great many poems, to have established this fact, that the same god Parganya, the god of clouds and thunder and lightning and rain, who was invoked in India a thousand years before India was discovered by Alexander, should have been remembered and believed in by Lituanian peasants on the frontier between East Prussia and Russia, not more than two hundred years ago, and should have retained its old name Parganya, which in Sanskrit meant "showering," under the form of *Perkuna*, which in Lituanian is a name and a name only, without any etymological meaning at all; nay, should live on, as some scholars assure us, in an abbreviated form in most

---

1. Grimm, l. c. p. 176, quoting from Joh. Gutslaff, "Kurzer Bericht und Unterricht von der falsch heilig genannten Bäche in Liefland Wöhhanda," Dorpat, 1644, pp. 362-364.
2. In modern Esthonian Pitkne, the Finnish Pitcainen(?).
3. On foreign influences in Esthonian stories, see "Ehstniche Märchen," von T. Kreutzwald, 1869, Vorwort (by Schiefner), p. iv.

Slavonic dialects, namely, in Old Slavonic as *Perun*, in Polish as *Piorun*, in Bohemian as *Peraun*, all meaning thunder or thunder-storm?[1]

Such facts strike me as if we saw the blood suddenly beginning to flow again through the veins of old mummies; or as if the Egyptian statues of black granite were suddenly to begin to speak again. Touched by the rays of modern science the old words – call them mummies or statues – begin indeed to live again, the old names of gods and heroes begin indeed to speak again.

All that is old becomes new, all that is new becomes old, and that one word, Parganya, seems, like a charm, to open before our eyes the cave or cottage in which the fathers of the Aryan race, our own fathers – whether we live on the Baltic or on the Indian Ocean – are seen gathered together, taking refuge from the buckets of Parganya, and saying, "Stop now, Parganya; thou hast sent rain; thou hast made the deserts passable, and hast made the plants to grow; and thou hast obtained praise from man."

* * *

We have still to consider the third class of gods, in addition to the gods of the earth and the sky, namely the gods of the highest heaven, more serene in their character than the active and fighting gods of the air and the clouds, and more remote from the eyes of man, and therefore more mysterious in the exercise of their power than the gods of the earth or the air.

---

1. Grimm suggests in his "Teutonic Mythology" that Parganya should be identified with the Gothic fairguni, or mountain. He imagines that from being regarded as the abode of the god it had finally been called by his name. Fergunna and Virgunià, two names of mountains in Germany, are relics of the name. The name of the god, if preserved in the Gothic, would have been Fairguneis; and indeed in the Old Norse language Fiörgynn is the father of Frigg, the wife of Odin, and Fiörgynnior, the Earth-goddess, is mother of Thor. Professor Zimmer takes the same view. Grimm thinks that the Greeks and Romans, by changing *f* into *h*, represented Fergunni by Hercynia, and, in fine, he traces the words *berg* and *burg* back to Parganya.—A. W.

The principal deity is here no doubt the bright sky itself, the old *Dyaus*, worshipped as we know by the Aryans before they broke up into separate people and languages, and surviving in Greece as Zeus, in Italy as Jupiter, Heaven-father, and among the Teutonic tribes as *Tŷr* and *Tiu*. In the Veda we saw him chiefly invoked in connection with the earth, as Dyâvâ-prithivî, Heaven and Earth. He is invoked by himself also, but he is a vanishing god, and his place is taken in most of the Vedic poems by the younger and more active god, *Indra*.

Another representative of the highest heaven, as covering, embracing, and shielding all things, is Varuna, a name derived from the root var, to cover, and identical with the Greek *Ouranos*. This god is one of the most interesting creations of the Hindu mind, because though we can still perceive the physical background from which he rises, the vast, starry, brilliant expanse above, his features, more than those of any of the Vedic gods, have become completely transfigured, and he stands before us as a god who watches over the world, punishes the evil-doer, and even forgives the sins of those who implore his pardon.

I shall read you one of the hymns addressed to him:[1]

"Let us be blessed in thy service, O Varuna, for we always think of thee and praise thee, greeting thee day by day, like the fires lighted on the altar, at the approach of the rich dawns." 2.

"O Varuna, our guide, let us stand in thy keeping, thou who are rich in heroes and praised far and wide! And you, unconquered sons of Aditi, deign to accept us as your friends, O gods!" 3.

"Âditya, the ruler, sent forth these rivers; they follow the law of Varuna. They tire not, they cease not; like birds they fly quickly everywhere." 4.

---

1. Rig-Veda II. 28.

"Take from me my sin, like a fetter, and we shall increase,
O Varuna, the spring of thy law. Let not the thread be cut
while I weave my song! Let not the form of the workman
break before the time! 5.

"Take far away from me this terror, O Varuna; Thou,
O righteous king, have mercy on me! Like as a rope from a
calf, remove from me my sin; for away from thee I am not
master even of the twinkling of an eye." 6.

"Do not strike us, Varuna, with weapons which at thy
will hurt the evil-doer. Let us not go where the light has
vanished! Scatter our enemies, that we may live." 7.

"We did formerly, O Varuna, and do now, and shall
in future also, sing praises to thee, O mighty one! For on
thee, unconquerable hero, rest all statutes, immovable, as if
established on a rock." 8.

"Move far away from me all self-committed guilt, and
may I not, O king, suffer for what others have committed!
Many dawns have not yet dawned; grant us to live in them,
O Varuna." 9.

You may have observed that in several verses of this hymn
Varuna was called Âditya, or son of Aditi. Now Aditi means *infini-
tude*, from *dita*, bound, and *a*, not, that is, not bound, not limited,
absolute, infinite. Aditi itself is now and then invoked in the Veda,
as the Beyond, as what is beyond the earth and the sky, and the sun
and the dawn – a most surprising conception in that early period of
religious thought. More frequently, however, than Aditi, we meet
with the Âdityas, literally the sons of Aditi, or the gods beyond the
visible earth and sky – in one sense, the infinite gods. One of them
is Varuna, others Mitra and Aryaman (Bhaga, Daksha, Amsa), most
of them abstract names, though pointing to heaven and the solar
light of heaven as their first, though almost forgotten source.

When Mitra and Varuna are invoked together, we can still
perceive dimly that they were meant originally for day and night,

light and darkness. But in their more personal and so to say dramatic aspect, day and night appear in the Vedic mythology as the two Asvins, the two horsemen.

Aditi, too, the infinite, still shows a few traces of her being originally connected with the boundless Dawn; but again, in her more personal and dramatic character, the Dawn is praised by the Vedic poets as Ushas, the Greek Eos, the beautiful maid of the morning, loved by the Asvins, loved by the sun, but vanishing before him at the very moment when he tries to embrace her with his golden rays. The sun himself, whom we saw reflected several times before in some of the divine personifications of the air and the sky and even of the earth, appears once more in his full personality, as the sun of the sky, under the names of Sûrya (Helios), Savitri, Pûshan, and Vishnu, and many more.

You see from all this how great a mistake it would be to attempt to reduce the whole of Aryan mythology to solar concepts, and to solar concepts only. We have seen how largely the earth, the air, and the sky have each contributed their share to the earliest religious and mythological treasury of the Vedic Aryans. Nevertheless, the Sun occupied in that ancient collection of Aryan thought, which we call Mythology, the same central and commanding position which, under different names, it still holds in our own thoughts.

What we call the Morning, the ancient Aryans called the Sun or the Dawn; "and there is no solemnity so deep to a rightly-thinking creature as that of the Dawn." (These are not my words, but the words of one of our greatest poets, one of the truest worshippers of Nature – John Ruskin.) What we call Noon, and Evening, and Night, what we call Spring and Winter, what we call Year, and Time, and Life, and Eternity – all this the ancient Aryans called *Sun*. And yet wise people wonder and say, How curious that the ancient Aryans should have had so many solar myths. Why, every time we say "Good-morning," we commit a solar myth. Every poet who sings about "the May driving the Winter from the field again" commits a solar myth. Every "Christmas number" of our newspapers

– ringing out the old year and ringing in the new – is brimful of solar myths. Be not afraid of solar myths, but whenever in ancient mythology you meet with a name that, according to the strictest phonetic rules (for this is a *sine qua non*), can be traced back to a word meaning sun, or dawn, or morning, or night, or spring or winter, accept it for what it was meant to be, and do not be greatly surprised, if a story told of a solar eponymos was originally a solar myth.

No one has more strongly protested against the extravagances of comparative mythologists in changing everything into solar legends, than I have; but if I read some of the arguments brought forward against this new science, I confess they remind me of nothing so much as of the arguments brought forward, centuries ago, against the existence of Antipodes! People then appealed to what is called Common Sense, which ought to teach everybody that Antipodes could not possibly exist, because they would tumble off. The best answer that astronomers could give, was, "Go and see." And I can give no better answer to those learned skeptics who try to ridicule the Science of Comparative Mythology—"Go and see!" that is, go and read the Veda, and before you have finished the first Mandala, I can promise you, you will no longer shake your wise heads at solar myths, whether in India, or in Greece, or in Italy, or even in England, where we see so little of the sun, and talk all the more about the weather – that is, about a solar myth.

We have thus seen from the hymns and prayers preserved to us in the Rig-Veda, how a large number of so-called Devas, bright and sunny beings, or gods, were called into existence, how the whole world was peopled with them, and every act of nature, whether on the earth or in the air or in the highest heaven, ascribed to their agency. When we say *it* thunders, they said Indra thunders; when we say, *it* rains, they said Parganya pours out his buckets; when we say, *it* dawns, they said the beautiful Ushas appears like a dancer, displaying her splendor; when we say; *it* grows dark, they said Sûrya unharnesses his steeds. The whole of nature was alive to the poets of the Veda, the presence of the gods was felt everywhere, and in that sentiment of the presence of the gods there was a germ of religious morality, sufficiently strong, it would seem, to restrain people from committing as it were before the eyes of their gods what they were ashamed to commit before the eyes of men. When speaking of Varuna, the old god of the sky, one poet says:[1]

"Varuna, the great lord of these worlds, sees as if he were near. If a man stands or walks or hides, if he goes to lie down or to get up, what two people sitting together whisper to each other, King Varuna knows it, he is there as the third.[2] This earth too belongs to Varuna, the King, and this wide sky with its ends far apart. The two seas (the sky and the ocean) are Varuna's loins; he is also contained in this small drop of water. He who should flee far beyond the sky, even he would not be rid of Varuna, the King.[3] His spies proceed from heaven toward this world; with thousand eyes they overlook this earth. King Varuna sees all this, what is between heaven and earth, and what is beyond. He has counted the twinklings of the eyes of men. As a player throws down the dice, he settles all things (irrevocably). May all thy fatal snares which stand spread out seven by seven and threefold, catch the man who tells a lie, may they pass by him who speaks the truth."

You see this is as beautiful, and in some respects as true, as anything in the Psalms. And yet we know that there never was such a Deva, or god, or such a thing as Varuna. We know it is a mere name,

---

1. Atharva-Veda IV. 16.
2. Psalm cxxxix. 1, 2, "O Lord, thou hast searched me and known me. Thou knowest my down sitting and mine uprising, thou understandest my thought afar off."
3. Psalm cxxxix. 9, "If I take the wings of the morning, and dwell in the uttermost parts of the sea; even there shall thy hand lead me, and thy right hand shall hold me."

meaning originally "covering or all-embracing," which was applied to the visible starry sky, and afterward, by a process perfectly intelligible, developed into the name of a Being, endowed with human and superhuman qualities.

And what applies to Varuna applies to all the other gods of the Veda and the Vedic religion, whether three in number, or thirty-three, or, as one poet said, "three thousand three hundred and thirty-nine gods."[1] They are all but names, quite as much as Jupiter and Apollo and Minerva; in fact, quite as much as all the gods of every religion who are called by such appellative titles.

Possibly, if anyone had said this during the Vedic age in India, or even during the Periklean age in Greece, he would have been called, like Sokrates, a blasphemer or an atheist. And yet nothing can be clearer or truer, and we shall see that some of the poets of the Veda too, and, still more, the later Vedântic philosopher, had a clear insight that it was so.

Only let us be careful in the use of that phrase "it is a mere name." No name is a mere name. Every name was originally meant for something; only it often failed to express what it was meant to express, and then became a weak or an empty name, or what we then call "a mere name." So it was with these names of the Vedic gods. They were all meant to express the *Beyond*, the Invisible behind the Visible, the Infinite within the Finite, the Supernatural above the Natural, the Divine, omnipresent, and omnipotent. They failed in expressing what, by its very nature, must always remain inexpressible. But that Inexpressible itself remained, and in spite of all these failures, it never succumbed, or vanished from the mind of the ancient thinkers and poets, but always called for new and better names, nay calls for them even now, and will call for them to the very end of man's existence upon earth.

---

1. Rig-veda III. 9, 9; X. 52, 6.

Lecture 7

Veda and Vedanta

I do not wonder that I should have been asked by some of my hearers to devote part of my last lecture to answering the question, how the Vedic literature could have been composed and preserved, if writing was unknown in India before 500 B.C., while the hymns of the Rig-Veda are said to date from 1500 B.C. Classical scholars naturally ask what is the date of our oldest MSS. of the Rig-Veda, and what is the evidence on which so high an antiquity is assigned to its contents. I shall try to answer this question as well as I can, and I shall begin with a humble confession that the oldest MSS. of the Rig-Veda, known to us at present, date not from 1500 B.C., but from about 1500 A.D.

We have therefore a gap of three thousand years, which it will require a strong arch of argument to bridge over.

But that is not all.

You may know how, in the beginning of this century, when the age of the Homeric poems was discussed, a German scholar, Frederick August Wolf, asked two momentous questions:

1. At what time did the Greeks first become acquainted
    with the alphabet and use it for inscriptions on public
    monuments, coins, shields, and for contracts, both public
    and private?[1]
2. At what time did the Greeks first think of using writing for
    literary purposes, and what materials did they employ for
    that purpose?

These two questions and the answers they elicited threw quite a
new light on the nebulous periods of Greek literature. A fact more
firmly established than any other in the ancient history of Greece is
that the Ionians learned the alphabet from the Phenicians. The
Ionians always called their letters Phenician letters,[2] and the very
name of Alphabet was a Phenician word. We can well understand
that the Phenicians should have taught the Ionians in Asia Minor a
knowledge of the alphabet, partly for commercial purposes, *i.e.* for
making contracts, partly for enabling them to use those useful little
sheets, called *Periplus*, or *Circumnavigations*, which at that time
were as precious to sailors as maps were to the adventurous seamen
of the middle ages. But from that to a written literature, in our
sense of the word, there is still a wide step. It is well known that the
Germans, particularly in the North, had their Runes for inscriptions on tombs, goblets, public monuments, but not for literary
purposes.[3] Even if a few Ionians at Miletus and other centres of
political and commercial life acquired the art of writing, where
could they find writing materials? and still more important, where
could they find readers? The Ionians, when they began to write, had to
be satisfied with a hide or pieces of leather, which they called *diphthera*,

1. On the early use of letters for public inscriptions, see Hayman, *Journal of
    Philology*, 1879, pp. 141, 142, 150; Hicks, "Manual of Greek Historical
    Inscriptions," pp. 1 seqq.
2. Herod, (v. 59) says: "I saw Phenician letters on certain tripods in a temple of
    the Ismenian Apollo at Thebes in Bœotia, the most of them like the Ionian
    letters."
3. Munch, "Die Nordisch Germanischen Völker," p. 240.

and until that was brought to the perfection of vellum or parchment, the occupation of an author cannot have been very agreeable.[1]

So far as we know at present the Ionians began to write about the middle of the sixth century B.C.; and, whatever may have been said to the contrary, Wolf's *dictum* still holds good that with them the beginning of a written literature was the same as the beginning of prose writing.

Writing at that time was an effort, and such an effort was made for some great purpose only. Hence the first written skins were what we should call Murray's Handbooks, called *Periegesis* or *Periodos*, or, if treating of sea-voyages, *Periplus*, that is, guide-books, books to lead travellers round a country or round a town. Connected with these itineraries were the accounts of the foundations of cities, the *Ktisis*. Such books existed in Asia Minor during the sixth and fifth centuries, and their writers were called by a general term, *Logographi*, or λόγιοι or λογοποιοί,[2] as opposed to ἀοιδοί, the poets. They were the forerunners of the Greek historians, and Herodotus (443 B.C.), the so-called father of history, made frequent use of their works.

The whole of this incipient literary activity belonged to Asia Minor. From "Guides through towns and countries," literature seems to have spread at an early time to Guides through life, or philosophical dicta, such as are ascribed to Anaximander the Ionian (610-547 B.C.[3]), and Pherekydes the Syrian (540 B.C.). These names carry us into the broad daylight of history, for Anaximander was the teacher of Anaximenes, Anaximenes of Anaxagoras, and Anaxagoras of Perikles. At that time writing was a recognized art, and its cultivation had been rendered possible chiefly through trade

---

1. Herod. (v. 58) says: "The Ionians from of old call βύβλος διφθέραι, because once, in default of the former, they used to employ the latter. And even down to my own time, many of the barbarians write on such diphtheræ."

2. Hekatæos and Kadmos of Miletos (520 B.C.), Charon of Lampsakos (504 B.C.), Xanthos the Lydian (463 B.C.), Pherekydes of Leros (480 B.C.), Hellanikos of Mitylene (450 B.C.), etc.

3. Lewis, "Astronomy," p. 92.

with Egypt and the importation of *papyros*. In the time of Æschylos
(500 B.C.) the idea of writing had become so familiar that he could
use it again and again in poetical metaphors,[1] and there seems little
reason why we should doubt that both Peisistratos (528 B.C.) and
Polykrates of Samos (523 B.C.) were among the first collectors of
Greek manuscripts.

In this manner the simple questions asked by Wolf helped to
reduce the history of ancient Greek literature to some kind of order,
particularly with reference to its first beginnings.

It would therefore seem but reasonable that the two first
questions to be asked by the students of Sanskrit literature should
have been:

1. At what time did the people of India become acquainted
    with an alphabet?
2. At what time did they first use such alphabet for literary
    purposes?

Curiously enough, however, these questions remained in abeyance for a long time, and, as a consequence, it was impossible to
introduce even the first elements of order into the chaos of ancient
Sanskrit literature.[2]

I can here state a few facts only. There are no inscriptions to
be found anywhere in India before the middle of the third century
B.C. These inscriptions are Buddhist, put up during the reign of
Asoka, the grandson of Kandragupta, who was the contemporary
of Seleucus, and at whose court in Patalibothra Megasthenes lived
as ambassador of Seleucus. Here, as you see, we are on historical
ground. In fact, there is little doubt that Asoka, the king who put
up these inscriptions in several parts of his vast kingdom, reigned
from 259-222 B.C.

---

1. See Hayman, *Journal of Philology*, 1879, p. 139.
2. See M. M., "History of Ancient Sanskrit Literature," pp. 497 seqq., "On the
   Introduction of Writing in India."

These inscriptions are written in two alphabets – one written from right to left, and clearly derived from an Aramæan, that is, a Semitic alphabet; the other written from left to right, and clearly an adaptation, and an artificial or systematic adaptation, of a Semitic alphabet to the requirements of an Indian language. That second alphabet became the source of all Indian alphabets, and of many alphabets carried chiefly by Buddhist teachers far beyond the limits of India, though it is possible that the earliest Tamil alphabet may have been directly derived from the same Semitic source which supplied both the *dextrorsum* and the *sinistrorsum* alphabets of India.

But writing for commercial purposes was known in India before that time. Megasthenes was no doubt quite right when he said that the Indians did not know letters,[1] that their laws were not written, and that they administered justice from memory. But Nearchus, the admiral of Alexander the Great, who sailed down the Indus (325 B.C.), and was therefore brought in contact with the merchants frequenting the maritime stations of India, was probably equally right in declaring that "the Indians wrote letters on cotton that had been well beaten together." These were no doubt commercial documents, contracts, it may be, with Phenician or Egyptian captains, and they would prove nothing as to the existence in India at that time of what we mean by a written literature. In fact, Nearchus himself affirms what Megasthenes said after him, namely that "the laws of the sophists in India were not written." If, at the same time, the Greek travellers in India speak of mile-stones, and of cattle marked by the Indians with various signs and also with numbers, all this would perfectly agree with what we know from other sources, that though the art of writing may have reached India before the time of Alexander's conquest, its employment for literary purposes cannot date from a much earlier time.

Here then we are brought face to face with a most startling fact. Writing was unknown in India before the fourth century before Christ,

---

1. M. M., "History of Ancient Sanskrit Literature," p. 515.

and yet we are asked to believe that the Vedic literature in its three well-defined periods, the Mantra, Brâhmana, and Sûtra periods, goes back to at least a thousand years before our era.

Now the Rig-Veda alone, which contains a collection of ten books of hymns addressed to various deities, consists of 1017 (1028) poems, 10,580 verses, and about 153,826 words.[1] How were these poems composed – for they are composed in very perfect metre – and how, after having been composed, were they handed down from 1500 before Christ to 1500 after Christ, the time to which most of our best Sanskrit MSS. belong?

Entirely by memory.[2] This may sound startling, but – what will sound still more startling, and yet is a fact that can easily be ascertained by anybody who doubts it – at the present moment, if every MS. of the Rig-Veda were lost, we should be able to recover the whole of it – from the memory of the Srotriyas in India. These native students learn the Veda by heart, and they learn it from the mouth of their Guru, never from a MS., still less from my printed edition – and after a time they teach it again to their pupils.

I have had such students in my room at Oxford, who not only could repeat these hymns, but who repeated them with the proper accents (for the Vedic Sanskrit has accents like Greek), nay, who, when looking through my printed edition of the Rig-Veda, could point out a misprint without the slightest hesitation.

I can tell you more. There are hardly any various readings in our MSS. of the Rig-Veda, but various schools in India have their own readings of certain passages, and they hand down those readings with great care. So, instead of collating MSS., as we do in Greek and Latin, I have asked some friends of mine to collate those

---

1. M. M., "Hibbert Lectures," p. 153.
2. Learning was anciently preserved by memory. The Jewish, or rather Chaldaic *Kabala*, or Tradition was not written for many centuries. The Druids of ancient Britain preserved their litanies in the same way, and to a Bard a good memory was indispensable, or he would have been refused initiation.—A. W.

Vedic students, who carry their own Rig-Veda in their memory, and to let me have the various readings from these living authorities.

Here then we are not dealing with theories, but with facts, which anybody may verify. The whole of the Rig-Veda, and a great deal more, still exists at the present moment in the oral tradition of a number of scholars who, if they liked, could write down every letter, and every accent, exactly as we find them in our old MSS. Of course, this learning by heart is carried on under a strict discipline; it is, in fact, considered as a sacred duty. A native friend of mine, himself a very distinguished Vedic scholar, tells me that a boy, who is to be brought up as a student of the Rig-Veda, has to spend about eight years in the house of his teacher. He has to learn ten books: first, the hymns of the Rig-Veda; then a prose treatise on sacrifices, called the Brâhmana; then the so-called Forest-book or Âranyaka; then the rules on domestic ceremonies; and lastly, six treatises on pronunciation, grammar, etymology, metre, astronomy, and ceremonial.

These ten books, it has been calculated, contain nearly 30,000 lines, each line reckoned as thirty-two syllables.

A pupil studies every day during the eight years of his theological apprenticeship, except on the holidays, which are called "non-reading days." There being 360 days in a lunar year, the eight years would give him 2880 days. Deduct from this 384 holidays, and you get 2496 working days during the eight years. If you divide the number of lines, 30,000, by the number of working days, you get about twelve lines to be learned each day, though much time is taken up, in addition, for practising and rehearsing what has been learned before.

Now this is the state of things at present, though I doubt whether it will last much longer, and I always impress on my friends in India, and therefore impress on those also who will soon be settled as civil servants in India, the duty of trying to learn all that can still be learned from those living libraries. Much ancient Sanskrit lore will be lost forever when that race of Srotriyas becomes extinct.

But now let us look back. About a thousand years ago a Chinese of the name of I-tsing, a Buddhist, went to India to learn Sanskrit, in order to be able to translate some of the sacred books of his own religion, which were originally written in Sanskrit, into Chinese. He left China in 671, arrived at Tâmralipti in India in 673, and went to the great College and Monastery of Nâlanda, where he studied Sanskrit. He returned to China in 695, and died in 703.[1]

In one of his works which we still possess in Chinese, he gives an account of what he saw in India, not only among his own co-re-ligionists, the Buddhists, but likewise among the Brâhmans.[2]

Of the Buddhist priests he says that after they have learned to recite the five and the ten precepts, they are taught the 400 hymns of Mâtriketa, and afterward the 150 hymns of the same poet. When they are able to recite these, they begin the study of the Sûtras of their Sacred Canon. They also learn by heart the Gâtakamâlâ,[3] which gives an account of Buddha in former states of existence. Speaking of what he calls the islands of the Southern Sea, which he visited after leaving India, I-tsing says: "There are more than ten islands in the South Sea. There both priests and laymen recite the Gâtakamâlâ, as they recite the hymns mentioned before; but it has not yet been translated into Chinese."

One of these stories, he proceeds to say, was versified by a king (Kié-zhih) and set to music, and was performed before the public with a band and dancing – evidently a Buddhist mystery play.

I-tsing then gives a short account of the system of education. Children, he says, learn the forty-nine letters and the 10,000 compound letters when they are six years old, and generally finish them in half a year. This corresponds to about 300 verses,

---

1. See my article on the date of the Kâsikâ in the *Indian Antiquary*, 1880, p. 305.
2. The translation of the most important passages in I-tsing's work was made for me by one of my Japanese pupils, K. Kasawara.
3. See Bunyiu Nanjio's "Catalogue of the Chinese Tripitaka," p. 372, where Âryasûra, who must have lived before 434 A.D., is mentioned as the author of the "Gâtakamâlâ."

each sloka of thirty-two syllables. It was originally taught by Mahesvara. At eight years, children begin to learn the grammar of Pânini, and know it after about eight months. It consists of 1000 slokas, called Sûtras.

Then follows the list of roots (dhâtu) and the three appendices (khila), consisting again of 1000 slokas. Boys begin the three appendices when they are ten years old, and finish them in three years.

When they have reached the age of fifteen, they begin to study a commentary on the grammar (Sûtra), and spend five years on learning it. And here I-tsing gives the following advice to his countrymen, many of whom came to India to learn Sanskrit, but seem to have learned it very imperfectly. "If men of China," he writes, "go to India, wishing to study there, they should first of all learn these grammatical works, and then only other subjects; if not, they will merely waste their labor. These works should be learned by heart. But this is suited for men of high quality only... They should study hard day and night, without letting a moment pass for idle repose. They should be like Confucius, through whose hard study the binding of his Yih-king was three times cut asunder, being worn away; and like Sui-shih, who used to read a book repeatedly one hundred times." Then follows a remark, more intelligible in Chinese than in English: "The hairs of a bull are counted by thousands, the horn of a unicorn is only one."

I-tsing then speaks of the high degree of perfection to which the memory of these students attained, both among Buddhists and heretics. "Such men," he says, "could commit to memory the contents of two volumes, learning them only once."

And then turning to the *heretics*, or what we should call the orthodox Brahmans, he says: "The Brâhmanas are regarded throughout the five divisions of India as the most respectable. They do not walk with the other three castes, and other mixed classes of people are still further dissociated from them. They revere their Scriptures, the four Vedas, containing about 100,000 verses... The Vedas are handed down from mouth to mouth, not written on paper. There are in every generation some intelligent Brâhmans who can recite those 100,000 verses... I myself saw such men."

Here then we have an eye-witness who, in the seventh century after Christ, visited India, learned Sanskrit, and spent about twenty years in different monasteries – a man who had no theories of his own about oral tradition, but who, on the contrary, as coming from China, was quite familiar with the idea of a written, nay, of a printed literature: and yet what does he say? "The Vedas are not written on paper, but handed down from mouth to mouth."

Now, I do not quite agree here with I-tsing. At all events, we must not conclude from what he says that there existed no Sanskrit MSS. at all at his time. We know they existed. We know that in the first century of our era Sanskrit MSS. were carried from India to China, and translated there. Most likely therefore there were MSS. of the Veda also in existence. But I-tsing, for all that, was right in supposing that these MSS. were not allowed to be used by students, and that they had always to learn the Veda by heart and from the mouth of a properly qualified teacher. The very fact that in the later law-books severe punishments are threatened against persons who copy the Veda or learn it from a MSS., shows that MSS. existed, and that their existence interfered seriously with the ancient privileges of the Brâhmans, as the only legitimate teachers of their sacred scriptures.

If now, after having heard this account of I-tsing, we go back for about another thousand years, we shall feel less skeptical in accepting the evidence which we find in the so-called Prâtisâkhyas, that is, collections of rules which, so far as we know at present, go back to the fifth century before our era, and which tell us almost exactly the same as what we can see in India at the present moment, namely that the education of children of the three twice-born castes, the Brâhmanas, Kshatriyas, and Vaisyas, consisted in their passing at least eight years in the house of a Guru, and learning by heart the ancient Vedic hymns.

The art of teaching had even at that early time been reduced to a perfect system, and at that time certainly there is not the slightest trace of anything, such as a book, or skin, or parchment, a sheet of paper, pen or ink, being known even by name to the people of India; while every expression connected with what we should call literature, points to a literature (we cannot help using that word) existing in memory only, and being handed down with the most scrupulous care by means of oral tradition.

I had to enter into these details because I know that, with our ideas of literature, it requires an effort to imagine the bare possibility of a large amount of poetry, and still more of prose, existing in any but a written form. And yet here too we only see what we see elsewhere, namely that man, before the great discoveries of civilization were made, was able by greater individual efforts to achieve what to us, accustomed to easier contrivances, seems almost impossible. So-called savages were able to chip flints, to get fire by rubbing sticks of wood, which baffles our handiest workmen. Are we to suppose that, if they wished to preserve some songs which, as they believed, had once secured them the favor of their gods, had brought rain from heaven, or led them on to victory, they would have found no means of doing so? We have only to read such accounts as, for instance, Mr. William Wyatt Gill has given us in his "Historical Sketches of Savage Life in Polynesia,"[1] to see how anxious even savages are to preserve the records of their ancient heroes, kings, and gods, particularly when the dignity or nobility of certain families depends on these songs, or when they contain what might be called the title-deeds to large estates. And that the Vedic Indians were not the only savages of antiquity who discovered the means of preserving a large literature by means of oral tradition, we may learn from Cæsar,[2] not a very credulous witness, who tells us that the "Druids were said to know a large number of verses by heart; that some of them spent twenty years in learning them,

---

1. Wellington, 1880.
2. De Bello Gall. vi. 14; "History of Ancient Sanskrit Literature," p. 506.

and that they considered it wrong to commit them to writing" –
exactly the same story which we hear in India.

We must return once more to the question of dates. We have
traced the existence of the Veda, as handed down by oral tradition, from our days to the days of I-tsing in the seventh century
after Christ, and again to the period of the Prâtisâkhyas, in the fifth
century before Christ.

In that fifth century B.C. took place the rise of Buddhism, a
religion built up on the ruins of the Vedic religion, and founded, so
to say, on the denial of the divine authority ascribed to the Veda by
all orthodox Brâhmans.

Whatever exists, therefore, of Vedic literature must be accommodated within the centuries preceding the rise of Buddhism, and
if I tell you that there are three periods of Vedic literature to be
accommodated, the third presupposing the second, and the second
the first, and that even that first period presents us with a collection, and a systematic collection of Vedic hymns, I think you will
agree with me that it is from no desire for an extreme antiquity, but
simply from a respect for facts, that students of the Veda have come
to the conclusion that these hymns, of which the MSS. do not carry
us back beyond the fifteenth century after Christ, took their origin
in the fifteenth century before Christ.

* * *

One fact I must mention once more, because I think it may carry
conviction even against the stoutest skepticism.

I mentioned that the earliest inscriptions discovered in India
belong to the reign of King Asoka, the grandson of Kandragupta, who
reigned from 259-222 before Christ. What is the language of those
inscriptions? Is it the Sanskrit of the Vedic hymns? Certainly not.
Is it the later Sanskrit of the Brâhmanas and Sûtras? Certainly not.
These inscriptions are written in the local dialects as then spoken in
India, and these local dialects differ from the grammatical Sanskrit
about as much as Italian does from Latin.

What follows from this? First, that the archaic Sanskrit of the Veda had ceased to be spoken before the third century B.C. Secondly, that even the later grammatical Sanskrit was no longer spoken and understood by the people at large; that Sanskrit therefore had ceased, nay, we may say, had long ceased to be the spoken language of the country when Buddhism arose, and that therefore the youth and manhood of the ancient Vedic language lie far beyond the period that gave birth to the teaching of Buddha, who, though he may have known Sanskrit, and even Vedic Sanskrit, insisted again and again on the duty that his disciples should preach his doctrines in the language of the people whom they wished to benefit.

* * *

And now, when the time allotted to me is nearly at an end, I find, as it always happens, that I have not been able to say one half of what I hoped to say as to the lessons to be learned by us in India, even with regard to this one branch of human knowledge only, the study of the origin of religion. I hope, however, I may have succeeded in showing you the entirely new aspect which the old problem of the *theogony*, or the origin and growth of the Devas or gods, assumes from the light thrown upon it by the Veda. Instead of positive theories, we now have positive facts, such as you look for in vain anywhere else; and though there is still a considerable interval between the Devas of the Veda, even in their highest form, and such concepts as Zeus, Apollon, and Athene, yet the chief riddle is solved, and we know now at last what stuff the gods of the ancient world were made of.

But this theogonic process is but one side of the ancient Vedic religion, and there are two other sides of at least the same importance and of even a deeper interest to us.

There are in fact three religions in the Veda, or, if I may say so, three naves in one great temple, reared, as it were, before our eyes by poets, prophets, and philosophers. Here too we can watch the work and the workmen. We have not to deal with hard formulas only, with unintelligible ceremonies, or petrified fetiches. We can see how the human mind arrives by a perfectly rational process at all its later irrationalities. This is what distinguishes the Veda from all other Sacred Books. Much, no doubt, in the Veda also, and in the Vedic ceremonial, is already old and unintelligible, hard, and petrified. But in many cases the development of names and concepts, their transition from the natural to the supernatural, from the individual to the general, is still going on, and it is for that very reason that we find it so difficult, nay almost impossible, to translate the growing thoughts of the Veda into the full-grown and more than full-grown language of our time.

Let us take one of the oldest words for god in the Veda, such as deva, the Latin *deus*. The dictionaries tell you that *deva* means god and gods, and so, no doubt, it does. But if we always translated *deva* in the Vedic hymns by god, we should not be translating, but completely transforming the thoughts of the Vedic poets. I do not mean only that *our* idea of God is totally different from the idea that was intended to be expressed by *deva*; but even the Greek and Roman concept of gods would be totally inadequate to convey the thoughts imbedded in the Vedic *deva*. *Deva* meant originally bright, and nothing else. Meaning bright, it was constantly used of the sky, the stars, the sun, the dawn, the day, the spring, the rivers, the earth; and when a poet wished to speak of all of these by one and the same word – by what we should call a general term – he called them *Devas*. When that had been done, *Deva* did no longer mean "the Bright ones," but the name comprehended all the qualities which the sky and the sun and the dawn shared in common, excluding only those that were peculiar to each.

Here you see how, by the simplest process, the *Devas*, the bright ones, might become and did become the *Devas*, the heavenly, the kind, the powerful, the invisible, the immortal – and, in the end, something very like the θεοί (or *dii*) of Greeks and Romans.

In this way one Beyond, the Beyond of Nature, was built up in the ancient religion of the Veda, and peopled with Devas, and Asuras, and Vasus, and Âdityas, all names for the bright solar, celestial, diurnal, and vernal powers of nature, without altogether excluding, however, even the dark and unfriendly powers, those of the night, of the dark clouds, or of winter, capable of mischief, but always destined in the end to succumb to the valor and strength of their bright antagonists.

* * *

We now come to the second nave of the Vedic temple, the second *Beyond* that was dimly perceived, and grasped and named by the ancient Rishis, namely the world of the Departed Spirits.[1]

There was in India, as elsewhere, another very early faith, springing up naturally in the hearts of the people, that their fathers and mothers, when they departed this life, departed to a Beyond, wherever it might be, either in the East from whence all the bright Devas seemed to come, or more commonly in the West, the land to which they seemed to go, called in the Veda the realm of Yama or the setting sun. The idea that beings which once had been, could ever cease to be, had not yet entered their minds; and from the belief that their fathers existed somewhere, though they could see them no more, there arose the belief in another Beyond, and the germs of another religion.

---

1. See De Coulanges, "The Ancient City," Book I. II. "We find this worship of the dead among the Hellenes, among the Latins, among the Sabines, among the Etruscans; we also find it among the Aryas of India. Mention is made of it in the hymns of the Rig-Veda. It is spoken of in the Laws of Manu as the most ancient worship among men... Before men had any notion of Indra or of Zeus, they adored the dead; they feared them, and addressed them prayers. It seems that the religious sentiment began in this way. It was perhaps while looking upon the dead that man first conceived the idea of the supernatural, and to have a hope beyond what he saw. Death was the first mystery, and it placed man on the track of other mysteries. It raised his thoughts from the visible to the invisible, from the transitory to the eternal, from the human to the divine."

The sacred fire represented the ancestors, and therefore was revered and kept carefully from profanation by the presence of a stranger.—A. W.

Nor was the actual power of the fathers quite imperceptible or extinct even after their death. Their presence continued to be felt in the ancient laws and customs of the family, most of which rested on their will and their authority. While their fathers were alive and strong, their will was law; and when, after their death, doubts or disputes arose on points of law or custom, it was but natural that the memory and the authority of the fathers should be appealed to settle such points – that the law should still be their will.

Thus Manu says (IV. 178): "On the path on which his fathers and grandfathers have walked, on that path of good men let him walk, and he will not go wrong."

In the same manner then in which, out of the bright powers of nature, the Devas or gods had arisen, there arose out of predicates shared in common by the departed, such as pit*ris*, fathers, *preta*, gone away, another general concept, what we should call *Manes*, the kind ones, *Ancestors*, *Shades*, *Spirits*, or *Ghosts*, whose worship was nowhere more fully developed than in India. That common name, Pit*ris* or *Fathers*, gradually attracted toward itself all that the fathers shared in common. It came to mean not only fathers, but invisible, kind, powerful, immortal, heavenly beings, and we can watch in the Veda, better perhaps than anywhere else, the inevitable, yet most touching metamorphosis of ancient thought – the love of the child for father and mother becoming transfigured into an instinctive belief in the immortality of the soul.

It is strange, and really more than strange, that not only should this important and prominent side of the ancient religion of the Hindus have been ignored, but that of late its very existence should have been doubted. I feel obliged, therefore, to add a few words in support of what I have said just now of the supreme importance of this belief in and this worship of ancestral spirits in India from the most ancient to the most modern times. Mr. Herbert Spencer, who has done so much in calling attention to ancestorship as a natural ingredient of religion among all savage nations, declares in the most emphatic manner,[1] "that he has seen it implied, that he has heard it in conversation, and that he now has it before him in print, that no Indo-European or Semitic nation, so far as we know, seems to have made a religion of the worship of the dead." I do not doubt his words, but I think that on so important a point, Mr. Herbert Spencer ought to have named his authorities. It seems to me almost impossible that anybody who has ever opened a book on India should have made such a statement. There are hymns in the Rig-Veda addressed to the Fathers. There are full descriptions of the worship due to the Fathers in the Brâhmanas and Sûtras. The epic poems, the law books, the Purânas, all are brimful of allusions to ancestral offerings. The whole social fabric of India, with its laws of inheritance and marriage,[2] rests on a belief in the Manes – and yet we are told that no Indo-European nation seems to have made a religion of the worship of the dead.

The Persians had their Fravashis, the Greeks their εἴδωλα, or rather their θεοὶ ϖατρῷοι and their δαίμονες,

ἐσθλοί, ἐϖιχθόνιοι, φύλακες θνητῶν ἀνθρώϖων;
ὀΐρα φυλάσσουσίν τε δίκας καὶ σχέτλια ἔργα,
ἠέρα ἑσσάμενοι ϖάντη φοιτῶντες ἐϖ᾽ αἶαν,
ϖλουτοδόται (Hesiodi Opera et Dies, vv. 122-126);[3]

---

1. "Principles of Sociology," p. 313.
2. "The Hindu Law of Inheritance is based upon the Hindu religion, and we must be cautious that in administering Hindu law we do not, by acting upon our notions derived from English law, inadvertently wound or offend the religious feelings of those who may be affected by our decisions."—Bengal Law Reports, 103.
3. "Earth-wandering demons, they their charge began,
    The ministers of good and guards of man;
    Veiled with a mantle of aërial light,
    O'er Earth's wide space they wing their hovering flight."

while among the Romans the *Lares familiars* and the *Divi Manes* were worshipped more zealously than any other gods.[1] Manu goes so far as to tell us in one place (III. 203): "An oblation by Brâhmans to their ancestor transcends an oblation to the deities;" and yet we are told that no Indo-European nation seems to have made a religion of the worship of the dead.

Such things ought really not to be, if there is to be any progress in historical research, and I cannot help thinking that what Mr. Herbert Spencer meant was probably no more than that some scholars did not admit that the worship of the dead formed the whole of the religion of any of the Indo-European nations. That, no doubt, is perfectly true, but it would be equally true, I believe, of almost any other religion. And on this point again the students of anthropology will learn more, I believe, from the Veda than from any other book.

In the Veda the Pitris, or fathers, are invoked together with the Devas, or gods, but they are not confounded with them. The Devas never become Pitris, and though such adjectives as *deva* are sometimes applied to the Pitris, and they are raised to the rank of the older classes of Devas (Manu III. 192, 284, Yâgñavalkya I. 268), it is easy to see that the Pitris and Devas had each their independent origin, and that they represent two totally distinct phases of the human mind in the creation of its objects of worship. This is a lesson which ought never to be forgotten.

We read in the Rig-Veda, VI. 52, 4: "May the rising Dawns protect me, may the flowing Rivers protect me, may the firm Mountains protect me, may the Fathers protect me at this invocation of the gods." Here nothing can be clearer than the separate existence of the Fathers, apart from the Dawns, the Rivers, and the Mountains, though they are included in one common Devahûti, however, or invocation of the gods.

---

1. Cicero, "De Leg." II. 9, 22, "Deorum manium jura sancta sunto; nos leto datos divos habento."

We must distinguish, however, from the very first, between two classes, or rather between two concepts of Fathers, the one comprising the distant, half-forgotten, and almost mythical ancestors of certain families or of what would have been to the poets of the Veda, the whole human race, the other consisting of the fathers who had but lately departed, and who were still, as it were, personally remembered and revered.

The old ancestors in general approach more nearly to the gods. They are often represented as having gone to the abode of Yama, the ruler of the departed, and to live there in company with some of the Devas (Rig-Veda VII. 76, 4, devânâm sadhamâdah; Rig-Veda X. 16, 1, devânâm vasanîh).

We sometimes read of the great-grandfathers being in heaven, the grandfathers in the sky, the fathers on the earth, the first in company with the Âdityas, the second with the Rudras, the last with the Vasus. All these are individual poetical conceptions.[1]

Yama himself is sometimes invoked as if he were one of the Fathers, the first of mortals that died or that trod the path of the Fathers (the pitriyâna, X. 2, 7) leading to the common sunset in the West.[2] Still his real Deva-like nature is never completely lost, and, as the god of the setting sun, he is indeed the leader of the Fathers, but not one of the Fathers himself.[3]

Many of the benefits which men enjoyed on earth were referred to the Fathers, as having first been procured and first enjoyed by them. They performed the first sacrifices, and secured the benefits arising from them. Even the great events in nature, such as the rising of the sun, the light of the day and the darkness of the night, were sometimes referred to them, and they were praised for having

---

1. See Atharva-Veda XVIII. 2, 49.
2. Rig-Veda X. 14, 1-2. He is called Vaivasvata, the solar (X. 58, 1), and even the son of Vivasvat (X. 14, 5). In a later phase of religious thought Yama is conceived as the first man (Atharva-Veda XVIII. 3, 13, as compared with Rig-Veda X. 14, 1).
3. Rig-Veda X. 14.

broken open the dark stable of the morning and having brought out the cows, that is, the days (X. 68, 11).[1] They were even praised for having adorned the night with stars, while in later writing the stars are said to be the lights of the good people who have entered into heaven.[2] Similar ideas, we know, prevailed among the ancient Persians, Greeks, and Romans. The Fathers are called in the Veda truthful (satyá), wise (suvidátra), righteous (ritávat), poets (kaví), leaders (pathikrít), and one of their most frequent epithets is somya, delighting in Soma, Soma being the ancient intoxicating beverage of the Vedic Rishis, which was believed to bestow immortality,[3] but which had been lost, or at all events had become difficult to obtain by the Aryans, after their migration into the Punjâb.[4]

The families of the Bhrigus, the Angiras, the Atharvans all have their Pitris or Fathers, who are invoked to sit down on the grass and to accept the offerings placed there for them. Even the name of Pitriyagña, sacrifice of the Fathers, occurs already in the hymns of the Rig-Veda.

The following is one of the hymns of the Rig-Veda by which those ancient Fathers were invited to come to their sacrifice (Rig-veda X. 15):[5]

1. "May the Soma-loving Fathers, the lowest, the highest, and the middle, arise. May the gentle and righteous Fathers who have come to life (again), protect us in these invocations!

2. "May this salutation be for the Fathers to-day, for those who have departed before or after; whether they now dwell in the sky above the earth, or among the blessed people.

---

1. In the Avesta many of these things are done by Ahura-Mazda with the help of the Fravashis.
2. See Satapatha Brâhmana I. 9, 3, 10; VI. 5, 4, 8.
3. Rig-Veda VIII. 48, 3: "We drank Soma, we became immortal, we went to the light, we found the gods;" VIII. 48, 12.
4. Rig-Veda IX. 97, 39.
5. A translation considerably differing from my own is given by Sarvâdhikâri in his "Tagore Lectures for 1880," p. 34.

3. "I invited the wise Fathers... may they come hither quickly, and sitting on the grass readily partake of the poured-out draught!

4. "Come hither to us with your help, you Fathers who sit on the grass! We have prepared these libations for you, accept them! Come hither with your most blessed protection, and give us health and wealth without fail!

5. "The Soma-loving Fathers have been called hither to their dear viands which are placed on the grass. Let them approach, let them listen, let them bless, let them protect us!

6. "Bending your knee and sitting on my right, accept all this sacrifice. Do not hurt us, O Fathers, for any wrong that we may have committed against you, men as we are.

7. "When you sit down on the lap of the red dawns, grant wealth to the generous mortal! O Fathers, give of your treasure to the sons of this man here, and bestow vigor here on us!

8. "May Yama, as a friend with friends, consume the offerings according to his wish, united with those old Soma-loving Fathers of ours, the Vasishthas, who arranged the Soma draught.

9. "Come hither, O Agni, with those wise and truthful Fathers who like to sit down near the hearth, who thirsted when yearning for the gods, who knew the sacrifice, and who were strong in praise with their songs.

10. "Come, O Agni, with those ancient fathers who like to sit down near the hearth, who forever praise the gods, the truthful, who eat and drink our oblations, making company with Indra and the gods.

11. "O Fathers, you who have been consumed by Agni, come here, sit down on your seats, you kind guides! Eat of the offerings which we have placed on the turf, and then grant us wealth and strong offspring!

12. "O Agni, OGâtavedas,[1] at our request thou hast carried the offerings, having first rendered them sweet. Thou gavest them to the Fathers, and they fed on their share. Eat also, O god, the proffered oblations!

13. "The Fathers who are here, and the Fathers who are not here, those whom we know, and those whom we know not, thou *Gâtavedas*, knowest how many they are, accept the well-made sacrifice with the sacrificial portions!

14. "To those who, whether burned by fire or not burned by fire, rejoice in their share in the midst of heaven, grant thou, O King, that their body may take that life which they wish for!"[2]

---

1. Cf. Max Müller, Rig-Veda, transl. vol. i. p. 24.

2. In a previous note will be found the statement by Professor De Coulanges, of Strasburg, that in India, as in other countries, a belief in the ancestral spirits came first, and a belief in divinities afterward. Professor Müller cites other arguments which might be employed in support of such a theory. The name of the oldest and greatest among the Devas, for instance, is not simply Dyaus, but Dyaush-pitâ, Heaven-Father; and there are several names of the same character, not only in Sanskrit, but in Greek and Latin also. Jupiter and Zeus Pater are forms of the appellation mentioned, and mean the Father in Heaven. It does certainly look as though Dyaus, the sky, had become personal and worshipped only after he had been raised to the category of a Pitri, a father; and that this predicate of Father must have been elaborated first before it could have been used, to comprehend Dyaus, the sky, Varuna, and other Devas. Professor Müller, however, denies that this is the whole truth in the case. The Vedic poets, he remarks, believed in Devas—gods, if we must so call them—literally, the bright ones; Pitris, fathers; and Manushyas, men, mortals. (Atharva-Veda, X. 6, 32.) Who came first and who came after it is difficult to say; but as soon as the three were placed side by side, the Devas certainly stood the highest, then followed the Pitris, and last came the mortals. Ancient thought did not comprehend the three under one concept, but it paved the way to it. The mortals after passing through death became Fathers, and the Fathers became the companions of the Devas.

    In Manu there is an advance beyond this point. The world, all that moves and rests, we are told (Manu III., 201), has been made by the Devas; but the Devas and Danavas were born of the Pitris, and the Pitris of the Rishis.

Distinct from the worship offered to these primitive ancestors, is the reverence which from an early time was felt to be due by children to their departed father, soon also to their grandfather, and great-grandfather. The ceremonies in which these more personal feelings found expression were of a more domestic character, and allowed therefore of greater local variety.

It would be quite impossible to give here even an abstract only of the minute regulations which have been preserved to us in the Brâhmanas, the Srauta, Grihya, and Sâmayâkârika Sûtras, the Law-books, and a mass of later manuals on the performance of endless rites, all intended to honor the Departed. Such are the minute prescriptions as to times and seasons, as to altars and offerings, as to the number and shape of the sacrificial vessels, as to the proper postures of the sacrificers, and the different arrangements of the vessels, that it is extremely difficult to catch hold of what we really care for, namely, the thoughts and intentions of those who first devised all these intricacies. Much has been written on this class of sacrifices by European scholars also, beginning with Colebrooke's excellent essays on "The Religious Ceremonies of the Hindus," first published in the "Asiatic Researches," vol. v. Calcutta, 1798. But when we ask the simple question, What was the thought from whence all this outward ceremonial sprang, and what was the natural craving of the human heart which it seemed to satisfy, we hardly get an intelligible answer anywhere. It is true that

---

Originally the Rishis were the poets of the Vedas, seven in number; and we are not told how they came to be placed above the Devas and Pitris. It does not, however, appear utterly beyond the power to solve. The Vedas were the production of the Rishis, and the Pitris, being perpetuated thus to human memory, became by a figure of speech their offspring. The Devas sprung from the Pitris, because it was usual to apotheosize the dead. "Our ancestors desired," says Cicero, "that the men who had quitted this life should be counted in the number of gods." Again, the conception of patrons or Pitris to each family and tribe naturally led to the idea of a Providence over all; and so the Pitri begat the Deva. This religion preceded and has outlasted the other.—A. W.

Srâddhas continue to be performed all over India to the present day, but we know how widely the modern ceremonial has diverged from the rules laid down in the old Sâstras, and it is quite clear from the descriptions given to us by recent travellers that no one can understand the purport even of these survivals of the old ceremonial, unless he understands Sanskrit and can read the old Sûtras. We are indeed told in full detail how the cakes were made which the Spirits wore supposed to eat, how many stalks of grass were to be used on which they had to be offered, how long each stalk ought to be, and in what direction it should be held. All the things which teach us nothing are explained to us in abundance, but the few things which the true scholar really cares for are passed over, as if they had no interest to us at all, and have to be discovered under heaps of rubbish.

In order to gain a little light, I think we ought to distinguish between—

1. The daily ancestral sacrifice, the Pitriyagña, as one of the five Great Sacrifices (Mahâyagñas);
2. The monthly ancestral sacrifice, the Pinda-pitri-yagña, as part of the New and Full-moon sacrifice;
3. The funeral ceremonies on the death of a householder;
4. The Agapes, or feasts of love and charity, commonly called Srâddhas, at which food and other charitable gifts were bestowed on deserving persons in memory of the deceased ancestors. The name of Srâddha belongs properly to this last class only, but it has been transferred to the second and third class of sacrifices also, because Srâddha formed an important part in them.

The daily Pitriyagña or Ancestor-worship is one of the five sacrifices, sometimes called the Great Sacrifices,[1] which every married man

1. Satapatha Brâhmana XI. 5, 6, 1; Taitt. Âr. II. 11, 10; Âsvalâyana Grihya-sûtras III. 1, 1; Pâraskara Grihya-sûtras II. 9, 1; Âpastamba, Dharma-sûtras, translated by Bühler, pp. 47 seq.

ought to perform day by day. They are mentioned in the Grihya-sûtras (Âsv. III. 1), as Devayagña, for the Devas, Bhûtayagña, for animals, etc., Pitriyagña, for the Fathers, Brahmayagña, for Brahman, *i.e.* study of the Veda, and Manushyayagña, for men, *i.e.* hospitality, etc. Manu (III. 70) tells us the same, namely, that a married man has five great religious duties to perform:

1. The Brahma-sacrifice, *i.e.* the studying and teaching of the Veda (sometimes called Ahuta).
2. The Pit*ri*-sacrifice, *i.e.* the offering of cakes and water to the Manes (sometimes called Prâsita).
3. The Deva-sacrifice, *i.e.* the offering of oblations to the gods (sometimes called Huta).
4. The Bhûta-sacrifice, *i.e.* the giving of food to living creatures (sometimes called Prahuta).
5. The Manushya-sacrifice, *i.e.* the receiving of guests with hospitality (sometimes called Brâhmya huta).[1]

performance of this daily Pitriyagña, seems to have been extremely simple. The householder had to put his sacred cord on the right shoulder, to say "Svadhâ to the Fathers," and to throw the remains of certain offerings toward the south.[2]

The human impulse to this sacrifice, if sacrifice it can be called, is clear enough. The five "great sacrifices" comprehended in early times the whole duty of man from day to day. They were connected with his daily meal.[3] When this meal was preparing, and before he could touch it himself, he was to offer something to the gods, a Vais-vadeva offering, in which the chief deities were Agni, fire, Soma the Visve Devas, Dhanvantari, the kind of Æsculapius, Kuhû and Anumati

---

1. In the Sânkhâyana Grihya (I. 5) four Pâka-yagñas are mentioned, called Huta, ahuta, prahuta, prâsita.
2. Âsv. Grihya-sûtras I. 3, 10.
3. Manu III. 117-118.

(phases of the moon), Pragâpati, lord of creatures, Dyâvâ-prithivî, Heaven and Earth, and Svishtakrit, the fire on the hearth.[1]

After having thus satisfied the gods in the four quarters, the householder had to throw some oblations into the open air, which were intended for animals, and in some cases for invisible beings, ghosts and such like. Then he was to remember the Departed, the Pitris, with some offerings; but even after having done this he was not yet to begin his own repast, unless he had also given something to strangers (atithis).

When all this had been fulfilled, and when, besides, the householder, as we should say, had said his daily prayers, or repeated what he had learned of the Veda, then and then only was he in harmony with the world that surrounded him, the five Great Sacrifices had been performed by him, and he was free from all the sins arising from a thoughtless and selfish life.

This Pitriyagña, as one of the five daily sacrifices, is described in the Brâhmanas, the Grihya and Sâmayâkârika Sûtras, and, of course,

1. See Des Coulanges, "Ancient City," I. 3. "Especially were the meals of the family religions acts. The god [the sacred fire] presided there. He had cooked the bread and prepared the food; a prayer, therefore, was due at the beginning and end of the repast. Before eating, they placed upon the altar the first fruits of the food; before drinking, they poured out a libation of wine. This was the god's portion. No one doubted that he was present, that he ate and drank; nor did they not see the flame increase as if it had been nourished by the provisions offered? Thus the meal was divided between the man and the god. It was a sacred ceremony, by which they held communion with each other... The religion of the sacred fire dates from the distant and dim epoch when there were yet no Greeks, no Italians, no Hindus, when there were only Aryas. When the tribes separated they carried this worship with them, some to the banks of the Ganges, others to the shores of the Mediterranean... Each group chose its own gods, but all preserved as an ancient legacy the first religion which they had known and practiced in the common cradle of their race."
   The fire in the house denoted the ancestor, or pitri, and in turn the serpent was revered as a living fire, and so an appropriate symbol of the First Father.—A. W.

in the legal Samhitâs. Rajendralâl Mitra[1] informs us that "orthodox Brâhmans to this day profess to observe all these five ceremonies, but that in reality only the offerings to the gods and manes are strictly observed, while the reading is completed by the repetition of the Gâyatrî only, and charity and feeding of animals are casual and uncertain."

Quite different from this simple daily ancestral offering is the Pitriyagña or Pinda-pitriyagña, which forms part of many of the statutable sacrifices, and, first of all, of the New and Full-moon sacrifice. Here again the human motive is intelligible enough. It was the contemplation of the regular course of nature, the discovery of order in the coming and going of the heavenly bodies, the growing confidence in some ruling power of the world which lifted man's thoughts from his daily work to higher regions, and filled his heart with a desire to approach these higher powers with praise, thanksgiving, and offerings. And it was at such moments as the waning of the moon that his thoughts would most naturally turn to those whose life had waned, whose bright faces were no longer visible on earth, his father's or ancestors. Therefore at the very beginning of the New-moon sacrifice, we are told in the Brâhmanas[2] and in the Srauta-sûtras, that a Pitriyagña, a sacrifice to the Fathers, has to be performed. A Karu or pie had to be prepared in the Dakshinâgni, the southern fire, and the offerings, consisting of water and round cakes (pindas), were specially dedicated to father, grandfather, and great-grandfather, while the wife of the sacrificer, if she wished for a son, was allowed to eat one of the cakes.[3]

Similar ancestral offerings took place during other sacrifices too, of which the New and Full-moon sacrifices form the general type.

---

1. "Taittirîyâranyaka," Preface, p. 23.
2. Mâsi mâsi vo 'sanam iti sruteh; Gobhilîya Grihya sûtras, p. 1055.
3. See "Pindapitriyagña," von Dr. O. Donner, 1870. The restriction to three ancestors, father, grandfather, and great-grandfather, occurs in the Vâgasaneyi-samhitâ, XIX. 36-37.

It may be quite true that these two kinds of ancestral sacrifices have the same object and share the same name, but their character is different; and if, as has often been the case, they are mixed up together, we lose the most important lessons which a study of the ancient ceremonial should teach us. I cannot describe the difference between these two Pitriyagñas more decisively than by pointing out that the former was performed by the father of a family, or, if we may say so, by a layman, the latter by a regular priest, or a class of priests, selected by the sacrificer to act in his behalf. As the Hindus themselves would put it, the former is a grihya, a domestic, the latter a srauta, a priestly ceremony.[1]

We now come to a third class of ceremonies which are likewise domestic and personal, but which differ from the two preceding ceremonies by their occasional character, I mean the funeral, as distinct from the ancestral ceremonies. In one respect these funeral ceremonies may represent an earlier phase of worship than the daily and monthly ancestral sacrifices. They lead up to them, and, as it were, prepare the departed for their future dignity as Pitris or Ancestors. On the other hand, the conception of Ancestors in general must have existed before any departed person could have been raised to that rank, and I therefore preferred to describe the ancestral sacrifices first.

Nor need I enter here very fully into the character of the special funeral ceremonies of India. I described them in a special paper, "On Sepulture and Sacrificial Customs in the Veda," nearly thirty years ago.[2] Their spirit is the same as that of the funeral ceremonies

1. There is, however, great variety in these matters, according to different sâkhâs. Thus, according to the Gobhila-sâkhâ, the Pinda Pitriyagña is to be considered as smârta, not as srauta (pinda-pitriyagñah khalv as makkhâkhâyâm nâsti); while others maintain that an agnimat should perform the smârta, asrautâgnimat the srauta Pitriyagña; see Gobhilîya Grihya-sûtras, p. 671. On page 667 we read: anagner amâvasyâsraddhâ, nânvâhâryam ity âdaraniyam.
2. "Über Todtenbestattung und Opfergebräuche im Veda," in "Zeitschrift der Deutschen Morgenländischen Gesellschaft," vol. ix. 1856.

of Greeks, Romans, Slavonic, and Teutonic nations, and the coincidences between them all are often most surprising.

In Vedic times the people in India both burned and buried their dead, and they did this with a certain solemnity, and, after a time, according to fixed rules. Their ideas about the status of the departed, after their body had been burned and their ashes buried, varied considerably, but in the main they seem to have believed in a life to come, not very different from our life on earth, and in the power of the departed to confer blessings on their descendants. It soon therefore became the interest of the survivors to secure the favor of their departed friends by observances and offerings which, at first, were the spontaneous manifestation of human feelings, but which soon became traditional, technical, in fact, ritual.

On the day on which the corpse had been burned, the relatives (samânodakas) bathed and poured out a handful of water to the deceased, pronouncing his name and that of his family.[1] At sunset they returned home, and, as was but natural, they were told to cook nothing during the first night, and to observe certain rules during the next day up to ten days, according to the character of the deceased. These were days of mourning, or, as they were afterward called, days of impurity, when the mourners withdrew from contact with the world, and shrank by a natural impulse from the ordinary occupations and pleasures of life.[2]

Then followed the collecting of the ashes on the 11th, 13th, or 15th day of the dark half of the moon. On returning from thence they bathed, and then offered what was called a Srâddha to the departed.

This word Srâddha, which meets us here for the first time, is full of interesting lessons, if only properly understood. First of all it should be noted that it is absent, not only from the hymns, but, so far as we know at present, even from the ancient Brâhmanas. It seems therefore a word of a more modern origin. There is a passage in

---

1. Asvalâyana Grihya-sûtras IV. 4, 10.
2. Manu V. 64-65.

Âpastamba's Dharma-sûtras which betrays, on the part of the author, a consciousness of the more modern origin of the Srâddhas:[1]

"Formerly men and gods lived together in this world. Then the gods in reward of their sacrifices went to heaven, but men were left behind. Those men who perform sacrifices in the same manner as the gods did, dwelt (after death) with the gods and Brahman in heaven. Now (seeing men left behind) Manu revealed this ceremony which is designated by the word Srâddha."

Srâddha has assumed many[2] meanings, and Manu,[3] for instance, uses it almost synonymously with pitriyagña. But its original meaning seems to have been "that which is given with sraddhâ or faith," *i.e.* charity bestowed on deserving persons, and, more particularly, on Brâhmanas. The gift was called srâddha, but the act itself also was called by the same name. The word is best explained by Nârâyana in his commentary on the Grihya-sûtras of Âsvalâyana (IV. 7), "Srâddha is that which is given in faith to Brâhmans for the sake of the Fathers."[4]

Such charitable gifts flowed most naturally and abundantly at the time of a man's death, or whenever his memory was revived by happy or unhappy events in a family, and hence Srâddha has become

---

1. Bühler, Âpastamba, "Sacred Books of the East," vol. ii., p. 138; also "Srâddhâkalpa," p. 890. Though the Srâddha is prescribed in the "Gobhilîya Grihya-sûtras," IV. 4, 2-3, it is not described there, but in a separate treatise, the Srâddha-kalpa.
2. As meaning the food, srâddha occurs in srâddhabhug and similar words. As meaning the sacrificial act, it is explained, yatraita *k* khraddhayâ dîyate tad eva karma srâddhasabdâbhidheyam. Pretam pitrîmska nirdisya bhogyamyat priyam âtmanah sraddhayâ dîyate yatra takkhrâddham parikîrtitam. "Gobhilîya Grihya-sûtras," p. 892. We also read sraddhânvitah srâddham kurvîta, "let a man perform the srâddha with faith;""Gobhilîya Grihya-sûtras," p. 1053.
3. Manu III. 82.
4. Pitrîn uddi*s*ya yad dîyate brâhmanebhyah sraddhayâ tak khrâdd ham.

the general name for ever so many sacred acts commemorative of the departed. We hear of Srâddhas not only at funerals, but at joyous events also, when presents were bestowed in the name of the family, and therefore in the name of the ancestors also, on all who had a right to that distinction.

It is a mistake therefore to look upon Srâddhas simply as offerings of water or cakes to the Fathers. An offering to the Fathers was, no doubt, a symbolic part of each Srâddha, but it's more important character was charity bestowed in memory of the Fathers.

This, in time, gave rise to much abuse, like the alms bestowed on the Church during the Middle Ages. But in the beginning the motive was excellent. It was simply a wish to benefit others, arising from the conviction, felt more strongly in the presence of death than at any other time, that as we can carry nothing out of this world, we ought to do as much good as possible in the world with our worldly goods. At Srâddhas the Brâhmanas were said to represent the sacrificial fire into which the gifts should be thrown.[1] If we translate here Brâhmanas by priests, we can easily understand why there should have been in later times so strong a feeling against Srâddhas. But priest is a very bad rendering of Brâhmana. The Brâhmanas were, socially and intellectually, a class of men of high breeding. They were a recognized and, no doubt, a most essential element in the ancient society of India. As they lived for others, and were excluded from most of the lucrative pursuits of life, it was a social, and it soon became a religious duty, that they should be supported by the community at large. Great care was taken that the recipients of such bounty as was bestowed at Srâddhas should be strangers, neither friends nor enemies, and in no way related to the family. Thus Âpastamba says: "The food eaten (at a Srâddha) by persons related to the giver is a gift offered to goblins. It reaches neither the Manes nor the Gods." A man who tried to curry favor

---

1. Âpastamba II. 16, 3, Brâhmanâs tv âhavanîyârthe.

by bestowing Srâddhika gifts, was called by an opprobrious name, a Srâddha-mitra.[1]

Without denying therefore that in later times the system of Srâddhas may have degenerated, I think we can perceive that it sprang from a pure source, and, what for our present purpose is even more important, from an intelligible source.

Let us now return to the passage in the Grihya-sûtras of Âsvalâyana, where we met for the first time with the name of Srâddha.[2] It was the Srâddha to be given for the sake of the Departed, after his ashes had been collected in an urn and buried. This Srâddha is called ekoddishta,[3] or, as we should say, personal. It was meant for one person only, not for the three ancestors, nor for all the ancestors. Its object was in fact to raise the departed to the rank of a Pitri, and this had to be achieved by Srâddha offerings continued during a whole year. This at least is the general, and, most likely, the original rule. Âpastamba says that the Srâddha for a deceased relative should be performed every day during the year, and that after that a monthly Srâddha only should be performed or none at all, that is, no more personal Srâddha,[4] because the departed shares henceforth in the regular Pârvana-srâddhas.[5] Sânkhâyana says the same,[6] namely that the personal Srâddha lasts for a year, and that then "the Fourth" is dropped, *i.e.* the great-grandfather was dropped, the grandfather became the great-grandfather, the father the grandfather, while the lately Departed occupied the father's place among

---

1. Manu III. 138, 140.
2. "Âsv. Grihya-sûtras" IV. 5, 8.
3. It is described as a vikriti of the Pârvana-srâddha in "Gobhilîya Grihya-sûtras," p. 1011.
4. One of the differences between the acts before and after the Sapindîkarana is noted by Sâlankâyana:—Sapindîkaranam yâvad rigudarbhaih pitrikriyâ Sapindîkaranâd ûrdhvam dvigunair vidhivad bhavet. "Gobhilîya Grihya-sûtras," p. 930.
5. "Gobhilîya Grihya-sûtras," p. 1023.
6. "Grihya-sûtras," ed. Oldenberg, p. 83.

the three principal Pitris.[1] This was called the Sapindîkarana, *i.e.* the elevating of the departed to the rank of an ancestor.

There are here, as elsewhere, many exceptions. Gobhila allows six months instead of a year, or even a Tripaksha,[2] *i.e.* three half-months; and lastly, any auspicious event (vriddhi) may become the occasion of the Sapindîkarana.[3]

The full number of Srâddhas necessary for the Sapindana is sometimes given as sixteen, viz., the first, then one in each of the twelve months, then two semestral ones, and lastly the Sapindana. But here too much variety is allowed, though, if the Sapindana takes place before the end of the year, the number of sixteen Srâddhas has still to be made up.[4]

When the Srâddha is offered on account of an auspicious event, such as a birth or a marriage, the fathers invoked are not the father, grandfather, and great-grandfather, who are sometimes called asru-mukha, with tearful faces, but the ancestors before them, and they are called nândîmukha, or joyful.[5]

Colebrooke,[6] to whom we owe an excellent description of what a Srâddha is in modern times, took evidently the same view. "The first set of funeral ceremonies," he writes, "is adapted to effect, by means of oblations, the re-embodying of the soul of the deceased, after burning his corpse. The apparent scope of the second set is to raise his shade from this world, where it would else, according to the notions of the Hindus, continue to roam among demons and evil spirits, up to heaven, and then deify him, as it were, among the manes of departed ancestors. For this end, a Srâddha should

---

1. A pratyâbdikam ekoddishtam on the anniversary of the deceased is mentioned by Gobhilîya, l. c. p. 1011.
2. "Gobhilîya Grihya-sûtras," p. 1039.
3. "Sânkh. Grihya," p. 83; "Gobh. Grihya," p. 1024. According to some authorities the ekoddishta is called nava, new, during ten days; navamisra, mixed, for six months; and purâna, old, afterward. "Gobhilîya Grihya-sûtras," p. 1020.
4. "Gobhilîya," l. c. p. 1032.
5. "Gobhilîya," l. c. p. 1047.
6. "Life and Essays," ii. p. 195.

regularly be offered to the deceased on the day after the mourning expires; twelve other Srâddhas *singly* to the deceased in twelve
successive months; similar obsequies at the end of the third fort-
night, and also in the sixth month, and in the twelfth; and the
oblation called Sapindana on the first anniversary of his decease.[1]
At this Sapindana Srâddha, which is the last of the ekoddishta srâddhas, four funeral cakes are offered to the deceased and his three
ancestors, that consecrated to the deceased being divided into three
portions and mixed with the other three cakes. The portion retained
is often offered to the deceased, and the act of union and fellowship
becomes complete."[2]

When this system of Srâddhas had once been started, it seems
to have spread very rapidly. We soon hear of the monthly Srâddha,
not only in memory of one person lately deceased, but as part of the
Pitriyagña, and as obligatory, not only on householders (agnimat),
but on other persons also, and, not only on the three upper castes,
but even, without hymns, on Sûdras,[3] and as to be performed,
not only on the day of New-Moon, but on other days also, whenever there was an opportunity. Gobhila seems to look upon the
Pindapitriyagña, as itself a Srâddha,[4] and the commentator holds
that, even if there are no pindas or cakes, the Brâhmans ought still
to be fed. This Srâddha, however, is distinguished from the other,

1. Colebrooke adds that in most provinces the periods for these sixteen ceremonies, and for the concluding obsequies entitled Sapindana, are anticipated, and
   the whole is completed on the second or third day; after which they are again
   performed at the proper times, but in honor of the whole set of progenitors
   instead of the deceased singly. It is this which Dr. Donner, in his learned paper
   on the "Pindapitriyagña" (p. 11), takes as the general rule.
2. See this subject most exhaustively treated, particularly in its bearings on the
   law of inheritance, in Rajkumar Sarvâdhikâri's "Tagore Law Lectures for
   1880," p. 93.
3. "Gobhilîya Grihya-sûtras," p. 892.
4. See p. 666, and p. 1008. Grihyakârah pindapitriyagñasya srâddhatvam âha.

the true Srâddha, called Anvâhârya, which follows it,[1] and which is properly known by the name of Pârvana Srâddha.

The same difficulties which confront us when we try to form a clear conception of the character of the various ancestral ceremonies, were felt by the Brâhmans themselves, as may be seen from the long discussions in the commentary on the Srâddha-kalpa[2] and froṁ the abusive language used by Kandrakânta Tarkâlankâra against Raghunandana. The question with them assumes the form of what is pradhâna (primary) and what is anga (secondary) in these sacrifices, and the final result arrived at is that sometimes the offering of cakes is pradhâna, as in the Pindapitriyagña, sometimes the feeding of Brâhmans only, as in the Nitya-srâddha, sometimes both, as in the Sapindikarana.

We may safely say, therefore, that not a day passed in the life of the ancient people of India on which they were not reminded of their ancestors, both near and distant, and showed their respect for them, partly by symbolic offerings to the Manes, partly by charitable gifts to deserving persons, chiefly Brâhmans. These offertories varied from the simplest, such as milk and fruits, to the costliest, such as gold and jewels. The feasts given to those who were invited to officiate òr assist at a Srâddha seem in some cases to have been very sumptuous,[3] and what is very important, the eating of meat, which in later times was strictly forbidden in many sects, must, when the Sûtras were written, have been fully recognized at these feasts, even to the killing and eating of a cow.[4]

---

1. Gobhila IV. 4, 3, itarad anvâhâryam. But the commentators add anagner amâvasyâsrâddham, nânvâhâryam. According to Gobhila there ought to be the Vaisvadeva offering and the Bali offering at the end of each Pârvana-srâddha; see "Gobhilîya Grihya-sûtras," p. 1005, but no Vaisvadeva at an ekoddishta srâddha, l. c. p. 1020.

2. L. c. pp. 1005-1010; "Nirnayasindhu," p. 270.

3. See Burnell, "The Law of Partition," p. 31.

4. Kalau tâvad gavâlambho mâmsadânam ka srâddhe nishiddham, Gobhilena tu madhyamâshtakâyâm vâstukarmani ka gavâlambho vihitah, mâmsa-

This shows that these Srâddhas, though, possibly of later date than the Pitriyagñas, belong nevertheless to a very early phase of Indian life. And though much may have been changed in the outward form of these ancient ancestral sacrifices, their original solemn character has remained unchanged. Even at present, when the worship of the ancient Devas is ridiculed by many who still take part in it, the worship of the ancestors and the offering of Srâddhas have maintained much of their old sacred character. They have sometimes been compared to the "communion" in the Christian Church, and it is certainly true that many natives speak of their funeral and ancestral ceremonies with a hushed voice and with real reverence. They alone seem still to impart to their life on earth a deeper significance and a higher prospect. I could go even a step further and express my belief, that the absence of such services for the dead and of ancestral commemorations is a real loss in our own religion. Almost every religion recognizes them as tokens of a loving memory offered to a father, to a mother, or even to a child, and though in many countries they may have proved a source of superstition, there runs through them all a deep well of living human faith that ought never to be allowed to perish. The early Christian Church had to sanction the ancient prayers for the Souls of the Departed, and in more southern countries the services on All Saints' and on All Souls' Day continue to satisfy a craving of the human heart which must be satisfied in every religion.[1] We, in the North, shrink from these open manifestations of grief, but our hearts know often a deeper bitterness; nay, there would seem to be a higher truth than we at first imagine in the belief of the ancients

---

karus kânvashtakyasrâddhe; Gobhilîya Grihya-sûtra, ed. "Kandrakânta Tarkâlankâra, Vigñapti," p. 8.

1. It may be seriously doubted whether prayers to the dead or for the dead satisfy any craving of the human heart. With us in "the North," a shrinking from "open manifestations of grief" has nothing whatever to do with the matter. Those who refuse to engage in such worship believe and teach that the dead are not gods and cannot be helped by our prayers. Reason, not feeling, prevents such worship.—AM. PUBS.

that the souls of our beloved ones leave us no rest, unless they are appeased by daily prayers, or, better still, by daily acts of goodness in remembrance of them.[1]

But there is still another Beyond that found expression in the ancient religion of India. Besides the Devas or Gods, and besides the Pitris or Fathers, there was a third world, without which the ancient religion of India could not have become what we see it in the Veda. That third Beyond was what the poets of the Veda call the Rita, and which I believe meant originally no more than "the straight line." It is applied to the straight line of the sun in its daily course, to the straight line followed by day and night, to the straight line that regulates the seasons, to the straight line which, in spite of many momentary deviations, was discovered to run through the whole realm of nature. We call that Rita, that straight, direct, or right line, when we apply it in a more general sense, *the Law of Nature*; and when we apply it to the moral world, we try to express the same idea again by speaking of the *Moral Law*, the law on which

---

1. A deeper idea than affection inspired this custom. Every kinsman was always such, living or dead; and hence the service of the dead was sacred and essential. The Srâddhas were adopted as the performance of such offices. There were twelve forms of this service: 1. The daily offering to ancestors. 2. The sraddha for a person lately deceased, and not yet included with the pitris. 3. The srâddha offered for a specific object. 4. The offering made on occasions of rejoicing. 5. The sraddha performed when the recently-departed has been incorporated among the Pitris. 6. The srâddha performed on a parvan-day, *i.e.*, new moon, the eighth day, fourteenth day, and full moon. 7. The sraddha performed in a house of assembly for the benefit of learned men. 8. Expiatory. 9. Part of some other ceremony. 10. Offered for the sake of the Devas. 11. Performed before going on a journey. 12. Srâddha for the sake of wealth. The srâddhas may be performed in one's own house, or in some secluded and pure place. The number performed each year by those who can afford it varies considerably; but ninety-six appears to be the more common. The most fervent are the twelve new-moon rites; four Yuga and fourteen Manu rites; twelve corresponding to the passages of the sun into the zodiacal mansions, etc.—A. W.

our life is founded, the eternal Law of Right and Reason, or, it may be, "that which makes for righteousness" both within us and without.[1] And thus, as a thoughtful look on nature led to the first perception of bright gods, and in the end of a God of light, as love of our parents was transfigured into piety and a belief in immortality, a recognition of the straight lines in the world without, and in the world within, was raised into the highest faith, a faith in a law that underlies everything, a law in which we may trust, whatever befall, a law which speaks within us with the divine voice of conscience, and tells us "this is rita," "this is right," "this is true," whatever the statutes of our ancestors, or even the voices of our bright gods, may say to the contrary.[2]

These three Beyonds are the three revelations of antiquity; and it is due almost entirely to the discovery of the Veda that we, in this nineteenth century of ours, have been allowed to watch again these early phases of thought and religion, which had passed away long before the beginnings of other literatures.[3] In the Veda an ancient city has been laid bare before our eyes which, in the history of all other religions, is filled up with rubbish, and built over by new architects. Some of the earliest and most instructive scenes of our distant childhood have risen once more above the horizon of

---

1. See "Hibbert Lectures," new ed. pp. 243-255.
2. The same concept is found in the Platonic Dialogue between Sokrates and Euthyphrôn. The philosopher asks the diviner to tell what is holy and what impiety. "That which is pleasing to the gods is holy, and that which is not pleasing to them is impious" promptly replies the mantis, "To be holy is to be just," said Sokrates; "Is the thing holy because they love it, or do they love it because it is holy?" Euthyphrôn hurried away in alarm. He had acknowledged unwittingly that holiness or justice was supreme above all gods; and this highest concept, this highest faith, he dared not entertain.—A. W.
3. In Chinese we find that the same three aspects of religion and their intimate relationship were recognized, as, for instance, when Confucius says to the Prince of Sung: "Honor the sky (worship of Devas), reverence the Manes (worship of Pitris); if you do this, sun and moon will keep their appointed time (Rita)." Happel, "Altchinesische Reichsreligion," p. 11.

our memory which, until thirty or forty years ago, seemed to have vanished forever.

* * *

Only a few words more to indicate at least how this religious growth in India contained at the same time the germs of Indian philosophy. Philosophy in India is, what it ought to be, not the denial, but the fulfilment of religion; it is the highest religion, and the oldest name of the oldest system of philosophy in India is *Vedânta*, that is, the end, the goal, the highest object of the Veda.

Let us return once more to that ancient theologian who lived in the fifth century B.C., and who told us that, even before his time, all the gods had been discovered to be but three gods, the gods of the *Earth*, the gods of the *Air*, and the gods of the *Sky*, invoked under various names. The same writer tells us that in reality there is but *one* God, but he does not call him the Lord, or the Highest God, the Creator, Ruler, and Preserver of all things, but he calls him Âtman, THE SELF. The one Âtman or Self, he says, is praised in many ways owing to the greatness of the godhead. And then he goes on to say: "The other gods are but so many members of the one Âtman, Self, and thus it has been said that the poets compose their praises according to the multiplicity of the natures of the beings whom they praise."

It is true, no doubt, that this is the language of a philosophical theologian, not of an ancient poet. Yet these philosophical reflections belong to the fifth century before our era, if not to an earlier date; and the first germs of such thoughts may be discovered in some of the Vedic hymns also. I have quoted already from the hymns such passages as[1]—"They speak of Mitra, Varuna, Agni; then he is the heavenly bird Garutmat; *that which is and is one* the poets call in various ways; they speak of Yama, Agni, Mâtarisvan."

---

1. Rig-Veda I. 164, 46; "Hibbert Lectures," p. 311.

In another hymn, in which the sun is likened to a bird, we read: "Wise poets represent by their words the bird who is one, in many ways."[1]

All this is still tinged with mythology; but there are other passages from which a purer light beams upon us, as when one poet asks:[2]

"Who saw him when he was first born, when he who has no bones bore him who has bones? Where was the breath, the blood, the Self of the world? Who went to ask this from any that knew it?"

Here, too, the expression is still helpless, but though the flesh is weak, the spirit is very willing. The expression, "He who has bones" is meant for that which has assumed consistency and form, the Visible, as opposed to that which has no bones, no body, no form, the Invisible, while "breath, blood, and self of the world" are but so many attempts at finding names and concepts for what is by necessity inconceivable, and therefore unnamable.

In the second period of Vedic literature, in the so-called Brâhmanas, and more particularly in what is called the Upanishads, or the Vedânta portion, these thoughts advance to perfect clearness and definiteness. Here the development of religious thought, which took its beginning in the hymns, attains to its fulfilment. The circle becomes complete. Instead of comprehending the One by many names, the many names are now comprehended to be the One. The old names are openly discarded; even such titles as Pragâpati, lord of creatures, Visvakarman, maker of all things, Dhâtri, creator, are put aside as inadequate. The name now used is an expression of nothing but the purest and highest subjectiveness – it is Âtman, the Self, far more abstract than our *Ego* – the Self of all things, the Self of all the old mythological gods – for they were not *mere* names, but names intended for something – lastly, the Self in which each

1. Rig-Veda X. 114, 5; "Hibbert Lectures," p. 313.
2. Rig-Veda I. 164, 4.

individual self must find rest, must come to himself, must find his own true Self.

You may remember that I spoke to you in my first lecture of a boy who insisted on being sacrificed by his father, and who, when he came to Yama, the ruler of the departed, was granted three boons, and who then requested, as his third boon, that Yama should tell him what became of man after death. That dialogue forms part of one of the Upanishads, it belongs to the Vedânta, the end of the Veda, the highest aim of the Veda. I shall read you a few extracts from it.

Yama, the King of the Departed, says:

"Men who are fools, dwelling in ignorance, though wise in their own sight, and puffed up with vain knowledge, go round and round, staggering to and fro, like blind led by the blind.

"The future never rises before the eyes of the careless child, deluded by the delusions of wealth. *This* is the world, he thinks; there is no other; thus he falls again and again under my sway (the sway of death).

"The wise, who by means of meditating on his *Self*, recognizes the Old (the old man within) who is difficult to see, who has entered into darkness, who is hidden in the cave, who dwells in the abyss, as God, he indeed leaves joy and sorrow far behind.

"That Self, the Knower, is not born, it dies not; it came from nothing, it never became anything. The Old man is unborn, from everlasting to everlasting; he is not killed, though the body be killed.

"That Self is smaller than small, greater than great; hidden in the heart of the creature. A man who has no more desires and no more griefs, sees the majesty of the Self by the grace of the creator.

"Though sitting still, he walks far; though lying down, he goes everywhere. Who save myself is able to know that God, who rejoices, and rejoices not?

"That Self cannot be gained by the Veda; nor by the understanding, nor by much learning. He whom the Self chooses, by him alone the Self can be gained.

"The Self chooses him as his own. But he who has not first turned away from his wickedness, who is not calm and subdued, or whose mind is not at rest, he can never obtain the Self, even by knowledge.

"No mortal lives by the breath that goes up and by the breath that goes down. We live by another, in whom both repose.

"Well then, I shall tell thee this mystery, the eternal word (Brahman), and what happens to the *Self,* after reaching death.

"Some are born again, as living beings, others enter into stocks and stones, according to their work, and according to their knowledge.

"But he, the Highest Person, who wakes in us while we are asleep, shaping one lovely sight after another, he indeed is called the Light, he is called Brahman, he alone is called the Immortal. All worlds are founded on it, and no one goes beyond. *This is that.*

"As the one fire, after it has entered the world, though one, becomes different according to what it burns, thus the One Self within all things, becomes different, according to whatever it enters, but it exists also apart.

"As the sun, the eye of the world, is not contaminated by the external impurities seen by the eye, thus the One Self within all things is never contaminated by the sufferings of the world, being himself apart.

"There is one eternal thinker, thinking non-eternal thoughts; he, though one, fulfils the desires of many. The wise who perceive Him within their Self, to them belongs eternal life, eternal peace.[1]

"Whatever there is, the whole world, when gone forth (from Brahman), trembles in his breath. That Brahman is a great terror, like a drawn sword. Those who know it, become immortal.

"He (Brahman) cannot be reached by speech, by mind, or by the eye. He cannot be apprehended, except by him who says, *He is.*

"When all desires that dwell in the heart cease, then the mortal becomes immortal, and obtains Brahman.

"When all the fetters of the heart here on earth are broken, when all that binds us to this life is undone, then the mortal becomes immortal – here my teaching ends."

This is what is called Vedânta, the Veda-end, the end of the Veda, and this is the religion or the philosophy, whichever you like to call it, that has lived on from about 500 B.C. to the present day. If the people of India can be said to have now any system of religion at all – apart from their ancestral sacrifices and their Srâddhas, and apart from mere caste-observances – it is to be found in the Vedânta philosophy, the leading tenets of which are known, to some extent in every village.[2] That great revival of religion, which was inaugurated some fifty years ago by Ram-Mohun Roy, and is now known as the Brahma-Samâg, under the leadership of my noble friend Keshub Chunder Sen, was chiefly founded on the Upanishads, and was Vedântic in spirit. There is, in fact, an unbroken continuity between the most modern and the most ancient phases of Hindu thought, extending over more than three thousand years.

---

1. Τὺ δὲ φρόνημα τοῦ πνεύματος ζωὴ καὶ εἰρήνη. See also Ruskin, "Sesame," p. 63.
2. Major Jacob, "Manual of Hindu Pantheism," Preface.

To the present day India acknowledges no higher authority in matters of religion, ceremonial, customs, and law than the *Veda*, and so long as India is India, nothing will extinguish that ancient spirit of Vedântism which is breathed by every Hindu from his earliest youth, and pervades in various forms the prayers even of the idolater, the speculations of the philosopher, and the proverbs of the beggar.

For purely practical reasons therefore – I mean for the very practical object of knowing something of the secret springs which determine the character, the thoughts and deeds of the lowest as well as of the highest among the people in India – an acquaintance with their religion, which is founded on the Veda, and with their philosophy, which is founded on the Vedânta, is highly desirable.

It is easy to make light of this, and to ask, as some statesmen have asked, even in Europe, What has religion, or what has philosophy, to do with politics? In India, in spite of all appearances to the contrary, and notwithstanding the indifference on religious matters so often paraded before the world by the Indians themselves, religion, and philosophy too, are great powers still. Read the account that has lately been published of two native statesmen, the administrators of two first-class states in Saurâshtra, Junâgadh, and Bhavnagar, Gokulaji and Gaurisankara,[1] and you will see whether the Vedânta is still a moral and a political power in India or not.

1. "Life and Letters of Gokulaji Sampattirâma Zâlâ and his views of the Vedânta, by Manassukharâma Sûryarâma Tripâthî." Bombay, 1881.

As a young man Gokulaji, the son of a good family, learned Persian and Sanskrit. His chief interest in life, in the midst of a most successful political career, was the "Vedânta." A little insight, we are told, into this knowledge turned his heart to higher objects, promising him freedom from grief, and blessedness, the highest aim of all. This was the turning-point of his inner life. When the celebrated Vedânti anchorite, Râma Bâvâ, visited Junâgadh, Gokulaji became his pupil. When another anchorite, Paramahansa Sakkidânanda, passed through Junâgadh on a pilgrimage to Girnar, Gokulaji was regularly initiated in the secrets of the Vedânta. He soon became highly proficient in it, and through the whole course of his life, whether in power or in disgrace, his

But I claim even more for the Vedânta, and I recommend its study, not only to the candidates for the Indian Civil Service, but to all true students of philosophy. It will bring before them a view of life, different from all other views of life which are placed before us in the History of Philosophy. You saw how behind all the Devas or gods, the authors of the Upanishads discovered the Âtman or Self. Of that Self they predicated three things only, that it is, that it perceives, and that it enjoys eternal bliss. All other predicates were negative: it is not this, it is not that – it is beyond anything that we can conceive or name.

But that Self, that Highest Self, the Paramâtman, could be discovered after a severe moral and intellectual discipline only, and those who had not yet discovered it were allowed to worship lower gods, and to employ more poetical names to satisfy their human wants. Those who knew the other gods to be but names or persons – *personae* or masks, in the true sense of the word – pratîkas, as they call them in Sanskrit – knew also that those who worshipped these names or persons, worshipped in truth the Highest Self, though ignorantly. This is a most characteristic feature in the religious history of India. Even in the Bhagavadgîtâ, a rather popular and exoteric exposition of Vedântic doctrines, the Supreme Lord or Bhagavat himself is introduced as saying: "Even those who worship idols, worship me."[1]

---

belief in the doctrines of the Vedânta supported him, and made him, in the opinion of English statesmen, the model of what a native statesman ought to be.

1. Professor Kuenen discovers a similar idea in the words placed in the mouth of Jehovah by the prophet Malachi, i. 14: "For I am a great King, and my name is feared among the heathen." "The reference," he says, "is distinctly to the adoration already offered to Yahweh by the people, whenever they serve their own gods with true reverence and honest zeal. (A1) Even in Deuteronomy the adoration of these other gods by the nations is represented as a dispensation of Yahweh. Malachi goes a step further, and accepts their worship as a tribute which in reality falls to Yahweh – to Him, the Only True. Thus the opposition between Yahweh and the other gods, and afterward between the one true God

But that was not all. As behind the names of Agni, Indra, and Pragâpati, and behind all the mythology of nature, the ancient sages of India had discovered the Âtman – let us call it the objective Self – they perceived also behind the veil of the body, behind the senses, behind the mind, and behind our reason (in fact behind the mythology of the soul, which we often call psychology), another Âtman, or the subjective Self. That Self too was to be discovered by a severe moral and intellectual discipline only, and those who wished to find it, who wished to know, not themselves, but their Self, had to cut far deeper than the senses, or the mind, or the reason, or the ordinary Ego. All these too were Devas, bright apparitions – mere names – yet names meant for something. Much that was most dear, that had seemed for a time their very self, had to be surrendered, before they could find the Self of Selves, the Old Man, the Looker-on, a subject independent of all personality, an existence independent of all life.

When that point had been reached, then the highest knowledge began to dawn, the Self within (the Pratyagâtman) was drawn toward the Highest Self (the Paramâtman), it found its true self in the Highest Self, and the oneness of the subjective with the objective Self was recognized as underlying all reality, as the dim dream of religion – as the pure light of philosophy.

This fundamental idea is worked out with systematic completeness in the Vedânta philosophy, and no one who can appreciate the lessons contained in Berkeley's philosophy, will read the Upanishads and the Brahmasûtras, and their commentaries without feeling a richer and a wiser man.

---

and the imaginary gods, makes room here for the still higher conception that the adoration of Yahweh is the essence and the truth of all religion." "Hibbert Lectures," p. 181.

    A1: There is, we believe, not the slightest authority for reading Malachi in this way; any reader of the Old Testament is competent to judge for himself.—AM. PUBS.

I admit that it requires patience, discrimination, and a certain amount of self-denial before we can discover the grains of solid gold in the dark mines of Eastern philosophy. It is far easier and far more amusing for shallow critics to point out what is absurd and ridiculous in the religion and philosophy of the ancient world than for the earnest student to discover truth and wisdom under strange disguises. Some progress, however, has been made, even during the short span of life that we can remember. The Sacred Books of the East are no longer a mere butt for the invectives of missionaries or the sarcasms of philosophers. They have at last been recognized as historical documents, ay, as the most ancient documents in the history of the human mind, and as palæontological records of an evolution that begins to elicit wider and deeper sympathies than the nebular formation of the planet on which we dwell for a season, or the organic development of that chrysalis which we call man.

If you think that I exaggerate, let me read you in conclusion what one of the greatest philosophical critics[1] – and certainly not a man given to admiring the thoughts of others – says of the Vedânta, and more particularly of the Upanishads. Schopenhauer writes:

"In the whole world there is no study so beneficial and so elevating as that of the Upanishads. It has been the solace of my life – it will be the solace of my death."[2]

* * *

I have thus tried, so far as it was possible in one course of lectures, to give you some idea of ancient India, of its ancient literature, and, more particularly, of its ancient religion. My object was, not merely to place names and facts before you, these you can find in

---

1. The author's enthusiasm has carried him beyond bounds. The weight to be given to Schopenhauer's opinion touching any religious subject may be measured by the following quotation: "The happiest moment of life is the completest forgetfulness of self in sleep, and the wretchedest is the most wakeful and conscious."—AM. PUBS.
2. "Sacred Books of the East," vol. i, "The Upanishads," translated by M. M.; Introduction, p. lxi.

many published books, but, if possible, to make you see and feel the general human interests that are involved in that ancient chapter of the history of the human race. I wished that the Veda and its religion and philosophy should not only seem to you curious or strange, but that you should feel that there was in them something that concerns ourselves, something of our own intellectual growth, some recollections, as it were, of our own childhood, or at least of the childhood of our own race. I feel convinced that, placed as we are here in this life, we have lessons to learn from the Veda, quite as important as the lessons we learn at school from Homer and Virgil, and lessons from the Vedânta quite as instructive as the systems of Plato or Spinoza.

I do not mean to say that everybody who wishes to know how the human race came to be what it is, how language came to be what it is, how religion came to be what it is, how manners, customs, laws, and forms of government came to be what they are, how we ourselves came to be what we are, must learn Sanskrit, and must study Vedic Sanskrit. But I _do_ believe that not to know what a study of Sanskrit, and particularly a study of the Veda, has already done for illuminating the darkest passages in the history of the human mind, of that mind on which we ourselves are feeding and living, is a misfortune, or, at all events, a loss, just as I should count it a loss to have passed through life without knowing something, however little, of the geological formation of the earth, or of the sun, and the moon, and the stars – and of the thought, or the will, or the law, that govern their movements.

BESTSELLING FICTION

- 1984 by George Orwell, ISBN: 9788193545836
- A Passage to India by E.M. Forster, ISBN: 9789391181772
- A Wrinkle in Time by Madeleine L'Engle, ISBN: 9789389440188
- Animal Farm by George Orwell, ISBN: 9789387669062
- Anthem by Ayn Rand, ISBN: 9789389157178
- As a Man Thinketh by James Allen, ISBN: 9789388118422
- Demian by Hermann Hesse, ISBN: 9789388118170
- Gitanjali by Rabindranath Tagore, ISBN: 9789387669079
- Lost Horizon by James Hilton, ISBN: 9789389440492
- Notes from the Underground by Fyodor Dostoyevsky, ISBN: 9789354990106
- Passing by Nella Larsen, ISBN: 9789389440508
- Poirot Investigates by Agatha Christie, ISBN: 9789354992179
- Siddhartha by Hermann Hesse, ISBN: 9789387669116
- Tender is the Night by F. Scott Fitzgerald, ISBN: 9789354994760
- The Call of the Wild by Jack London, ISBN: 9789354990427
- The Greatest Short Stories of Leo Tolstoy, ISBN: 9789389157932
- The Jungle Book by Rudyard Kipling, ISBN: 9789387669338
- The Little Prince by Antoine de Saint-Exupéry, ISBN: 9789389440027
- The Murder on the Links by Agatha Christie, ISBN: 9789390492442
- The Mysterious Affair at Styles by Agatha Christie, ISBN: 9789354993084
- The Prophet by Kahlil Gibran, ISBN: 9789388118453
- The Railway Children by E Nesbit, ISBN: 9789354990199
- The Secret of Chimneys by Agatha Christie, ISBN: 9789354991684
- The Sun Also Rises by Ernest Hemingway, ISBN: 9789354990229
- Walden and Civil Disobedience by Henry D. Thoreau, ISBN: 9789354994135

Search the book by its ISBN

HARDCOVER NON-FICTION

- 12 Years A Slave by Solomon Northup, ISBN: 9789354993985
- 51 Must Know Facts About Albert Einstein by GP Editors, ISBN: 9789354992285
- 51 Must Know Facts About Brain by GP Editors, ISBN: 9789354994654
- A Theory of Human Motivation by A.H. Maslow, ISBN: 9789354994005
- Becoming a Writer by Dorothea Brande, ISBN: 9789389157192
- Believe in Yourself by Joseph Murphy, ISBN: 9789388118439
- Beyond Good and Evil by Friedrich Nietzsche, ISBN: 9789389157871
- Chanakya Neeti by Chanakya, ISBN: 9789390492916
- Creative Mind and Success by Ernest Holmes, ISBN: 9789354991141
- Feeling is the Secret by Neville Goddard, ISBN: 9789389157208
- Five Chimneys by Olga Lengyel, ISBN: 9789354994043
- Five Lessons by Neville Goddard, ISBN: 9789354994050
- Gravity by George Gamow, ISBN: 9789388118705
- Great Speeches of Abraham Lincoln, ISBN: 9789387669154
- How to Attract Money by Joseph Murphy, ISBN: 9789388118446
- How to Develop Self Confidence and... by Dale Carnegie, ISBN: 9789388118286
- How to Enjoy Your Life and Your Job by Dale Carnegie, ISBN: 9789388118293
- How to Own Your Own Mind by Napoleon Hill, ISBN: 9789354994067
- How to Stop Worrying and Start Living by Dale.Carnegie, ISBN: 9789387669161
- How to Win Friends and Influ. People by Dale Carnegie, ISBN: 9789387669178
- If You Want to Write by Brenda Ueland, ISBN: 9789389157895
- Illustrated Bio. of William Shakespeare by Manju Gupta, ISBN: 9789387669246
- Life in Corona by NK Sondhi, ISBN: 9789354994081
- Madhubala by Manju Gupta, ISBN: 9789387669253
- Mahatma Gandhi by Romain Rolland, ISBN: 9789354994722

HARDCOVER NON-FICTION

- Meditation and Its Methods by Swami Vivekananda, ISBN: 9789389157987
- Meditations by Marcus Aurelius, ISBN: 9789388118781
- Mein Kampf by Adolf Hitler, ISBN: 9789387669260
- Memory by William Walker Atkinson, ISBN: 9789354990069
- My Inventions: An Autobiography by Nikola Tesla, ISBN: 9789388118187
- My Life : Albert Einstein by GP Editors, ISBN: 9789389157901
- My Life : Dilip Kumar by GP Editors, ISBN: 9789389157994
- Nationalism by Rabindranath Tagore, ISBN: 9789354992025
- State and Revolution by Vladimir Ilich Lenin, ISBN: 9789354990113
- Stolen Legacy by George J.M. James, ISBN: 9789354994753
- Success Through a Positive Mental Attitude by N. Hill, ISBN: 9789390492909
- Tao Te Ching by Lao Tzu, ISBN: 9789354992629
- The Alchemy of Happiness by Al-Ghazzali, ISBN: 9789388118309
- The Art of Living by Epictetus, ISBN: 9789389440539
- The Art of Public Speaking by Dale Carnegie, ISBN: 9789388118477
- The Autobio. of a Yogi by Paramahansa Yogananda, ISBN: 9789387669192
- The Autobiography of Benjamin Franklin, ISBN: 9789389440003
- The Complete Prophecies of Nostradamus, ISBN: 9789354994432
- The Dynamic Laws of Prosperity by Catherine Ponder, ISBN: 9789388118194
- The Elements of Style by William Strunk, ISBN: 9789389157222
- The Federalist Papers by Alexander Hamilton, ISBN: 9789354992841
- The Interpretation of Dreams by Sigmund Freud, ISBN: 9789354992926
- The Kybalion: Philo. of Egypt & Greece by Three Initiates, ISBN: 9789354994845
- The Law and the Promise by Neville Goddard, ISBN: 9789354994852
- The Light of Asia by Sir Edwin Arnold, ISBN: 9789387669130

Search the book by its ISBN

HARDCOVER NON-FICTION

- The Miracles of Your Mind by Joseph Murphy, ISBN: 9789387669215
- The Path of Prosperity by James Allen, ISBN: 9789388118323
- The Power of Awareness by Neville Goddard, ISBN: 9789388118330
- The Power of Concentration by Theron Q. Dumont, ISBN: 9789388118224
- The Problem of Increasing Human Energy by Nikola Tesla, ISBN: 9789354990182
- The Problems of Philosophy by Bertrand Russell, ISBN: 9789354994500
- The Quick & Easy Way to Effec. Speaking by Dale Carnegie, ISBN: 9789388118347
- The Science of Being Great by Wallace D. Wattles, ISBN: 9789389440249
- The Science of Being Well by Wallace D. Wattles, ISBN: 9789389440256
- The Science of Mind by Ernest Holmes, ISBN: 9789354990809
- The Secret of Imagining by Neville Goddard, ISBN: 9789389440041
- The Seven Laws of Teaching by John Milton Gregory, ISBN: 9789388118460
- The Story of My Life by Helen Keller, ISBN: 9789389157956
- The Success System that Never Fails by W.C. Stone, ISBN: 9789389440058
- The Ultimate Guide To Success by Julia Seton, ISBN: 9789354993947
- The Wit and Wisdom of Gandhi by Mahatma Gandhi, ISBN: 9789389440560
- The Yoga Sutras of Patanjali by Patanjali, ISBN: 9789389157963
- Think and Grow Rich by Napoleon Hill, ISBN: 9789387669352
- Thoughts are Things by Prentice Mulford, ISBN: 9789354994562
- Up From Slavery by Booker T. Washington, ISBN: 9789389440270
- Value, Price, and Profit by Karl Marx, ISBN: 9789389440065
- Wake Up and Live by Dorothea Brande, ISBN: 9789388118255
- Who were the Shudras by Dr. B.R. Ambedkar, ISBN: 9789354990243
- You Can by George Matthew Adams, ISBN: 9789354995606
- Your Faith is Your Fortune by Neville Goddard, ISBN: 9789389157260

Search the book by its ISBN